PRAISE FOR *TRIAL BY FIRE*

"Michael doesn't just talk the talk and walk the walk. He is an arsonist in the law. His corporate smack downs are the stuff of legend. This is a must read for anyone even remotely interested in the subject."
—Mark Geragos, CNN Legal Correspondent and criminal defense lawyer, inducted into the Trial Lawyers Hall of Fame in 2016

"Justice is not naturally occurring. It is not random. Look behind most stories where true justice has prevailed and you will typically find a tenacious, uncompromising individual who struggled and sacrificed mightily to bring about the birth of justice. Michael Burg is one of those individuals. For thirty years he has shown up in courtrooms from New York to Los Angeles with one goal in mind—Justice. This book gives you a look behind those stories."
—Mike Papantonio, trial attorney instrumental in the tobacco and asbestos litigation, inducted into the Trial Lawyers Hall of Fame in 2015

"He's always prepared. He knows his material; he's very bright; he's very dogged and yet cooperative with opposing counsel. He is also extremely cooperative with the court and well respected by fellow attorneys on the plaintiff's side. His leadership was extremely important in resolving about 2,000 to 2,500 cases. He played a role in coordinating state courts and the ultimate resolution of the cases by settlement."
—The Honorable David Katz, U. S. District Court judge for the Northern District of Ohio

"Michael Burg is an attorney who exemplifies the mission of the American Association for Justice—promoting a fair and effective justice system, and supporting the work of attorneys in their efforts to ensure that any person who is injured by the misconduct or negligence of others can obtain justice in America's courtrooms, even when taking on the most powerful interests. This book demonstrates the lengths to which he is willing to go in order to achieve that result! He is a true defender of the American justice system."

—Lisa Blue Baron, past president, American Association for Justice, inducted into the Trial Lawyers Hall of Fame in 2015

"Just imagine a modern day hero—one who protects the innocent . . . one who is a fierce warrior in battles for the underprivileged . . . one who embraces righteous causes for the good of mankind . . . and one who is the standard bearer for courage in the courtroom. Mike Burg is that ultimate advocate. *Trial by Fire* **is more than a book**— it is a work of art, methodology, and inspiration! It is the ultimate must read for all who seek to be leaders, managers, mothers and fathers and advocates and coaches and the keepers of the promise to make this a better world. It is for doctors, lawyers, environmentalists, workers of all kinds . . . an action book—a life book . . . a "lessons-learned" book! In *Trial by Fire*, Mike Burg teaches us what it really means to become an 'OBSTACLEIST!'"

—John F. Romano, trial attorney, inducted into the Trial Lawyers Hall of Fame in 2016

TRIAL

BY

FIRE

TRIAL BY FIRE

ONE MAN'S BATTLE TO END
CORPORATE GREED AND SAVE LIVES

MIKE BURG

WITH JOSH YOUNG

BenBella Books, Inc.
Dallas, Texas

BenBella

BenBella Books, Inc.
PO Box 572028
Dallas, TX 75357-2028
www.benbellabooks.com
Send feedback to feedback@benbellabooks.com

Printed in the United States of America
10 9 8 7 6 5 4 3 2 1

Library of Congress Cataloging-in-Publication Data is available upon request.
ISBN 978-1-942952-56-5

Editing by Dori Perrucci
Copyediting by Patricia Connolly
Proofreading by Chris Gage and James Fraleigh
Indexing by Amy Murphy Indexing & Editorial

Text design and composition by Aaron Edmiston
Cover design by Faceout Studio, Kara Davison
Jacket design by Sarah Dombrowsky
Printed by Lake Book Manufacturing

Distributed by Perseus Distribution
www.perseusdistribution.com

To place orders through Perseus Distribution:
Tel: (800) 343-4499
Fax: (800) 351-5073
E-mail: orderentry@perseusbooks.com

**Special discounts for bulk sales (minimum of 25 copies) are available.
Please contact Aida Herrera at aida@benbellabooks.com.**

To my mother, Phyllis, and my father, Sydney. They always told me I could be successful at anything I did. They taught me by example to fight for what was right. My father was the most honest and ethical person I ever knew. He told me, "Don't chase the money. Be the best lawyer and the money will follow." He was right.

CONTENTS

Foreword by Alan K. Simpson   xiii

PROLOGUE
Just a Touch of Crazy   1

CHAPTER 1
Making a Difference in People's Lives   13

CHAPTER 2
Surviving the Rough-and-Tumble Windy City   19

CHAPTER 3
Toughening Up   33

CHAPTER 4
Adventures in the Sports Trade   39

CHAPTER 5
The Working Life   57

CHAPTER 6
The Client from Central Casting   65

CHAPTER 7
A Young Prospector Takes to Denver   73

CHAPTER 8

Clearing the Bar 83

CHAPTER 9

"Row, Row, Row Your Boat Gently"—to the Court 95

CHAPTER 10

So a Lawyer Walks into a Comedy Club 103

CHAPTER 11

Forced Out on My Own 111

CHAPTER 12

Flying Solo 121

CHAPTER 13

A Matter of Principle 131

CHAPTER 14

Bloodied but Still Fighting 139

CHAPTER 15

Ready for My Close-Up 149

CHAPTER 16

Hollywood Calling . . . 157

CHAPTER 17

Return to Reality 169

CHAPTER 18

Blazing Mad 181

CHAPTER 19

Winning Cases 193

CHAPTER 20
On the Brink   207

CHAPTER 21
Steamboat Springs Explodes   215

CHAPTER 22
Ready for Trial   223

CHAPTER 23
Another Town Explodes!   233

CHAPTER 24
Meet the Simpsons!   245

CHAPTER 25
Mass Torts: The World Series of Law   251

CHAPTER 26
The "Crap and Vomit" Case   263

CHAPTER 27
Not So Fine Wine   277

EPILOGUE
The Role of a Lifetime   281

Index   289

Acknowledgments   297

About the Authors   299

FOREWORD

I have met many a fine lawyer in my life—thanks to my roles in practicing law and holding public offices—but of all these lawyers, no one compares to Mike Burg. He has a fire burning inside of him, a tenacity that cannot be dented, and a drive to bring justice for his clients that makes him the powerfully successful lawyer that he is. Aside from Mike's fierce determination to champion every case he takes on, he's a damn hard worker—one of the most vital traits any successful person or lawyer can ever possess. It takes one to know one!

I always worked my butt off for the simple purpose of trying not to make an ass of myself. There's no other goal or noble aspiration to the task—it's that we want to be the best at what we do, and we want to keep doing it—and that takes real effort and courage—to keep your integrity and protect your good name.

All my life, my good name is all that I have had. I've worked hard every day to create and uphold my reputation. When I first met Mike and discussed becoming his firm's partner, I had already pissed off more people than Mike Burg ever would, simply because that is the clear nature of exercising strong political leadership. Mike wanted the firm to be called "Simpson Burg." I laughed and told him that sounded like the name of some small Western town. Besides, I don't need my name on anything—"So let it be Burg Simpson."

My dad used to say, "If you're damned if you do and damned if you don't—then DO"—and that's what I've always tried to do. So when we talked about lending my name to his fine firm, I said very clearly, "All I have is my good name, so if I do this with you, don't screw it up."

So far so good. I didn't want much to do with the day-to-day law business itself. People see the Burg Simpson name and ask me how the firm is doing and I simply and confidently tell them that Mike and his able crew are taking good care of everything—quite beautifully!

Mike and I share another trait that makes us cut from the same cloth—an ego. We both have "walls of fame"—framed pictures, documents, and awards in our offices that stand as landmarks on our paths in life. Having an ego is part of what a successful life is all about. If you don't have an ego, it's best to stay out of the game of life. Ego doesn't mean boasting and arrogance; it means self-worth and pride in what you are doing and what you've accomplished.

On my "wall of fame," I have handwritten letters from Presidents Eisenhower, Nixon, Carter, Reagan, Bush, and Clinton; pictures with Presidents Johnson and Clinton; as well as notes and photos from Ted Kennedy, Colin Powell, Mack Baldridge, Dick Cheney, "Tip" O'Neill, Howard Baker, Bob Dole, and Father Ted Hesburgh among many others. These are persons I am proud to have formed relationships with, and I can see why Mike is proud of his connections, too. He should be! Hell, if I were one of the very few plaintiffs' attorneys to be presented the Clarence Darrow Award and be named one of the America's top 50 leading trial attorneys by *The Legal 500*, I'd probably put that plaque up for a big sale on eBay!

Mike is mighty proud of what he has done, and rightly so. It's one thing to gain connections and achievements from sheer good luck, or through inheritance or legacy—surely there is little hard work required for those (un)accomplishments. But when you have worked so diligently for your awards and honors, I would not blame a guy for wearing them around on a T-shirt for all the world to see.

Above all, Mike Burg cares about human beings. He is a worldly, humanitarian man, even with all his lofty accomplishments. He loves to be with the humans. He can talk frankly about getting the shit knocked out of him while coming through the scraps as a kid in an ethnically and religiously difficult time. He relates *to people* eas-ily; he is very endearing and exceedingly convincing. He has earned every single ounce of recognition he has received, and he's justifi-ably proud of it, especially since his rise did not follow a most con-ventional trajectory.

Like Mike, while I valued formal schooling, it was not my strong suit. I was told that Mike struggled in school and faced some trou-ble because of that. In the corridors of power in Washington, DC, I used to tell the big-guy and gal swells who had attended Harvard, Yale, Berkeley, and Princeton that I was eighteenth in my law class. They'd say, "Oh really, that's amazing . . . How many were in the class?" I'd promptly reply, "Eighteen." I have found that grades and school marks don't really matter once you break into the big leagues of any chosen field, as Mike has found, too. No one asks you in a jury trial what your grade average was. What matters are your results.

Having come to know Mike so well over these past years, it is ever more clear that he is brilliant, wise, and fierce, and you would want him watching your back. When he is in the courtroom fight-ing a case, he has a burning deep in his gut, like that in a nuclear submarine, fueling every fiber of his brain and body. Mike is a pow-erful production of raw guts, zeal, and fire. He nurtures this incen-diary, explosive, and dynamic force just below the surface, often to the point that the opposition might not know what's coming—but the minute the judge hits the gavel, his universe opens like a fish taking oxygen from water. That is the kind of energy Mike gains from a courtroom, and it is that very same passion that brought him from the most modest makings of early life to the very pinnacle of American law.

I am so proud that my name has been honored by this very honest and reputable law firm led by Mike Burg, who has risen to the very top among his peers and thus carried his name—and mine—without blemish.

—ALAN K. SIMPSON
Former U.S. Senator (R-Wyoming)

PROLOGUE

JUST A TOUCH OF CRAZY

Iam not like most lawyers. The image of a lawyer conjures up a stone-faced professional in a stiff suit, with no sense of humor, and perhaps a blood lust for justice or money, which in some cases are considered interchangeable. But while I fight for justice and large verdicts for my clients, I am not that lawyer.

What differentiates me from the all-business types are my personal experiences, my unwavering personal commitment to fight for the underdog at all costs, and my undeniably explosive personality, complete with theatrics, eccentricities, excitement, a sense of humor—and maybe just a touch of crazy. My younger brother, Peter, also a lawyer, calls me Forrest Gump. I take that as a huge compliment, because Forrest was both adventurous and smart.

For a time I worked as a model and actor. I auditioned for the lead role in the TV series *Breaking Away*, based on the 1979 movie. I even tried my hand at stand-up comedy in Denver, performing a couple of acts away from a local comedian named Roseanne Barr, who made it big. These experiences seemingly have nothing to do with the practice of law, but they have informed the way I practice law today.

As noted above, I am just a little bit crazy, and I insist on having fun when practicing law. You can see that in the photographs displayed on the walls of my office.

Everything that surrounds me tells a piece of the story of the lawyer that I am today. Some of the photos and plaques show my legal accomplishments, my family, and my eccentricities. Some have a tinge of ego, while others convey a sense of amazement that I've made it this far.

The strangest photo by far is of the Fabulous Kangaroos, which represents the "full-on Mike Burg." It stems from the only case Peter and I have ever tried together. The case involved another lawyer. He was suing our clients, who were also friends of ours, for millions of dollars in a securities matter. Just as the opposing lawyers were ready to put on their case, I went up to the lead lawyer and said, "You may not be old enough to remember the Fabulous Kangaroos, but they were the greatest Australian tag-team world champions of all time. My brother and I are gonna act just like them here over the next two weeks."

The lawyer gave me a strange look.

"I'm going to be tagging him, he's going to be jumping into the ring, taking on witnesses, then he's gonna tag me and I'll be back in the ring," I said, raising my voice. "We're gonna be all over this courtroom! You'll never know who's coming at you!"

The lawyer freaked out. He was certain I was crazy.

On my birthday, a month after we won the case, Peter gave me a framed picture of the Fabulous Kangaroos.

I also have a picture of the Marx Brothers that dates from when I was growing up in Chicago along with Peter and my older brother, Frank. Family is very important to me, both personally and professionally. As Jews, we lived in a small, Jewish section of the city, and we stuck together. We also had a good time together. I'm not sure we were quite as entertaining Chico, Harpo, and Groucho, but we tried.

Frank is now a safety expert in the Chicago area who often testifies at trials as an expert witness. Peter is an equal shareholder in the

The Real Fabulous Kangaroo Brothers

law firm. When he joined my firm, I was on the verge of going out of business, and he basically kept us afloat with the insurance clients he brought in. In 2013, my brother and I were named Outstanding Alumni by the University of Denver Sturm College of Law, so I keep a picture of that on my wall, too.

I also have several pictures of my wife, Kathy, and our children from earlier marriages: Kathy's children, Reese and Samantha, and my sons, Scott and Stephen, together on vacation in places like the Great Wall of China, Mexico, and Vancouver. One of my favorite family pictures is with Scott at the annual major league baseball game in Denver before the city landed the Rockies. One year we went to a Cubs game at the old Mile High Stadium and ended up on the cover of the *Denver Post* magazine. Scott now runs a successful hedge fund in Steamboat Springs, Colorado. My younger son, Stephen, is a lawyer and a shareholder in the firm.

Currently we have sixty lawyers in our firm, with offices in five cities. Leadership is a quality I value highly. I try to lead by example, but rather than have a sign about leadership, I have a photo on my wall of Robert F. Kennedy, who served as U.S. Attorney General when his brother John was president. In the photo, taken by the acclaimed *Life* photographer Harry Benson, RFK is campaigning for president just days before he was assassinated. I bought the photo at a New York charity event for the RFK Foundation, which is run by his daughter Kerry. The photo serves as a constant reminder of leadership because of the work that Kennedy did during the Civil Rights era.

The cornerstone of my personal philosophy is, I never give up. I have always said that no matter how many times you get knocked down in life, you've got to get back up. To remind me of this, a law partner of mine, Bill Simpson, gave me a picture of Jack Dempsey being knocked out of the ring in the first round by Luis Angel Firpo in their September 1923 bout at the Polo Grounds in New York—in front of eighty thousand people. Dempsey was pushed back into the ring by the sportswriters. He then knocked Firpo out in the next round to become world champion.

I've been knocked out of the ring plenty of times but, like Dempsey, I always get back in.

My son Scott and me on the cover of *Denver Post* magazine
(Damian Strohmeyer/Denver Post/Getty Images)

So, what is a lawyer anyway? First of all, a lawyer is not someone who finds the truth and then buries it, as the clichéd one-liner states. A lawyer is not, to paraphrase the writer Mario Puzo, someone who can steal more with a briefcase than a thousand mobsters can steal with guns. Nor do (all) lawyers spend most of their time shoveling smoke, as the great Supreme Court Justice Oliver Wendell Holmes proclaimed.

It is nearly impossible to describe succinctly exactly what a lawyer does or how a lawyer performs his or her occupation. The role of an attorney varies significantly across legal jurisdictions, as well as across various practice areas, which can range from criminal defense to insurance to real estate. Every lawyer brings to the table a different background, personality, education, and breadth of knowledge, and chooses to use his or her tools in different ways. But being an attorney brings with it a common set of denominators:

> *Lawyers are the protectors of justice.*
> *Lawyers are the protectors of civil rights.*
> *Lawyers are the protectors of America's judicial system—the most*
> *   important and powerful system of justice in the world.*
> *Lawyers take on the immense responsibility of using their talents and*
> *   skills to protect the citizens of this country against the negligence*
> *   of others.*

Any lawyer who does not subscribe to this doctrine should carefully examine the reasons why he or she decided to become a member of one of the most honorable professions that exists today.

Part of our job as lawyers is to educate society about exactly what it is we do, why we do it, and how the citizens of this country benefit from what we do. We really do protect people—most of us anyway. Our job is to do the right thing: to help those who need to be helped, and to make sure that everyone has equal access to the legal system.

I've worked on a wide variety of cases, from complicated First Amendment rights to cases as simple as a dog bite or a car accident. Some of these cases are about seeking justice for one person, while others affect thousands—and even hundreds of thousands—as is the situation with a sweeping action I filed against twenty-eight California wineries in March 2015.

What I've learned is that most people who come to me for help genuinely need help. They are not after a fast buck. They are not trying to game the system or get something for nothing. These are people who simply want to be made whole. They want their lives to go on the way they had gone on for years, but in a way that becomes impossible because of a circumstance in which they find themselves, often through no fault of their own. A man injured in a snowmobile accident who becomes a paraplegic doesn't want a fancy car or Italian loafers. He simply wants to be able to take a shower by himself. He wants to be able to drive to his job so he can provide for his family.

I have always made it my primary goal as a lawyer to fight for Everyman. I don't say this with a sense of noblesse oblige. I believe it with every fiber of my body. The government does not do this anymore. Congress is largely in the back pocket of big business. Regulatory agencies are overwhelmed, and there is a revolving door between the agencies and the businesses they monitor. The only way the common person can get any traction when wronged is to hire a lawyer.

Clarence Darrow was one of the greatest trial lawyers in U.S. history. His storied career had a huge influence on me. I was honored when I was chosen to receive the Clarence Darrow Award at the 2013 Mass Torts Made Perfect conference. The award is the highest honor given to lawyers who take on cases involving thousands of plaintiffs wronged by big business. The award, featuring Darrow's picture, hangs across from my desk.

In contrast to the Darrow picture, but in keeping with the myriad of clients I've been fortunate enough to represent, on the wall behind my desk is an original Yogi Bear cartoon. I have been blessed to have had more interesting clients than most lawyers, from professional athletes to spunky car dealers—even the Little Rascals! Yes, my firm and I represented the Little Rascals in a lawsuit against King World for using their likenesses for a cartoon without compensating them.

As part of the Little Rascals case, I took the deposition of Bob Singer, an animator who worked on the series (a deposition is sworn testimony that is given during the workup of the case, and used in fact finding). Singer was one of the creators of Yogi Bear, my all-time favorite cartoon. He took a liking to me because I was so fascinated with his animation process. At one point, he asked if there was anything he could do for me. I told him about my passion for Yogi Bear. When the case was over, he sent me an original cartoon.

There have been many other rewards: in the early nineties, I attended a celebrity charity golf tournament with Walter Davis, a former standout for the Phoenix Suns, whom I became friends with through a mutual acquaintance. Walter had invited me to play in his tournament he organized every year. Michael Jordan, then in his heyday with the Chicago Bulls, was playing in the tournament. Of course, everyone wanted to play in Michael's foursome.

Walter decided that rather than having the big-money guys play with Michael—and I certainly wasn't a big-money guy back then— he would have a couple of his friends play with him. So Walter paired me, a friend of mine, and former U.S. Vice President Dan Quayle's brother with Michael.

Playing golf with Michael Jordan was the most nerve-wracking experience of my life. Thousands of people were watching because Michael was in our foursome. To add to the pressure, Michael also had side bets going with the other All-Stars, such as Charles Barkley. Throughout the round, Michael kept pressing us to do better. "Come on guys, you're costing me a fortune here," he said.

At the end of the round, we headed to the hot dog stand. Michael had no cash, so I bought him a hot dog to make up for my poor showing.

My career has led me to some lofty places. One was the annual Alfalfa Club dinner held in Washington, DC. The Alfalfa Club was

Wrapping up a round of golf with Michael Jordan

originally founded in 1913 as a way to celebrate the birthday of Confederate Civil War General Robert E. Lee. The name Alfalfa Club comes from the fact that the alfalfa plant is apparently willing to do anything for a drink! Members include prominent politicians, former presidents, and various members of the business community. Today it is a social organization that exists solely for the purpose of holding an annual dinner every January. The current U.S. president generally gives the remarks for the dinner. At the 1999 dinner, I found myself included in this "Who's Who" of the political and business world.

It was quite a scene. The room was packed with the greatest concentration of true power imaginable at a small dinner—former President George Bush; former Secretaries of State James Baker and Henry Kissinger; former Defense Secretary and soon to be Vice President Dick Cheney; Condoleezza Rice; nearly a quorum of U.S.

senators, including Mitch McConnell, John Danforth, and David Boren; Colin Powell; Ben Bradlee, then-editor of *The Washington Post*; Warren Buffett; and three Supreme Court justices—among others.

I chatted with Rice, who was soon to become Bush 43's National Security Adviser and eventually Secretary of State. "Condi," as she is known, and I had gone to college at the same time at the University of Denver. She was a freshman and I was a senior, but we had a political science seminar together. She had entered college at sixteen. Clearly, she was super smart, and she let everyone know it. She was also an accomplished ice skater and pianist. When I mentioned those days to her, she laughed me off. "Oh, Denver, that was a long time ago," she said.

I also ended up in a conversation with former President H. W. Bush. He told me that if his son were elected, he would bring the country together and govern with a steady hand. Later, the forty-first president and I exchanged letters on the topic of his son. He wrote, "He won't let you down."

As I looked around that room, I couldn't help but wonder, how did Denver lawyer Mike Burg end up there?

GEORGE BUSH

February 15, 2000

Dear Michael,

Thanks for your good letter.

I am glad you enjoyed the Alfalfa Club Dinner. I think it is always the best dinner in Washington every year.

I appreciate your kind words about George. He's a good man, and he won't let you down.

Warm regards,

Mr. Michael S. Burg
Burg Simpson Eldredge & Hersh, P.C.
40 Inverness Drive East
Englewood, CO 80112

P. O. BOX 79798 · HOUSTON, TEXAS 77279-9798
PHONE (713) 686-1188 · FAX (713) 683-0801

Bush 41 promoting Bush 43 to me

CHAPTER 1

MAKING A DIFFERENCE
IN PEOPLE'S LIVES

Gadolinium (Gd) is a chemical element that appears on the periodic table with the atomic number 64. Aside from being used to clean nuclear waste plants, it also serves a medical purpose. Because of its paramagnetic properties, gadolinium solutions are sometimes used as contrast agents during magnetic resonance imaging, commonly known as MRIs. When you get an MRI, contrast dye is often used so that the scans light up to show tumors and other problems. Gadolinium is the magnetic agent often utilized for such imaging.

But hold on. Gadolinium is also used as a *nuclear cleaning agent*. So while it works wonders in MRIs, it is also highly toxic. In order for gadolinium to be used safely in humans, it must be encapsulated in a layer of protective molecules to avoid becoming embedded in the body's tissue before it can be discharged. I always thought of it as a ferocious tiger in a cage; if the tiger gets out of the cage, then it is going to wreak havoc on the body.

A normal, healthy person will discharge the solution within twenty-four to forty-eight hours. However, for those with renal failure or compromised renal function, it can take longer and result in dangerous complications like nephrogenic systemic fibrosis (NSF), a rare nodular inflammatory disease, which is entirely man-made and did not exist until the 1990s when gadolinium was first used as a contrast agent for MRIs on people with end-stage renal disease.

We know all of this now, but when we first took on the case in early 2007, we did not really know what the problems were. Clients were coming to us with this very rare disorder; only after we continued our investigation into the drug were we able to get to the bottom of the issue. Our firm, along with our co-counsel and medical experts, concluded that the formulas weren't stable enough to keep the tiger in the cage.

The case was complex. Many of the best patents for contrast agents used in MRIs had already been taken, leaving big companies like General Electric (GE) to develop their own contrast agents in conjunction with their multimillion-dollar MRI machines. GE and Bayer came up with their own formulas separately.

Unfortunately, there was a problem with various formulas and their ability to maintain the stability of the molecules encapsulating the gadolinium. The chelate, or covering, around the gadolinium would separate, freeing the gadolinium to be absorbed into the tissue, where it then became a major problem.

Most vulnerable to this problem were people with decreased renal function or those with renal failure who were on dialysis. For them, diagnostic MRIs with contrast that used gadolinium opened up the potential for exposure to NSF.

NSF is one of the most horrific and painful diseases I have ever had the displeasure to know about. NSF essentially turns your body into stone. It causes fibrosis (scarring) of the skin, joints, eyes, and internal organs. Seeing this happen to a person is tragic. It has been described as akin to Lou Gehrig's disease, with excruciating pain.

Take one client, a fifty-five-year-old man, who had his fractured ankle imaged. After the MRI, he went home to wait for the results. Six weeks later, he was in a nursing home, unable to move his arms or legs due to the severity of NSF caused by the gadolinium that had been absorbed into his tissue. His skin felt like cold, hard marble. He was, in practical terms, an immobile statue that could breathe, think, and feel the pain of what his body was enduring.

We had about a thousand cases of NSF, and more than half of our clients died premature deaths—painful, unnecessary, premature deaths.

It was the most awful thing we had ever seen in the arena of mass torts, and probably remains the worst I have seen to this day. Mass tort cases are civil actions brought against a single entity or entities that has done damage to multiple people. Unlike a class action, where a small group of people act as representatives for the entire group, in a mass tort case, cases are filed individually, then grouped together in one jurisdiction for efficiency and for the purpose of pre-trial discovery and workup, as well as "bellwether" or limited trials. Bellwether trials are single trials involving one individual whose case is considered to be representative of multiple cases. Liability is then established as a whole, followed by individual damages being assessed.

My brother Peter was the co-lead lawyer in this case with Troy Rafferty, a partner with Levin Papantonio, a prominent firm in Pensacola, Florida, that we often work with on mass tort cases. Like other mass tort cases, there were a number of firms involved, but we were in the leadership position that led the way for other firms to settle their cases.

With gadolinium, we had some 20 million pages of documents to review. Our files were so large they had to be housed in a document depository, which allows you to store documents in one location, both electronically and in hard copy, and limit access to the documents, as needed. Lawyers from all over the country flew to Denver to comb through our files. They went through millions of pages of documents over the course of a few months, trained to keep their eyes peeled for contradictory information and puzzle pieces that did not fit.

As they proceeded, several of our research lawyers reported a few emails referring to an email file referencing a vacation spot. They were perplexed, so they brought the documents to us.

One case went to trial because GE refused to properly compensate the victim. Our colleagues at Ashcraft & Gerel tried the case and won it. The victim was awarded $5 million, a verdict later affirmed by the Sixth Circuit Court of Appeals.

We settled nearly all of our cases, 150 in total. More often than not, there is a confidentiality clause in settlement documents required by the defendants. When we settle a case, we do so because we believe that option, even with confidentiality, to be in our clients' best interest.

The settlements were fraught with complications and independent variables. Most of our clients were older people, in their sixties and seventies, with end-stage renal failure. They were all looking to settle on a deadline: before they died. Each case was worth multiple millions of dollars in our opinion, and they wanted the money so they could pass it on to their children and grandchildren. Plus, in most states, the value of a case decreases significantly after death, so all of these factors contributed to the settlement dynamics.

The gadolinium case was a great triumph for us because we were able to discover and legally eradicate a man-made disease within a relatively short period of time.

We were involved in other important mass tort cases, such as the birth control pill Yaz/Yasmin. The case started in 2007, with the first settlements from Bayer beginning in 2009. We still have some settlements that will be paid out during 2016. The total amount paid will add up to about $2 billion, plus or minus a bit, as the total compensation for the injured women.

I was co-lead counsel on the case. In my opinion, Yaz has no reason to exist other than for its maker, Bayer, to make money. There were already many safe birth control pills that had been around since the '60s and '70s, made by many manufacturers, and Bayer alone had two. The only reason I can think of to develop something new was for a bigger market share. Bayer also marketed the drug for uses other than birth control, such as alleviating premenstrual syndrome (PMS) and clearing up acne.

After Yaz came Pradaxa, a blood thinner and preventative medication for strokes and blood clots. On Pradaxa, Seth Katz was co-lead lawyer. Seth has been a shareholder with Burg Simpson since 2005. He is an expert in the area of pharmaceutical litigation, and a key player in our mass tort practice.

We discovered that Boehringer Ingelheim, the manufacturing company, was destroying documents along the way. The judge levied a $1 million fine against the company, saying the fine would only get worse if they continued. Amazingly, this was the *third* time Boehringer Ingelheim had been caught destroying documents. In May 2014, a $650 million settlement was negotiated in Pradaxa, and in 2015 this case was brought to a conclusion as a result of the global settlement and payment to the injured men and women.

The one common thread was that the drug companies often did not play it straight. At least Bayer had the good sense to come forward as soon as they were caught.

I am incredibly proud of the work we do on mass torts. We are helping to level the playing field for the average person who is harmed by drug companies seeking profits over the health of its customers. The only part I don't like is that I seldom meet individual clients. It's not that I want them to thank my firm for the work we do—I want to thank *them* for continually reminding me that taking huge chances on these cases makes a difference in people's lives.

CHAPTER 2

SURVIVING THE
ROUGH-AND-TUMBLE WINDY CITY

There was a time when it looked as though I might not have any kind of future, let alone one as a trial lawyer. Chance and grace played no part in my life, particularly at a young age. Back then, it was pure survival.

Rewind to 1952. When I was just two years old, the first and possibly most dangerous challenge of my life posed itself to me. Baby Mickey Burg began to wail, alerting his mother to a serious problem. In toddler speak, I communicated to my mother that I had pains— very bad pains—in my stomach. Maybe it was maternal intuition, or perhaps my mother was erring on the safe side, but she claims to have known that something was very, very wrong.

She rushed me to Dr. Rambar, the local pediatrician, a nice, middle-aged man with round glasses. He told her to take me to the hospital immediately. In the emergency room, what appeared as nothing more than a common stomach ache turned out to be a much more serious condition, one that if left untreated would have killed me.

The ER doctors informed my mother I had a perforated bowel that had caused sepsis to occur. (Sepsis is a life-threatening condition, the process by which chemicals in the bloodstream are released to fight an infection but result in inflammation and can cause multiple organ failure.) The doctors were not sure of the extent of the sepsis, but they cautioned my utterly panicked mother that the situation was dire. They told her that they weren't sure I was going to make it, but they promised to do the best they could.

I spent the next four weeks in the hospital, struggling first for life and then to recover. Even though I was so young, I would remember those days for the rest of my life in fighting for the underdog, because in that moment I *was* the underdog. I've never forgotten that feeling of helplessness and of not having any control over my own life.

Those were deep thoughts for a two-year-old. It took me years to be able to understand and articulate them. But as I did, those sentiments developed into a driving force that would permeate every aspect of my future life: namely, that if I could help someone, I should do so.

I had been born a month premature and a slight five pounds on a cold, wintry night on March 12, 1950. My parents, Sydney and Phyllis, were at a dinner party. Their second child was not due for at least a month, but he was apparently anxious to see the world. In the middle of the dinner party, my mother went into labor, and my parents scrambled to get to the hospital.

Just prior to midnight on March 12, Michael S. Burg was born. I was an early present for Phyllis Burg's father, Jules Shapiro, whose birthday was also March 12.

I was scrawny but healthy. My father used to say I looked like a little chicken. My older brother, Frank, was already two years old and wasn't enthusiastic about having anyone else enter his world.

Two years later, still underweight, I fought my way back from sepsis and was eventually given a clean bill of health. I was released from the hospital after four weeks and sent home. However, after my stint in the hospital, my life dramatically changed. For years, I had fears of getting hurt. I was afraid of being in any kind of danger. I was afraid of going back to the hospital, and most afraid that the next time I would not come out.

⋙⋘

Maybe my early hospital experience made me scared to grow up in a neighborhood that was rougher than most. Life wasn't easy on the South Side of Chicago in the 1950s. All around us were reminders of racial and economic tension.

Like so many children who grew up in major American cities, my life felt controlled to some degree by the surrounding neighborhoods. The area around us slowly degenerated during my elementary school years. Gangs and the drug trade moved in, along with an exponential increase in the crime rate.

The dividing line on the South Side was 67th Street, a long avenue of shops, restaurants, taverns, and movie theaters. The West Side was made up of white middle-class neighborhoods; the East Side was made up of "Negro" neighborhoods. (This was many years before *African American* became the preferred term.) Like much of Chicago at the time, the entire area went from middle class to poor in the span of a couple of blocks.

On the surface, the Burgs didn't have it too bad. We lived in an apartment building of middle-class white families. My father, Sydney Burg, worked as a salesman at Gold Seal Liquors. Having grown up during the Great Depression, he had a diligent work ethic that he passed on to my brothers and me. I have great respect for the way my father worked all his life; his work ethic would later inform my own. Starting from age thirteen, my father went out and got a job to help support his family when money was tight. He still managed to stay in school while he worked.

During my childhood, my father would typically leave our apartment early in the morning. Although, every now and then he would

Phyllis and Syd Burg

sit down for a quick breakfast of eggs, bacon, and toast with the rest of us. Most nights he wouldn't return home until after we had already eaten dinner, which meant that he was usually absent from family meals. This was necessary to put food on the table, but it was also a compulsion because hard work was ingrained in him.

My father was constantly offering us tidbits of advice about work, such as: "If you think it's hard today, wait till tomorrow; it's only gonna get harder." He did not share many details of his work with us, but we were all grateful for everything he did.

I saw that his hard work paid off. He was able to provide a good life for my mother, brothers, and me. Our apartment on 73rd and Ridgelan was nice, but not overdone. It was a typical Chicago-style apartment—long and narrow, with two bedrooms and a kitchen all off a central, dimly lit hallway. Though it was modest, from the time I was born until 1960, it was home. I shared a room with Frank, and then also with Peter, after he graduated from the crib in my parents' room.

We Burgs were a tight-knit group, and we made life on the South Side fun for each other. We always looked out for each other; above all, since we were short of money, we always kept an eye out for good deals.

I remember one day in kindergarten when I was on my way to school with Frank. We were wearing our shoes that we had gotten with our father on Roosevelt Road. These were not ordinary shoes; they were factory rejects deemed unsuitable for sale in regular shoe stores. The defects were small, a missing lace loop or small irregularity on the toes. But because they were cheaper, my father reasoned buying them would be a good way to save a few bucks. Unfortunately, everybody knew of our humble footwear. Every time we sat cross-legged on the floor during circle time at school, they could see the words *Factory Rejects* stamped on the soles of our shoes. The other kids duly assigned us our nicknames: the Burg Boys were branded the factory rejects of our elementary school.

Now, what little kid wants to be known as a factory reject? Not me; that was for sure. Frank and I returned home that first afternoon with tears in our eyes. Our mom immediately made the decision that we would never wear our factory reject shoes again. Into the trash bin they went.

Growing up on the South Side in the 1950s was even more challenging as a Jewish kid. My brothers and I did not make our Bar Mitzvahs, though we were all confirmed. At the time, my mother didn't believe that, number one, you were really a man at thirteen, and, number two, she didn't think you should have a party that was equivalent to a wedding. But here we were, Frank, Mike, and Pete, three Jewish kids with Italian names. We had been named after my father's Italian friends. Nobody ever told us straight out that we were named for those guys, but we had our suspicions. All the other Jewish kids in our neighborhood had names like Joshua, David, and Adam.

The Burg Brothers

Even with our not-so-Jewish first names, our last name gave us away. We lived in a Waspy area with lots of Catholic schools and adults who openly disapproved of me because my last name was Burg. The kids caught onto it, too.

During my daily lunch break at school, I liked to cross the street to get lunch from a little sandwich shop called Sal's Market with the money my parents gave me for food. One day, a group of fifth and sixth graders from a nearby Catholic school approached me as I was about to enter Sal's for my cheee sandwich.

These guys were not actually very big but they towered over me like titans, and they came up to me in a pack of four or five. They were all dressed in the matching Catholic school uniform of khakis, button-downs, sweater vests, and loafers. Here I was one tier up from factory reject shoes, sneakers that were so beaten up that the sole was starting to split away at the toe.

All I wanted was my sandwich, but as soon as these guys got within five feet of me I knew there would be trouble. The tallest one, a kid with pale skin, light eyes, and jet-black hair, bared his teeth like an angry dog and said, "You little kike, give us your lunch money."

At first I just shook my head, my eyes wide and fearful. I imagined the sounds of ambulance sirens careening toward me, a puddle of beaten up Mickey Burg pulp on the ground, as those jerks ran away, waving my three dollars like a victory flag.

"What, cat got your tongue, rat?" said another one.

The tall leader of the group took a step toward me. "You deaf or something? Give us your money right now or we'll beat the living crap outta you," he demanded.

I wasn't stupid. I knew when I was outnumbered. I quickly handed over the money and hightailed it out of there. It was frustrating for me, even then, to feel powerless and to be left wanting to do something. Under those circumstances, there was nothing I felt I could do. Had I tried to fight, they would have kicked me to pieces. Had I tried to reason, they probably would have done the same thing.

I never went back to Sal's for lunch again because I was so scared of getting yelled at, of being made to feel small and inferior, or of being beaten up. As much as I wanted to stand up for myself, it wasn't possible facing five older neighborhood delinquents.

There were constant reminders that I was different because of my heritage and religion. In the late 1950s, my parents began looking for a house for us in the suburbs. Suburban living in Chicago exploded after Mayor Richard J. Daley was elected in 1955. The city underwent massive infrastructure changes. The Tri-State, East-West, and Northwest Tollways connecting Wisconsin, Chicago, and Indiana, and the Calumet Skyway, connecting Chicago with the Indiana Toll Road, were opened in 1958. The Kennedy and Eisenhower Expressways connecting the suburbs to downtown were finished in 1960. Ultimately, under Mayor Daley, the city's expressway system increased from 53 to 506 miles.

None of the new highways were as pretty as Lake Shore Drive, which snakes north of the city along Lake Michigan, but they achieved their desired result, which was reshaping the entire region by creating new business centers and connecting the suburbs with the city. Prior to the expressway system, there was very little mobility between South Side and all the other pockets north and west of the city.

Living frugally had allowed my parents to save enough money for a house in the suburbs. They didn't see the point of spending money on frivolous things like vacations and nice restaurant dinners. Instead, they saved their money so their boys could one day have a yard to play in and get a good education.

My parents looked in the Wilmette area north of downtown, where several new housing developments were going up in the late 1950s. After a few weeks of house hunting, my parents found a place that they thought we could make into a home.

My father contacted the builder, James Crabb, who informed my parents that while his homes were indeed for sale, they would not be sold to any Jews. "You ought to look somewhere else," he said. And so my parents did. There was no protest, no argument. That was just the way it was in the 1950s. Long after World War II, anti-Semitism lived on, and still does to this day.

My mother, though she let it go at the time, held onto the encounter. Years later in my adulthood, my mother was at a dinner party. She met an older man, the very same James Crabb. Making small talk, he mentioned that he was a builder and he asked her where she lived. My mother told him where she lived, and he told her that was close to where he used to build houses.

"I know exactly who you are," she said in a loud voice for all the people in the room to hear. "Years ago my husband and I wanted to buy a house from you, but you wouldn't sell to Jews!"

I loved that about my mother. She always spoke her mind—even if it meant killing the mood of the dinner party.

Years later, she confronted Frank Sinatra—for a very different reason. It happened in Palm Springs, Sinatra's other hangout. I was with my mother and my Great Aunt Eva at Dominic's restaurant. The three of us were eating, dipping our fries in ketchup, when in walked a guy who looked eerily like Frank Sinatra, surrounded by bodyguards. He took a seat at the bar. From the reaction, he clearly was the Chairman of the Board.

My mother saw him immediately. Across the restaurant, she started yelling, "Frank! Frank! Over here!"

Sinatra, sitting at the bar, black-clad bodyguards huddled around him, twisted his head over his shoulder to scope out which crazy lady was squawking his name. My mother, the insistent one that she is, did not give up trying to get his attention.

The bodyguards began eyeing her irritably, as she said, "Wait! I've got a reason! I know Lenny Garmica! I know him!"

To my amazement, Sinatra turned and said dismissively over his shoulder, "Everybody knows Lenny Garmica."

But hey, at least my mother got Sinatra to speak to her, I thought. However, she wasn't satisfied.

"No, I'm from Chicago, I really know Lenny Garmica. We went to school together," she shot back.

That really got his attention. Incredibly, Sinatra got up from the bar and sauntered over to our table. He sat down at the open chair, stared directly into my shocked mother's eyes, and asked, "How do you know Lenny?"

"Like I said, I went to high school with him," she replied calmly.

My great aunt was sitting there, completely starstruck. My mother pointed to her and said to Sinatra, "She's your biggest fan, you know."

Sinatra turned those blue eyes of his over to my great aunt and leaned in. She looked like she was about to die of a joyful heart attack. He planted a kiss on her cheek. He pulled back and said, "Any friend of Lenny Garmica's is a friend of mine."

He got up and returned to the bar. My mom smiled.

By 1960, my parents and their three sons had settled in a house in Wilmette. It turned out to be just a few blocks away from Crabb's house that my parents had liked so much. It was the first time for all of us living in a house instead of an apartment, and boy was there space!

In the 1960s, the North Shore was an interesting place to live. Most of the wealthiest people lived in Winnetka and Kenilworth. These areas were lined with houses that looked more like mansions, complete with idyllic front yards with grass that looked too green to be real.

While there were some wealthy people living in Wilmette, my family was on the poorer side of town. Our three-story house was probably around 1,600 square feet and had four small bedrooms. But the upside was that my brothers and I could each have our own rooms, which was exciting for all three of us.

My family was more than proud to live in that house, in that neighborhood, even if it wasn't a mansion. It didn't bother us that many of our neighbors were better off than we were. I remember riding my battered bike while some other kids in the neighborhood zoomed around on brand-new Schwinns, the paint sleek and shiny. When I played football in the park with some of the other boys in my neighborhood, they donned their gleaming new football helmets. I wore an appropriately sized helmet over my head for protection— made of cardboard.

Some of them made fun of me. I remember them chiding me, saying, "Ha-ha, Mickey Burg can't even afford a real helmet," or a new bike, or a new baseball bat, or new shoes. Whatever it was, little Mickey Burg was always getting pushed around and laughed at.

But I dealt with it. In my mind, it was just the way things were, although as I got older I grew increasingly fed up with it. It was the same with being treated so badly for being a Jew. Not long after we moved to Wilmette, we started running into trouble with some kids from Winnetka and Kenilworth. They would run around in a gang they called the Ridge Runners and look for Jewish kids to push around. Their name for these biweekly beating sessions was "Jew roundups."

This bunch of prep school jerks would wander to West Wilmette, where the houses were smaller and more Jewish families lived, and look for groups of younger kids to torment. One day, they spotted me and my friends and attacked us with chains and sticks. I was lucky enough to escape to a neighbor's house, unhurt. But a few of my friends weren't as lucky. They were beaten badly and had bruises and cuts to show for it.

Frank, tough kid that he was, fought back. He and his crew went after the guys and beat the hell out of them. I was proud of him for defending our honor, but whether I was a chickenshit or just being smart and playing it safe, I did not like bullying in any form. Sadly, because we were regarded as merely Jews, and just kids at that, nobody seemed to care.

Even the local adults were terrible to us. We couldn't go trick-or-treating in Indian Hills, a neighborhood of yet more mansions that was maybe five blocks from our house. One Halloween, we crossed the line and tried to get candy there. Dressed up in an oversized jersey, I rang the doorbell of one of the mansions. A prim-faced, curly haired woman answered the door and said, "You little Jews stay out of this neighborhood. Go home."

While I could not change my last name or my heritage, I could at least try to dress like everybody else. At the time, Gant shirts were the trend in boys clothing. All of the kids in my neighborhood had them. In retrospect they were nothing special, just another brand of button-downs and polo shirts, but I desperately wanted one. I felt that was the only way I could fit in with the other kids.

Convinced this was the only way to be accepted, one day after school I took my case to my mother. This was a huge moment for me, a certain turning point in my life. My mom was sitting at the kitchen table with a cup of coffee, reading the paper, a common way to find her at that time of the afternoon.

"Mom," I asked sweetly, "could I please, please get a Gant shirt? For my birthday or something?"

"Why?" my mother replied, glancing up from her paper to look at me over her glasses.

"Because all of my friends have them," I said, withholding the real reason. "And they look nice. And I just want one. Just one!"

"I don't think so, Mickey," my mother said, returning her gaze to the paper but speaking seamlessly. "I can buy three shirts from Kresge's for the price of a Gant shirt. You can save up money and buy one for yourself one day. I'm not buying it for you, so forget it."

My mother was a great woman, but she never was a soft one. If she had something to say, she said it—and without a filter. So that was that; no Gant shirt for me.

I fumed when she called me Mickey—in fact, when anybody called me Mickey, which everybody did. My name was Michael, but everyone around me had decided, for some unknown reason that was never shared with me, that I would be Mickey, not Michael or even Mike. Every time someone called me Mickey, I thought of Mickey Mouse, of rodents, and vermin, and of being a Jew. So in seventh grade, I decided that I was no longer Mickey Burg.

One night at the dinner table I stood up. "From now on, call me Michael or Mike," I announced. Everybody laughed! My whole family bantered back and forth, chuckling among themselves at my proclamation to free myself from my nickname. But somehow it worked.

Perhaps it was my delivery. From that point forward, they respected my wish. And so the name change stuck. Today when people ask if they should call me Mike or Michael, I tell them either works because I have been called worse!

That was the beginning of my push to rise up from being the underdog all the time. It was the first time I had stood up for myself, and the result—small as it may seem—buoyed my much-needed confidence. And you surely needed that in Chicago—it was a tough-guy's town.

CHAPTER 3

TOUGHENING UP

The downtown area and the suburbs were two different worlds in the 1960s, despite the fact that they were connected by a system of elaborate freeways. Business was done downtown and left behind as men commuted back home to their grassy yards in the suburbs. But some of the downtown ethos seeped into the outer areas. While I was not fully conscious of this feeling, it somehow rubbed off on me, and a tougher, brasher, and worldlier Michael Burg emerged.

Around the time of my name change, there were some other changes going on, too. For one thing, I was *tall*. At fourteen, I was at least a head taller than almost every other guy in my class. I had reached the height of six feet two inches and weighed in at 190 pounds. The following year I grew another half-inch, and that was that.

To take advantage of my height and to increase my popularity, I took up basketball. I was instantly deemed a star. The game was easy for me. Every time I got the ball, I would hold it high over my head, out of the defender's reach, and shoot. It was a sure-fire offensive strategy that made me the centerpiece of the team.

While I felt like a champion on the court, in the classroom my grades were weak. Until I became a basketball star, I had been a great student, motivated and earning good grades. But then along came my seventh-grade teacher, Mrs. Douglas.

Mrs. Douglas was an older teacher with hands like harpy claws who took pleasure in marking Fs at the top of all of my papers. She said it was because she couldn't read my handwriting, which, according to her, was unacceptable, regardless of how good the thoughts on the page were. Could I really help it that I had the natural penmanship of a chicken?

She was downright cruel. She told me, in no uncertain terms, that I would never amount to anything. She said that I would be a loser for the rest of my life, and that no one would want anyone to work for them who wrote like I did.

This crushed my spirit. I was devastated. I stopped turning in my homework. What was the use of turning in my homework if every paper was going to be dismissed with an F anyway?

At the end of the year, the school notified my parents that I was being held back. My mother, being my mother, contested this strongly. She went to the school office and arranged a conference with the principal and Mrs. Douglas. In court, when I write on the easel in closing arguments, I tell the jury the story of Mrs. Douglas' prophecy, but I add that she was right about becoming a loser—I became a lawyer! It always gets a chuckle out of the jury.

Though I was never certain what my mom said, she was able to talk the administration into letting me pass and advance to the eighth grade. However, because I had stopped turning in my homework, punishment awaited me in the Burg household.

My parents sat me down and confronted me about the homework situation. Even after I explained everything, and despite the fact that they understood, my father had me bend over and smacked me good on the rear with his brown leather belt. This was normal punishment for not getting good grades in the Burg house, and it was a lesson that we all remembered. It reminded us that every day we had to do the best we could, or there would be consequences. Not turning in my homework was definitely not the best I could have done, and from then on, I tried my hardest in the classroom.

Basketball, however, was the salvation for my self-esteem. Even though I went by Michael then, the bullied Mickey Burg, who had his lunch money stolen and had handwriting so atrocious no one could read it, still existed, and he needed a boost. Basketball provided that for me. Because of my height, I could make things happen on the basketball court that I could not make happen anywhere else.

I set up a hoop in the driveway at my house and shot baskets for hours every day, pushing myself to become as good as I possibly could. I practiced in the summer, the fall, and even in the winter when the brutal Chicago air would make my skin raw and my fingertips bleed.

I loved basketball because it was my escape, my place of freedom. The better I became at basketball, the more sports I explored. I soon took up every sport I could—basketball, football, baseball, you name it.

I became a huge fan as well. I loved to listen to the Loyola Ramblers' college basketball games on the radio. This was in the days of just three networks, long before ESPN. Most games were not televised. At night, I would listen to a transistor radio using earplugs so my parents couldn't hear.

Red Rush, a radio personality whose voice growled with excitement, would describe the Ramblers by giving hilarious plugs to the sponsor, Gonnella Bread. He would say, "Loyola makes the baskets, Gonnella makes the bread. G-O-double-N-E-double-L-A, GONNELLA," and "Swisheroo, it went through, like a loaf of Gonnella hard white!"

It was as exciting as it was funny and it was a great way to pass the time.

I remember when the Loyola Ramblers won the 1963 NCAA championship in overtime over the Cincinnati Bearcats. I was ecstatic. I dreamed of the day when I would play college basketball as a Rambler. I reasoned that if I kept growing, maybe to six-eight or six-nine, I might even make it to the NBA. But as my mother used to say, "You can plan, and God laughs," and I never grew another inch past six-two-and-a-half.

By the time freshman year in high school rolled around, the football coaches had all taken interest in me because I was so big. I was, by far, the biggest kid in the entire school, not just in height but in build, too. Playing so much basketball had toned me.

I enjoyed the idea of being recruited by the football team. When the coaches approached me, I saw another athletic dream unfolding before my eyes. "I want to be the tight end," I told them. The coaches, Mr. Malinsky and Mr. Chicowski, masochists both, said, "Sure thing, sure thing."

But they were lying straight through their teeth. When they got me on the field that fall, they slotted me as offensive tackle. I was bitter. I hated playing where the coaches told me to play, and I even thought about quitting. In fact, I really *wanted* to quit, but everyone I talked to told me to clam up, listen to the coaches, and stick it out.

Despite having virtually no knowledge of the sport, my own father said to me, "Burgs don't quit." So I stayed on the team and hated every minute of it. I would come home bruised and hurt after practice. The problem was that I never really wanted to hurt anybody, let alone get hurt myself.

Once the season finally ended, it was time for me to get back in the game—back into *my* game. Basketball tryouts were just around the corner. Unfortunately, my grades had not much improved since my run-in with Mrs. Douglas. I ended up getting a C, two Ds, and an F (in algebra).

My mom and dad told me that I could not try out for the basketball team because my grades were so bad. Obediently, I stayed home on the afternoon of tryouts, struggling over word problems, trying to solve for unfindable X. My career with the Ramblers and beyond was waylaid by algebra. Much later in my career, though,

I got something out of being a jock. My firm founded Pro Line
Management, a sports agency. We represented mostly NFL players
and, at one time, had over twenty players on our client rolls. We also
represented famed NBA referee Earl Strom and some other basketball players, so my years as a jock ended up paying off.

CHAPTER 4

ADVENTURES IN THE SPORTS TRADE

Growing up, sports were my safety net. They allowed me to stand out. Because I was tall, I was the centerpiece of my junior high school basketball team. As a Jew, I was something of an outcast, and sports gave me an outlet for my frustrations, a place where I could compete on a level playing field.

I was also a huge fan. I loved the Chicago Cubs best of all. Whether it was listening to the play-by-play on the radio or on the special occasion when my family would go out to the stadium for a game, the Cubs have held a place in my heart all these years.

My father never had time for sports. As a salesman who worked 7 A.M. to 8 P.M. most days, he was preoccupied with Gold Seal Liquors and his financial responsibilities. Unlike a lot of young boys, my introduction to sports did not come from my father. My mother didn't care much about sports, either. I was the only one in my family who was really a sports junkie.

Even though my father was not a sports fan, his boss was. I remember one time when his boss invited us to a White Sox game at Comiskey Park on the South Side. They were fantastic seats, front row, right behind the catcher. My father's employers were clearly well connected. I remember my parents lecturing us on the way there, telling me and my brothers how well-behaved we had to be, like perfect little robots, because they didn't want us to embarrass them in front of the boss.

It was when I got a little older, in junior high, that basketball became my thing. At fifteen, I was fully grown. I scored something like 70 points at one of our games. My teammates just kept passing the ball to me. Because I towered above the defense, nearly every time I had the ball, I was able to score and I just kept scoring. I was Wilt Chamberlain every time they passed me the ball.

I still had dreams of growing another two or three inches and playing in the NBA. I wanted to be the greatest basketball player there ever was. In my head I was always emulating players like Nate Thurmond or Walt Bellamy. But fate didn't have the same plans for me. I tried out for the team my sophomore year, and to my disappointment I was picked last. Even worse, the last one on the sophomore team was also the manager. I hated that extra responsibility and how it took away from my playing time. I would practice with them, but when they left court at the end of practice, I would have to stay and pick up the balls, clean the equipment, and gather up the towels.

My junior year I didn't try out for the basketball team because I had been so disheartened by the situation from the previous year. Instead of trying out for the high school team, I played in a church league, and I actually did really well there. I was a good shooter; I could make shots from the outside.

In college, I was able to walk onto the University of Denver's freshman basketball team. I lasted for about half the season before my knees began to give me serious trouble. Basketball at Denver was also a struggle because I was the shortest guy on the team. I played defense in a few games, but after the first half of the season I mostly rode the bench.

Even after I dropped off the team, I stayed friends with several of the guys. I actually tutored one of my teammates, Dave "Stretch" Bustion. He went on to be an All-American. I later ended up helping him with one of his contracts when he signed with the former Denver Rockets.

When I went to law school, I stayed in contact with the athletes I knew from college, and after I graduated I contacted some of my old athlete friends to learn what it took to be a sports lawyer. I got in touch with Rick Bragnalo and Tom Peluso, two Denver college hockey players, and asked them to let me represent them.

The main thing I learned was that at the time there was virtually no room for negotiation in sports law. A player earned X amount for playing in the minors or Y amount for playing in the pros, with no flexibility. But that would eventually change.

Between my jobs at Denver law firms, my love of sports propelled me to become a sports agent. In the mid-1980s, for a little while, I taught classes on sports management at the University of Denver. But I became a sports agent thanks to Vance Johnson, Ricky Nattiel, and Mark Jackson, the three Denver Broncos wide receivers nicknamed "The Three Amigos." I had met Vance first, and in the process of looking for work, I contacted them.

These three were originally being managed by an agent named John Maloney based out of San Francisco. Maloney, it appeared to us, had not been properly accounting for money owed to all three of the guys. I filed a lawsuit against Maloney that was eventually settled. Maloney paid them back all the money they were owed. The guys were so impressed with how I handled their case that they asked me to be their agent.

The Three Amigos were at the height of their careers in Denver when I handled them. They ended up playing in three Super Bowls in the 1980s, though they unfortunately lost all of them.

I negotiated contracts for Vance Johnson with Denver, and then with Minnesota, when he was traded. Vance was unexpectedly cut by Minnesota during preseason. I went back to the Broncos general manager, John Beake, and coach, Wade Phillips, and persuaded them to bring Vance back to Denver.

I also represented Vance against HBO over a matter of "inde-cency." HBO produced *Inside the NFL*, where they took their cam-eras into the locker rooms. In one of the shots panning the locker room, Vance was standing butt naked. Now, maybe if the camera had only captured his behind it wouldn't have been so bad. Instead, there was a very clear shot of Vance's penis broadcast for everyone to see on HBO.

The unbelievable thing was that HBO had three days before the program aired to edit the footage and cut the shot out, but for some reason they left it in. Vance was outraged. We sued in the federal court for negligence and for damages.

The funny thing was, Vance was known as a notorious wom-anizer with quite the track record. Everybody joked, "What's he suing for? Everyone's already seen his penis anyway." But we sued nonetheless.

The judge overseeing the case was the admirable Judge Sherman Finesilver, a wonderful man. As the case moved forward, he ordered the top executives from Time Warner, HBO's parent company, to come to Denver for a conference. Once these big shots were gathered in the courtroom, Judge Finesilver leaned over the bench and said, "You know, everyone here in Denver is a Broncos fan, and you should be very, very much aware of that. I'd recom-mend you settle this case." We ended up conferencing all day. By the evening, we reached a very favorable confidential settlement for Vance.

After it was all over, the judge ducked under his desk and pulled out three footballs. "Would you autograph these for me, please, Mr. Johnson?" he asked. Not even judges are exempt from the fanaticism of sports.

I, too, came away with some nice memorabilia from Vance. He gave me a ball from an incredible game where the Broncos were behind 20 points, but managed to make a comeback and win the game. Vance scored the winning touchdown. It was an honor to get that game ball, all painted up and with Vance's name on it. He also gave me his helmet, marked with his number, 82, and his gloves from one of the Super Bowls.

Vance later wrote a book titled *The Vance*. Other than himself, I am one of the only people he had something nice to say about.

Denver Bronco great Vance Johnson's helmet

Signed game ball from Vance Johnson

As mentioned earlier, when we decided to expand around 1995, the firm formed our own agency, Pro Line Management. We brought in Robb Nelson, a former Dallas Cowboys player turned agent, and Kevin Robinson, who had played football at Columbia University, to handle the day-to-day operations because they knew both sides of the sports world.

Our new agency consisted of Robb and Kevin, who were both registered agents with the NFL, myself, and my brother Peter, who also became registered agents. Once we had our initial team together, we went after it big time. We brought in several specialized trainers to work with our athletes. We hired Anthony Munoz, a Hall of Fame offensive tackle, to help our offensive linemen on technique, Louie Wright, a Denver Broncos All-Star defensive back, to work with the defensive backs, and Terry Nugent as our quarterback coach.

In addition to the trainers, we provided a workout facility. The first year the location was in Phoenix. By the second year, we had an indoor facility in Denver. We were able to provide these athletes with all of the resources they needed. Many of our clients were fifth- or sixth-round draft picks or even free agents. Half of the NFL rosters are made up of free agents. In fact, it was better for the players to be free agents, because then they had the freedom to look at all the different teams and decide which would be the best fit.

After the draft ended, we converted our conference room into a phone room where all four of us took calls from different teams about our free agents. We represented several notable players, including Ralph Tamm, who ended up with two Super Bowl rings.

One of our most famous clients was Marcellus Wiley, one of the top defensive lineman in the NFL. He had played in college at Columbia with Kevin Robinson.

Wiley was originally represented by Brad Blank. But when the NFL Players Association reduced the maximum amount an agent

Ralph Tamm

could collect on a contract from 5 percent to 3.5 percent, Blank
raised his fees to balance out his profits. Wiley let him go.

Without Blank, Wiley needed to find new representation, which
brought him to us. We flew him to Denver, and I put him up in my
home. We wined and dined him, and at the end of the night, he

agreed to sign on with us. I pulled out the contract, he signed, and we all celebrated.

This was big news for us because up until then we had been struggling. We had thrown millions of dollars into Pro Line Management, but we hadn't seen much in return. Wiley was set to be one of the top free agents that year, so we knew he meant big money.

Then Wiley turned the tables on us. A week after we signed him, we received a letter from him saying that he was firing us and going back to Brad Blank. It was clear that he had only used us as leverage to push Blank to lower his fees.

The whole thing made me sick to my stomach. It was an act of pure manipulation and deception, which runs sharply against my moral compass as a lawyer. Losing Marcellus Wiley wasn't as crippling as it might have been for other agencies. The most players we ever had in the NFL at one time was probably somewhere around twenty, while most agents are lucky if they have one or two players. In that regard, we were still doing just fine.

It was great that we had so much interest in our agency from all these up-and-coming athletic stars, but unfortunately, negotiating with the general managers (GMs) could be a giant pain in the ass. It was often difficult to come to an agreement and strike a balance between what we needed and what the GMs wanted.

Aaron Dalan, especially, was a great client. He was a free agent who came from University of Washington and had a wonderful, loving, and supportive family. At seven feet tall and 320 pounds he was huge. But he was also an academic All-American. He always talked about how he wanted to go to medical school one day, and he did.

Not long after he became our client, we landed him a really good deal with a nice-sized signing bonus with the Oakland Raiders. Aaron called us in the middle of training camp and told us he didn't want to play anymore. The next call came from Bruce Allen, the Raiders' GM. Bruce started screaming at me so loudly that I had to hold the phone away from my ear. He went on and on about how

the kid was walking out on the legendary Oakland Raiders. He tried
to bully me to get Aaron back to training camp.

"Bruce, Bruce, Bruce," I said into the phone, trying to reel him
back in from his ranting, "Aaron has been saying he wants to go to
medical school since we signed him. I can't talk him out of the future
that he wants."

"But he's signed!" Allen roared into the phone.

"Tough luck," I said.

Allen was furious, but I figured that was his problem.

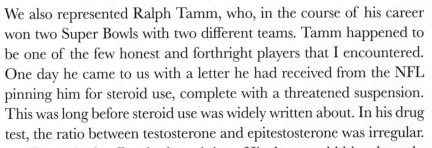

We also represented Ralph Tamm, who, in the course of his career
won two Super Bowls with two different teams. Tamm happened to
be one of the few honest and forthright players that I encountered.
One day he came to us with a letter he had received from the NFL
pinning him for steroid use, complete with a threatened suspension.
This was long before steroid use was widely written about. In his drug
test, the ratio between testosterone and epitestosterone was irregular.

Tamm had suffered a knee injury. His doctor told him that taking the supplement androstenedione would heal his knee faster. At
the time, it was not banned by the NFL. However, it had clearly
thrown off Tamm's testosterone balance to the point where he had
been red-flagged.

After I heard Tamm's story, I hired a toxicologist to put together
a report on the effect of androstenedione on the balance between
testosterone and epitestosterone. This was long before Major League
Baseball player Mark McGwire announced that he had used the
steroid.

I sent a letter to the NFL denying their claim. Our defense
was based on the fact that the substance that had caused Tamm to
fail the drug test was not, in fact, banned. He wasn't trying to use
performance-enhancing drugs; rather he was just trying to heal a
knee injury. The league scheduled a hearing in New York.

The expert toxicologist and I arrived at the NFL offices in New York with a PowerPoint presentation from my toxicologist. Commissioner Paul Tagliabue would hear the appeal and render judgment. At that time, no player had ever won an appeal on any drug suspension.

When I walked into the hearing room, Tagliabue was seated at the table. He stood up to greet me. I was taken aback. I'm over six feet two, but he towered over me, standing at least six feet eight.

"Wow, I never knew how tall you were!" I blurted out.

Tagliabue looked at me with an expression that read: what kind of a country bumpkin lawyer are we going to be dealing with?

The hearing was very informal. We put on our case. Tamm testified about his knee injury and his doctor's recommendations for getting him back on the field quickly. I took them through the toxicologist's findings. After about two-and-a-half hours, I rested our case.

The league officials then requested a break before they put on their case. They returned forty-five minutes later. The commissioner told us that he believed what Tamm was saying and informed us that he was dismissing the charges against him. Then he delivered the coup de grace that rippled across the league.

"As of now, we are banning androstenedione as a supplement that can be taken by any of the players," Tagliabue announced. I was floored. Our toxicologist's report had changed the league's policy on androstenedione, a ban that remains in place to this day.

That afternoon, the NFL issued a press release on the ban. When I returned to Denver the following day, I had calls from at least five other agents whose clients were facing similar charges. They were all asking me to represent them. I declined. Unlike Ralph Tamm, whom I trusted when he told me that he had not been trying to gain an unfair advantage by taking the steroid, I had learned not to trust the word of most of the players.

At Pro Line Management, we strove to be better than the average agents. We tried to run our business the right way, the honorable way. I attended the NFL Players Association meetings to keep current on what was going on in the bigger realm of the league, but I also learned a lot about how corrupt the NFL can be. Everyone is competing to sign young athletes who are really no more than kids. Some haven't even turned twenty-one. And here they are getting showered with money, trucks, hookers, drugs—all in violation of the rules.

The entire process was as dirty and corrupt as any political scene. Several college coaches asked me for money to steer their players over to Pro Line. The players themselves were no better. They lied through their teeth without so much as an ounce of remorse. Everyone was out for himself, and few people had any loyalties.

One year we signed a center from the University of Wisconsin, a Colorado native. He injured himself before the draft. He was all set up to be a second-round pick, but the injury took a big hit on his draft stock, and he ended up a free agent.

Here's the way the free agent process works: if a team needs a center, they have a list already formulated of the top five or six centers available. As soon as the draft is over, they start calling us to sign the free agents.

Jeff Fisher, then the head coach of the Tennessee Titans, called us after the draft one year. This was unusual, because the head coach typically doesn't make the calls, but here was Fisher, talking to me, saying, "Look, this kid would have been a third- or fourth-rounder, so we will pay top free agent money for him."

We ended up negotiating a six-figure signing bonus—much more than what you would typically get for a free agent. Next we called up the player and told him how badly Tennessee wanted him.

"Fisher called from Tennessee," I told him. "You're his number one priority."

The kid replied, "Gee, I really don't want to play in Tennessee."

"Look, man," I said to him, "this is a great deal with great money in it for you." I outlined it for him and that piqued his interest. Finally, he agreed.

I called Fisher back, and we arranged for him to fax me the contract. Before the fax arrived, the Chicago Bears called and said they wanted the guy. I told them I had just made a deal with Tennessee. The Bears rep said, "He hasn't signed anything yet, has he?"

"No, but I gave Tennessee my word," I said.

"Listen, I've got news for you, I just spoke to the kid, and he told me he wants to play for Chicago," the Bears rep said. "We'll match all the terms. But the main thing is, he doesn't want to play for Tennessee." Negotiations with all of these independent parties can get very messy for sure.

I called the player and asked him what he was doing. I sternly reminded him that I had made a deal with Tennessee on his okay.

"Either I go to the Bears or I'm going to get myself a new agent," he said. "You decide what you want to do."

I was in a tough predicament. I didn't want to break my word with Fisher, but I didn't want to lose the client either. I called Fisher and told him the deal was off. He swore at me like no one has ever sworn at me before.

"No, no, you're right," I conceded to him. "I would be pissed too. Not my fault though. What can I do? The kid doesn't want to sign with you. It's not happening." I felt bad, but I had to do what I had to do. That was business.

Years later, I spotted Jeff Fisher in a St. Louis airport and felt I had to go talk to him. I walked up to him and said, "You probably won't remember this, but I used to be a sports agent. I got out of it for a lot of reasons, too dirty, too crazy, too fucked up. The whole business was so dirty and corrupt that it made me crazy. But I wanted to apologize to you. You swore at me, and I deserved it."

He cocked his head to the side, staring at me before he opened his mouth and said, "I don't remember the incident, but I'll tell you this: it has gotten even worse now than it was back then. You should be happy you're out."

>₩<

We got out of the sports agency in 1999 because it stopped making sense as a business. We stayed in for about four years, a short but exciting run. We had four training camps, and plenty of our free agents were ready to turn the corner and make an impact in the pros.

Peter and me with Dr. J.

It ended when our two young agents, Kevin and Robb, waltzed into my office one day demanding $100,000 salaries. They were already making a modest salary, but we as a firm were losing money on the venture.

Peter and I talked to our partner Kerry Jardine, who is the managing partner at the firm, as well as some of the other partners in the firm. Initially, we were going to ask our partners for more money to pay our young guys a better salary, but talking to Kerry opened our eyes. We realized that for four years we had been slaving away, spending money, traveling all over the country, hiring more and more people to feed this beast. It had been four big, rough, pounding years. The verdict: "This is total madness. We can't do it anymore."

After the meeting, we called in the two young guys. We told them we had some bad news. Clearly, they were merely expecting us to say that we could not pay them more. But I told them we were closing up shop. If they wanted the clients, they could have them.

In the end, one of the guys tried to take the clients with him and do it himself. Unfortunately, he didn't have the financial wherewithal, and he eventually closed up shop, too.

Long after my sports agency phase came to a close, I was roped back into the sports world for another hurrah. My firm represented a man, Joe Santos, who had managed Nenê Hilario, an NBA player. Nenê's manager had discovered him in Brazil, brought him to America, and did everything from doing his laundry to helping Nenê's family back in Brazil. Joe had dedicated his life, 24/7, to Nenê, and ultimately brought him to basketball stardom. He had an agreement that said he was entitled to a certain percentage of Nenê's profit, but Nenê had fired him and refused to pay. He came to me to help him enforce his contract.

The situation was depressing. The manager had been with Nenê literally from the start. He went down to Brazil and lived with Nenê's family in their small hut of a house. The manager took Nenê everywhere with him, introduced him to a U.S. lifestyle, exposed him to the NBA, and essentially helped pave the way for Nenê's life and career. But when it came time for Nenê to live up to his obligation and fulfill the contract with his manager, he refused. At the time, he was with the Denver Nuggets. He had played with them for a couple of years, but never really compensated the manager who had conjured him from the dust and set him on his path to stardom.

There was an arbitration provision in the contract, which meant that any legal action would be settled outside of a courtroom by a third-party arbitrator. So we started the arbitration process. Both sides agreed to select an arbitrator named Ann Frick. At the time, she was in private practice. She is now a district court judge.

Nenê was represented by a couple of lawyers from Los Angeles, as well as a local lawyer from Denver. His lawyers were obviously lying about certain things and trying to create a smoke screen, based on their failure to produce certain documents.

The question at hand was whether Nenê was entitled to continue to play without giving his manager a cut. There were also some questions about how much time the manager had spent working for Nenê and his girlfriend. Frankly, it seemed as though he was less of a manager and more of a manservant.

As the evidence came into the arbitration through testimony, it was so overwhelming that it seemed obvious that Judge Frick would rule in our favor. But the next thing we knew, the other side made a motion to disqualify the arbitrator. We were never sure who was behind that, although it came through the American Arbitration Association (AAA). The AAA disqualified Judge Frick, but cited no reason. While I can't prove it, it seemed clear to me that Nenê's lawyers had been hired by the NBA. We felt that they were working on behalf of the NBA to protect him.

Of course, we demanded to know what their reasons were. But their response was: we don't have to tell you. The AAA appointed a new arbitrator, a former judge from Idaho. When the new arbitrator showed up, the first words out of my mouth were "We object to you."

The guy laughed me off. He told me that he had all the power and that I could not appeal his decision. It was soon clear that he was not going to rule in our favor.

I did, however, rattle Nenê's cage during the deposition. Nenê was a cocky guy who acted like he was the greatest basketball player in the world. He even told me how good he was during the deposition, saying that he had been an All-Star.

I stopped him. "Wait a second, you've never been an All-Star, have you?" I asked.

"I was in the pre-All-Star game," he said. As a first-year player, he had made a pre-All-Star game.

"But that's not really an All-Star," I said. "You testified two minutes ago that you were an All-Star. And you're not an All-Star. And I doubt you will ever be an All-Star. You're under perjury here. I don't care what country you come from, you have to understand the American rules."

He was fuming. I could tell from the steely set of his jaw and the iciness in his eyes that he wanted to deck me. Suddenly, everyone leaped to their feet. The air was tense. He had been rubbed the wrong way; I had just proved that he was a liar—on top of cheating his manager out of the money he was owed.

The arbitrator completely ignored our case and decided against us. We went to the district court to find out on what grounds Judge Frick was removed. The district court judge did not rule in our favor, and the court of appeals refused to hear the case. Nenê walked away without living up to his commitment.

There are, without a doubt, some crossovers between sports and law, just as there are crossovers between acting and law, and stand-up comedy and law. As far as sports go, competing is a big part of it.

I was always a big competitor. I hated to lose. This is a trait that many successful people share—they hate losing or failing. More important than hating to lose, though, is loving to win. I was not so much motivated by a fear of losing as a fierce desire to win—to prove to myself that I was the best.

One thing about lawyers is that a lot of them are motivated by not losing. When I am working on a case, I try not to think of losing at all—I only think about winning. It applies to sports, too. I never thought, "I don't want to lose"; it was always, "I want to win—badly." And not only, "I want to win," it was also, "How do I win?" tempered with "How do I play fairly?" To me, that's where sports meets the law: how do you play fairly *and* win?

CHAPTER 5

THE WORKING LIFE

High school was not a breeze for me. There were multiple tracks for students at my high school; level 2 was the easiest track, and level 5 the hardest, reserved only for the brightest of the bright, the geniuses who would go on to Ivy League colleges and earn six-figure salaries straight after graduation—or at least that was how it was portrayed. I struggled to get decent grades even in my level 2 classes, which at New Trier High were known as "Classes for Dummies."

I had other problems, too. I could not get a girl to let me take her out for ice cream, never mind kiss her. The guys I hung out with were all rich Jewish kids, to whom I could not relate. I never felt like I fit in anywhere in high school, and consequently ended up spending most of my four years as a loner.

I did have my family, though. With my father's encouragement, I got a job. My father strongly believed that his sons should start working as soon as possible. He knew that this would allow us to begin to grow up, to learn about making money, taking responsibility, and seeing what the real world would be like.

One of my first jobs was making popcorn and cotton candy at a local fair. To this day, I cannot ever eat cotton candy. I refer to it as "diabetes on a stick," because from making it, I know how much sugar is in there.

I had several other odd jobs during high school. I worked as a bagger at a grocery store, as a tie salesman at Marshall Fields, and in the Gold Seal Liquors warehouse. After working at all of them, I knew definitively that I did not want to do any of these jobs for a living when I grew up.

Of all my jobs, the one I remember the most was when I worked in the liquor warehouse. I would also work on the delivery truck sometimes, helping to offload cases from the truck and then bring them into the stores. Back in the warehouse, I would pitch in with whatever needed doing, whether it was jumping on the assembly line or collecting broken bottles with a man named Jake Spakone.

Jake was a short guy who had been around for a while and was in charge of the warehouse. He was feisty, either because he was short or because he always had his guard up, though it wasn't clear what for. I remember noticing an oddly placed bulge in his pants. Jake always packed. At first, it scared me to have a gun so close to me, not to mention on someone as jittery as Jake. But once I got to know him, Jake didn't seem such a bad guy, so one time I pointed to the bulge and asked him, "What's that for?"

He smiled. "Ya never know when ya need it," he said.

That exchange was one of my first clues that Gold Seal Liquors was, well, not the *cleanest* company there had ever been. I later learned that, as a result of a federal inquiry, Joe Fusco sold his interest in Gold Seal to Milt Friedman but continued in the liquor business.

To us, Fusco was the man. My mother used to tell stories. Fusco had offered to pay for the hospital bill if my mother had a baby within the first year of marriage. Miraculously, my brother Frank was born eleven months after the wedding. Fusco made good on his promise. He set my mother up in a giant maternity suite at the hospital postdelivery and had the room filled with flowers. Fusco cared about us, especially about my parents, and he wanted to do everything he could to help them and their family.

The summer that I worked for Gold Seal Liquors was a crazy one. I was sixteen, a big kid, albeit an innocent one who never got into any kind of trouble. Yet here I was, working for a somewhat shady corporation. Jake was packing all the time. Then out of the blue, Friedman's big-shot son, Laurie, took over the company. I started to realize that something might be fishy.

Laurie usually looked like he had just stepped off the plane from a blowout weekend in Vegas. He was trim and fit, suspiciously tan for Chicago, and always dressed to the nines in a sharp suit, no matter the season. You could tell, just from looking at him, that Laurie was *somebody*—or that he was trying to make himself into a somebody.

He also wore transitional lenses, the kind that turn dark when you step outside. Nobody had those lenses back then, nobody. But he did.

Laurie was married to a woman named Tootsie. Whether that was her real name or a nickname, I knew that Laurie had a wife named Tootsie. Somehow, it didn't surprise me. We ended up seeing Laurie and Tootsie a fair amount because my mom and Tootsie had grown up in the same neighborhood, and so my parents would hang out with them.

One normal day in the warehouse, Jake Spakone, packing as usual, approached me while I was on a break. "Look, Laurie Friedman's driver is out for the day, so we need somebody to drive him home."

"Me?" I said, confused as to why the boss would want anyone to drive him home at 3 P.M.

"We trust you," Jake went on. "We want you to do it."

I had no idea what was going on, but what else was I supposed to do except say yes? It turned out that Laurie had gotten plastered at lunch, though possibly it could have been at breakfast. In any event, he was drunk and he needed someone to drive him home and put him to bed.

I went out front. Parked at the curb was a shiny black Lincoln Town Car. This was one of the nicest, biggest cars I had ever seen. I had certainly never driven anything like it before.

Jake dropped the keys into my hand, told me Laurie's address, and gave me a knowing look and a pat on the shoulder. "Get him home," he said.

With my orders set, I unlocked the car with a series of bleeps. I got in and found myself sitting high behind the wheel, back pressed against the plush leather seat. At my fingertips was a control board that seemed as complex and high tech as a spaceship.

The next thing I knew, the back door was being pulled open. In poured Laurie, sprawling out across the back seat and struggling to right himself. Even though he was blind drunk, he still looked like a businessman, though his tie was loosened and his shirt had a few buttons undone. Jake sat Laurie upright and tugged the seat belt over him before slamming the door and giving the car two taps like actors did on TV shows.

It was go time. I cruised around for a while, enjoying the sheer luxury of the car, glancing into the rearview mirror every now and then to check on Laurie. His head was lolling around, and his sunglasses had fallen to the tip of his nose. He looked pretty passed out, but when I merged onto the Edens Expressway to head north to his neighborhood, he seemed to rouse himself. There was a surprising amount of traffic on the road; so here we were, sitting in bumper to bumper on a blazing hot day, air conditioner cranked. Finally, Laurie spoke up.

At first, I had no idea what he was trying to say. It sounded like slurred, mumbled garbage. But after a few "Whats?"and "Huhs?" he figured out how to enunciate. "I gotta get out," he said deliberately. "I gotta go pee."

"Uh, what?" I said, almost laughing, until I heard the click of the seat belt release. I thought, now? Seriously? Of all the times to have to pee!

In seconds, he was out of the car, walking along the shoulder of the highway—actually he was stumbling—past the other cars stuck in traffic.

"Mr. Friedman!" I screamed. "Mr. Friedman! Get back here! Get back in the car!"

I was scared that he was going get hit by a truck. Looking ahead and seeing that nobody was moving, I threw the car into park and leaped out into the heat of the Chicago summer day, screaming, "Mr. Friedman! Mr. Friedman! Get back here!"

I chased him down for about a quarter of a mile. He sashayed into some nearby bushes and, like a dog searching for the proper spot to mark his territory, found a place to relieve himself.

"I'm sorry, Mickey," he said, arm slung over my shoulder as I led him back to the car. "I just really had to go. You understand."

"Sure thing, boss," I said, pretty sure that he wouldn't remember any of this.

I got him back into the car and slammed the door shut. We sat in traffic for another half hour before we started moving again. He told me that he couldn't go home because Tootsie would be mad at him.

With Laurie nowhere near sober, I decided to drive around my neighborhood until he pulled himself together. I ended up taking him back to my house so he could lie down, drink some water, and talk to my mother for a bit. He didn't like that decision much, but he wasn't really in a position to argue.

My mother talked to him for a while. When my dad came home from work, he insisted on driving Laurie home. I wasn't too upset to let my dad finish up the day's job for me.

One of the perks of being in the liquor business was that my father knew other big players in the liquor business, notably in Las Vegas. On my twenty-first birthday, my parents surprised me with a special family trip to Vegas.

We stayed at the Stardust Hotel, an old-school, Rat Pack–type place. On our first night, my family and I hit the strip to see Debbie Reynolds' sold-out show. It was in a large casino venue. Through Gold Seal, my dad had scored us great seats, front and center of the stage.

Debbie Reynolds was amazing. She was funny, the consummate entertainer. All of a sudden, in the middle of her act, she paused for a beat, looked around the audience, and said, "I understand that we have a twenty-first birthday in the house!"

My jaw dropped. She couldn't have meant me, could she?

Sure enough, after some cheering and whooping from the crowd, Debbie Reynolds turned her eyes directly to me and said, "Isn't that right, Michael?"

I could have died. I was so ecstatic and overwhelmed that I couldn't help but laugh. I looked over at my parents, who flashed me faux-innocent smiles and shrugs before looking back up at Debbie, who was looming over me on the stage.

She reached out her hand and pulled me up on stage with her. Wow, there were a lot of people in the audience! She sang "Happy Birthday" directly to me, on stage, in front of everybody. It was heart stopping, to say the least. I certainly felt like I was getting the ultimate VIP treatment, and I relished it.

The next night it was the same deal at Totie Fields' show. She was doing a comedy act. After the birthday shout-out to me, she declared, "Boy, have I got a girl for you! My daughter is perfect. You'll love her."

Just like the night before, I found myself being pulled up onto the stage, and I thought to myself, "Twice? Really?" And of course, I began wondering what her daughter looked like, though I never found out.

What didn't happen in Vegas, stayed in Vegas.

Over the years, the more I thought about it, the more I was convinced that "something" was going on at Gold Seal. I never suspected my father of being involved in any shady business; my dad
was the straightest guy in the world. But companies in the liquor
business at the time were later shown to be not on the up and up.

Admittedly, I probably saw the entire Gold Seal operation
through the lens of a kid who loved mob movies. Many years later, I
defended a guy who was much closer to the genuine article.

CHAPTER 6

THE CLIENT FROM CENTRAL CASTING

One of my most memorable clients was R. Douglas Spedding. He was about twenty years older than me. When I first met Doug, in the late 1980s, I was a young, struggling lawyer with minimal worldly success. He owned Spedding Chevrolet in Denver and multiple car dealerships around the country. He was one of the most successful car dealers in the United States. After he opened a dealership in Denver, he had read about my case victories representing another car dealer and sought me out. Car dealers are always in need of trial lawyers for the inevitable litigation that is part of their business.

He had a reputation that preceded him. It was said that he was tied in with the boys, you know, involved in some mob or undercover business. Whether these rumors were true or not, I have no idea.

We met so he could interview me. The interview was more like a free-flowing conversation. Right from the start, we joked and bantered. We talked for forty minutes and hit it off.

"Hey, kid," he said near the end, "I'm going to hire you."

As thrilled as I was to have a high-profile client, I needed to make sure that I would get my due payment, so I started spitting numbers at him to make sure he knew what he was in for. I told him I needed $150 an hour. He laughed.

"Kid, for as much as you're going to learn, you ought to be paying me!"

"You're probably right, Doug, but unfortunately for you it doesn't quite work that way," I said. Doug told me that if I lasted working for him for six months—which many lawyers didn't—I'd work for him for life.

That was the beginning of our twenty-year relationship, until his death in 2007.

Doug had been accused of doing some sketchy stuff just before I met him, namely rolling back odometers on his used cars. Of course, when I asked him about it he said, "No, no, no, no, I told them that when they went after me for doing it."

"What about your employees?" I asked.

"Oh yeah, all the time!" he replied.

Terrific, I thought. It turned out that the authorities had tried to prosecute him for this, but there was no federal or state law against it. However, after his case came to trial, Colorado passed a law to make it a crime.

The state was constantly after Doug for something, trying to figure out how they could revoke his license. In all the years that I worked for him, he never told me anything that was not true. He was always honest with me and treated me incredibly well. He was one of the best, and certainly most colorful, clients I have ever had.

Doug was very generous with us and treated not only me but my family very well. My kids grew up spending their summers working for him at the dealership. When my wife, Kathy, turned fifty, Doug said, "Hey, kid, take your wife on the jet for a spin."

Of course, Doug Spedding had a private jet. When my son Scott turned twenty-one, Doug gave us the jet for a trip to Las Vegas. He was always very casual, with a half-smile and a look on his face like he wasn't doing anything more than lending us his lawn mower. "Take it, take it," he'd say.

Doug was also the reason that I got my first cell phone. He told me if I didn't get a cell phone, one of those big, bulky, original cell phones of the 1980s, he would have to find a new lawyer. Though I had been planning to hold out until phones were cheaper, not to mention smaller, for him I relented.

Doug owned a bunch of stuff. Along with several dealerships, he owned the Denver Gold, a team in the now defunct U.S. Football League. He and Donald Trump, who owned the New York Generals, used to bet on the games, and it would always piss Trump off when Spedding won—Spedding won a lot.

I won almost every case I ever tried for him, with the exception of one case against the state. As I say, the state was constantly trying to shut him down. Someone would complain to the state's motor vehicle department, and then the administrators there would have to decide if the complaint was founded or unfounded. No notice was ever given to Doug about the complaints. Eventually, all those complaints built up, and together they made for a pretty convincing case to have his license revoked.

When the administrative hearing on his license was held, it was like walking into a buzz saw, or rather a rigged proceeding. We had no chance. Citing the accretion of violations, the state suspended his license to sell cars.

Doug was incensed. He sent me a letter that essentially said, "Don't you ever win?" I pushed back. At that point, I had already represented him for a number of years and had won at least fifteen cases for him. I fired off a letter listing all of the cases I had won. I also told him that I would get this decision overturned. I angrily licked, stamped, and mailed the letter.

A few days passed, and I realized that I still hadn't heard from him. I called his assistant and asked if my letter had been received. She said, yes, he has it. I asked what he thought of it. She told me that she had heard him laughing in his office after he read it.

I fought the case. I actually pushed it all the way up to the Colorado Supreme Court. The court ruled in our favor, citing a lack of due process. It said, in essence, that it was not fair for the state to let hidden complaints build up and then use them against somebody. The ruling led to the Motor Vehicle Administration reworking and revamping the entire system, so that dealers could see complaints against them as they took place and they could respond.

I also handled the sales of Spedding's dealerships. In one transaction, he sold five of his dealerships to a company called C-Car, which in turn was sold to Auto Nation for in excess of $80 million. Spedding had a real knack for making money.

One of the strangest cases I ever worked on was for Doug Spedding. Doug had met a guy named Tom Rant and decided to go into business with him. Doug made a deal with Rant to buy a Toyota dealership in San Diego from him. The two of them drew up a one-page contract (which Doug didn't run by me). Doug put down $2.5 million and gave Rant a hold on the money until the deal closed. Then things went awry.

Doug called me and told me there was a problem. Rant was refusing to sell him the dealership—and refusing to return the down payment. I took a look at the agreement, which was not a very solid legal document. I told Doug we should meet with Rant.

We hopped on Spedding's private jet and flew to San Diego, where Rant lived. When we landed, Doug turned to me and said, "You wait on the plane, I'll be back."

"I thought you wanted a lawyer with you?" I said.

"Eh," he mumbled under his breath. "Let me see if I can work this out without getting my lawyer involved. One last chance."

An hour later, he returned to the plane. I could tell from the look on his face that it had not gone as planned. He was furious.

"Ya know, in the old days this guy would be in the Detroit River by now," Spedding declared.

Rant had told Doug that because Doug had enough money already, he did not need to return the $2.5 million. Of course, this was patently absurd. It looked like we would be suing Rant after all.

Clearly, the $2.5 million was Spedding's money. Rant's defense was that he was holding the money for the benefit of Spedding. That begged the obvious question: what benefit? It wasn't clear how Rant and his lawyers would be able to convince a jury to let Rant keep the money. It belied common sense, and I planned to exploit that fully.

The trial was held in San Diego in state court. Since I was from out of state, going into the trial I was regarded as a complete unknown with no credibility.

The judge tried to push my buttons on the first day. He wondered aloud if I was just some big-shot lawyer from out of state, hired by a local firm. He also told me that he didn't like litigators. "They're a bunch of paper pushers," he said. "And what are you?"

"I'm a trial lawyer, Judge," I said.

"I guess we're gonna find out," he said ominously, in a half-joking voice. I wasn't quite sure what to make of him.

The trial got underway. Rant's lawyers brought in an expert who went over the details of the flimsy contract that Rant and Spedding had both signed. Basically, he said that Rant could do whatever he wanted with the money, and Spedding didn't have any right to it, because there was nothing in the document about returning the money.

After their expert lawyer had finished up his spiel, I questioned him.

"Let me ask you a question," I began. "If Mr. Rant goes to the Mirage Hotel in Las Vegas and puts this $2.5 million on the line, and some other guy at the craps table throws a seven and he loses it, is the Mirage still holding $2.5 million on behalf of Mr. Spedding?"

The point landed with the jury. I kept harping on the fact that the entire case was absurd. My client had put down money on a transaction that did not happen. The other party could not simply "hold"—as Rant's lawyers put it—my client's money forever.

Before the jury was sent to deliberations, the judge called the lawyers into chambers. He looked at Rant's lawyer, a San Diego local, and asked what he thought. The lawyer said, "This was a nonsense case, Judge."

The judge laughed. "But Mr. Burg here has been crushing you like a grape for this entire lawsuit!" he said. "I advise you to settle it, or I'm going to direct verdict in his favor."

Rant's lawyer and I went outside to try to settle the case, but we couldn't come to an agreement. We came back in and the judge kept his word. He issued a directed verdict for Spedding for the $2.5 million, plus interest and all costs imaginable. He also levied a judgment lien on Rant's house in Lake Tahoe.

Not surprisingly, it turned out that Rant was leveraged to the hilt financially. He was basically broke, though he had a number of assets, including the San Diego dealership that Doug had tried to buy, and a number of houses. In the end, we managed to force the sale of one of Rant's houses to satisfy the judgment.

For years, Spedding continued to deal his cars, and I continued to do his legal work until he passed away. He was the minister of fun, loved by everyone. At his funeral, people showed up from all over the country to pay their respects. It was a beautiful service, wonderfully decorated with white flowers everywhere.

In the middle of the service, the priest rose to speak. In a trembling voice, he said that he was aware that many of us had worked for Doug, been fired by Doug, and crossed paths with Doug. He said that if any of us knew Doug well, then we knew that this was an honor that Doug would appreciate. He fell silent. Seconds later, the sounds of Frank Sinatra singing "My Way" began to filter through the church, right in the middle of the funeral.

It was classic Spedding. His gathered friends and family ate it up. After seeing the response, I decided that I want the same thing at my funeral service—an unexpected moment of lightness delivered by Sinatra.

CHAPTER 7

A YOUNG PROSPECTOR
TAKES TO DENVER

Denver was founded by a group of mining prospectors during the Pike's Peak gold rush in the 1850s and '60s, and the town burgeoned from there, adding stores, saloons, and gambling locales to service the miners. Denver was midway between the coasts, which meant it attracted new immigrants willing to seek out something different with the prospect of finding something great, and in the early days, that meant something lucrative.

From the moment I set foot in Denver, I knew it was perfect for me. I wasn't trying to reinvent myself as much as I was seeking a place that I could become myself. The city immediately became one of my favorite places in the entire world, and the place I call home today.

I was enchanted by the physical beauty and the majesty of the place. In contrast to Chicago, with its closed-in feeling of tall buildings, and its frigid lake-effect winds, Denver had a seemingly infinite blue sky and sweeping mountain vistas. Something about Denver spoke endless possibilities to me as a young man, and it still does. I felt like it was my town, the place where I belonged.

I visited Denver for the first time on a college visit with my mother in the late '60s. I had narrowed down my college choices to the University of Denver and the University of Arizona. Initially, Ohio State was my top choice, but I was rejected due to my poor grades, which left Denver and Arizona as possibilities.

Of the three Burg brothers, I was looking like the underachiever. My younger brother, Peter, was hands down the smartest. He got straight As all through school and went on to win a merit scholarship to Pomona College. He was the president of the high school in his sophomore and junior years. He was the one that our parents looked upon as the bright, shining light in the family. Like me, my older brother, Frank, had his academic struggles in high school, but he ended up at the University of Wisconsin studying psychology. He would go on to earn great grades there and begin a future as one of the most respected experts in the field of safety.

So, with my older brother ahead of me doing well, and my younger brother behind me doing well, I wasn't quite sure what was going to happen to me in college. All I knew was that I was ready to escape the bitter cold of Chicago, and for that, Arizona was the front-runner.

However, when I looked over my class list for the fall of 1968, I saw that it had ROTC requirements, and that made me think twice. The Vietnam War was in full swing. Back then, it did not make any sense to me that we were in Vietnam. I even knew some guys from high school who had gone to fight. I made up my mind that I was not going to spend my first year of college marching and learning to shoot a rifle. And so I decided that I needed to check out one of my other options, the University of Denver.

My mother and I boarded a plane for Denver on a freezing Chicago day in late January. The wind chill was twenty-five below zero, and the wind was whipping off the lake in that miserable, intolerable way that it did every winter day.

I had always thought of Denver as a cold, snowy place, but when the plane landed at Stapleton International Airport, I stepped outside to an unexpectedly beautiful blue sky, sunshine, and a balmy temperature of sixty degrees. In January!

Right then I made up my mind. It didn't matter what the school looked like or if the student body seemed weird, I was going to matriculate at the University of Denver. If I could have those beautiful mountains and sixty degrees in late January, this was the place for me. But first I had to successfully finish high school.

Academically, high school had seemed like a total bust until my junior year when I took a political science elective that had kids of all different academic levels. Being in level 2 and level 3 classes basically guaranteed you a C, because the teachers pegged you as a dummy. But in political science, I was with level 4 and level 5 kids, so teachers could not make any assumptions about intelligence. Rather, they graded justly, based on what I wrote.

It turned out that I wasn't such a dummy after all. I got an A in political science, the hardest class I took in my four years of high school. From that moment on, I understood that if I worked hard and ditched the idea of predetermined futures and intelligence levels, I could succeed. Why limit myself like that? My grades improved in my junior and senior years, and I decided that when I went to college, I wanted to study political science and history, which was another subject in which I discovered I could do well.

My GPA had risen to 2.8 on a 4.0 scale, thanks to all of my newly earned As and Bs my senior year, but I had not yet shed my reputation as a C student. When another guy from my school who had been accepted at the University of Denver got word that we would be in the same class, he came up to me and said, "Wow, I didn't think you were smart enough to get into DU."

I will never forget the sting of those words. They provided yet another motivation for me to prove myself.

In my final year of high school, I finally started to come into my own, to understand who I was and what I wanted to stand for. It happened on all levels.

Consider the tale of Mike Fabry, a 240-pound linebacker on the football team. A big guy with a brutish face and dumb, vacant eyes, Fabry was playing for the other team in a church league basketball game I was playing in. Given his size, he was easy to spot.

During the game, I saw that he was throwing guys around, knocking them down. In the second half, I watched Fabry give one of my pals a shove and knock him to the floor of the court. I had had enough. Even though Fabry hadn't even touched me, I was sick of watching him bully some of my smaller friends. I confronted him and told him to stop. He got right up in my face and said, "Make me."

After the game, Fabry and I went out into the Chicago cold, to a nearby parking lot. My friends all gathered behind me. We faced off like two boxers in a ring. My fists were up, ready to go, and adrenaline was coursing through my veins.

I was ready to take a stand. I thought I could take this guy. He was big, but so was I. I psyched myself up, bouncing on the balls of my feet, taunting Fabry with my eyes. In a flash, he barreled at me, tackled me to the ground, got on top of me, and punched me in the face multiple times. Finally, the other kids pulled him off me.

Even though I walked away with a bloody lip and a black eye, I felt a serene sense of accomplishment. I, Michael Burg, had stood up to this bully for something I believed in. I had stood up for the underdog—my smaller friends. No longer was I afraid of getting beat up for facing down bullies, like those Catholic school kids who took my lunch money all those years ago. It was the beginning of a change that would carry me through the rest of my life, fighting for the underdog and going after the bully. And boy, was it satisfying.

My mother was hesitant to send me to the University of Denver. Growing up, she'd had some nasty experiences with anti-Semites in Colorado. When my mother was a little girl, she and her family visited Colorado, where there were some hotels that at that time did not allow Jews. They had tried to stay at two high-end resorts, the Broadmoor in Colorado Springs and the Brown Palace Hotel in Denver, but were refused rooms in both. Being rejected from these places had left a bad taste in her mouth. But quite frankly, in the 1920s and 1930s, the state was pretty much run by the Ku Klux Klan, which had helped elect the state's governor. By the time I arrived in Denver, it was an entirely different place.

I took to the University of Denver immediately. I actually had a few buddies from high school there with me. At first I wasn't thrilled, because I wanted to have a fresh start—new place, new people—but it turned out to be good to have familiar faces around.

I adjusted academically with flying colors. My first quarter at Denver, I pulled straight As. For a guy who had struggled academically for the majority of my high school career, this changed the way I thought about myself. I began to think, "Oh my goodness, maybe I'm not an idiot after all." In my four years of school at Denver, I only ever earned one C. The rest were all As and Bs, exceptional by my high school standards.

I also joined the Phi Sigma Delta fraternity and was eventually elected vice president of the pledge class. There was camaraderie and raucous fun, but being hazed and harassed by some of the older jerks reminded me of the way the older kids in the neighborhood treated me when I was a kid.

Fraternity parties were a blast. To this day, I remain friends with some of the guys I met there, but frat life did not become a cornerstone of my college experience.

There were other major changes in my life. After a long, dry spell in my love life in high school, I finally started dating in college. There were some beautiful women in Denver, and now that I was a good student and a frat boy, my confidence was riding high.

My sophomore year I began dating a woman whom I will call Sue-Anne from Colorado Women's College. Her father was the mayor of a major city in the Northwest, so her family was well connected. One beautiful, temperate day, we were hanging out together. By this time, I had a car with me at college, so I suggested that we make it a date out and take an overnight road trip to Yellowstone Park, where neither of us had ever been. She agreed that sounded very romantic.

We got into the car and set out for Yellowstone. We laughed and talked the entire way. But when we hit Casper, Wyoming, we ran into a blizzard. This was long before the days of smartphone weather apps. Neither of us had thought to check the forecast because back in Denver it had been an absolutely spectacular day.

Now we were stuck in a blizzard. It was a whiteout, with snow blowing so hard at the windshield that I could barely see past the hood of the car. Worse, I was driving a Camaro, which did not have snow tires. I decided to turn back, but the police had put up a roadblock. They were going car to car, telling drivers that the road to Denver was closed until the storm passed.

My date's face turned dark and cloudy. She was not at all happy with the situation. I tried to keep the mood light by cracking jokes. I even put The Beatles' "Here Comes the Sun" on the eight-track player in my car, thinking that would make her smile.

We backtracked as far as we could to Cheyenne, Wyoming. I had very little money, just enough for an inexpensive meal, but I did have my father's Amoco gas station credit card. I drove around looking for a motel where we could ride out the storm. Eventually, I spotted a place called Little America, a combination gas station and motel. It looked a little questionable from the outside, but we desperately needed a place to stay.

Sue-Anne and I walked into the lobby that somehow reminded me of the Bates Motel in Alfred Hitchcock's movie *Psycho*. There was a chubby, bored-looking guy behind the counter, who thankfully didn't look too threatening to me. I walked up to the desk.

"Does this card work for a room?" I asked, holding out my Amoco credit card.

Sue-Anne was standing right beside me. The guy looked from me to her and back to me, then down to the Amoco card. He eyeballed the card and nodded his head. "Yeah, it works," he said. "You two on your honeymoon?"

I laughed awkwardly. "Yeah, that's right," I said. "Honeymoon in a blizzard."

"We have the honeymoon suite for the same price as a regular room, but whatever you want to do is cool with me," he said.

Sue-Anne and I exchanged a look. The honeymoon suite sounded pretty good to us, especially for the same price. I nodded yes. The desk clerk took the card and gave us the key. We headed to our room.

Now, the honeymoon suite in the Little America does not compare to the honeymoon suite at Caesars Palace, but it was a bigger-than-average room with a king-sized bed and a semi-clean-looking Jacuzzi tub. It would work for the night.

We decided to venture back out into the storm to find a place to eat dinner. When we returned to the honeymoon suite, the room phone was ringing.

"That's weird," I said, genuinely confused and wondering who would be calling us at the Little America.

I picked up the phone. It was my mother! She was hysterically yelling into the phone, "What are you, married now?" My dad was on an extension yelling as well. "Don't you understand the Mann Act?" he said. "You know you just took a girl under the age of twenty-one across the state line, right?"

I explained the situation and the poor planning that led to our plight. My parents insisted that we stay in separate rooms. They also sternly added that they were finished paying for my school, I was done in Denver, and I had better be ready to transfer closer to home.

Those threats later turned out to be a product of their hysterics of the moment—of them picturing a prominent Northwestern political family coming after me for violating that Mann Act with their daughter. Whatever the Mann Act was.

As soon as I hung up the phone, there was a knock on the door. I opened it. Two police officers were staring at me. They explained that they were investigating a report that a stolen credit card had been used to pay for the room. Clearly, the desk clerk who had been so nice as to give us the honeymoon suite had reported us to the police.

We eventually made it back to Denver, but I never saw Sue-Anne again after that weekend.

Despite that experience, I developed a reputation as a guy who delivered on his promises. My junior year I was living far from the campus with three other guys, Eddie Silberman, Bruce Nathanson, and Scott Feldman. Nearby was a place called the House of Pies, which sold nothing but pies. You name it, cherry pies, cream pies, chocolate, coconut—if it was a pie, they had it. One Sunday nights, there was always a debate of who was going to make the pie run.

I volunteered. As I was leaving, I asked the guys if they wanted anything else. Bruce quipped, "Yeah, four women! Four nice, young, cute women."

I stopped. "All right, what's it worth if I can bring back four lovely ladies with the pie?"

They all agreed on fifty bucks each. Given that I was twenty years old and had no gainful employment, the prospect of the money sounded better than banana cream pie. Off I went.

Near the House of Pies was a local bar called the College Inn, which was near the Colorado University campus hospital. I knew that the nurses from the hospital went there to unwind after their shifts, so after picking up a pie, I made that my first stop.

I walked in and sure enough I spotted four young ladies sitting in a booth sharing a pitcher of beer. I went over to them and told them the situation: I had been sent out for a pie and four ladies by my roommates, and I explained that the ladies carried a fifty dollar reward each for me. I added that we were all fresh-faced, nice young men.

They went for it! Next thing I know, they were following me home.

When we arrived, I told them to stay behind me. I opened the door and announced I had the pie. Bruce started to say something about the women, but I stopped him midsentence.

"And by the way, I've got four really great ladies," I said.

We all hung out and talked. None of them really dated or anything, but it was still fun. I got my hundred and fifty bucks, and more important, my roommates never doubted me again.

❧

My senior year at the University of Denver, I met Debbie White. Debbie and I became serious very quickly, escalating from drink dates to dinners to meeting the parents and, eventually, talk of marriage.

Debbie was a tall, beautiful, dark-haired woman with a refined, New England quality about her, a lightness and a grace. She was from Stamford, Connecticut, a pretty, albeit incredibly Catholic, area. The house she grew up in was a mansion, at least by my Wilmette standards. It was situated directly on the Long Island Sound and I thought it had a certain Gatsby-esque quality.

The Whites belonged to the Stamford Yacht Club. At the time, the club had no Jewish members. Her parents, even though they were very different from me, were good, kind people, and they accepted me for who I was.

As my college career drew to a close, I decided that I would go to law school. I began looking around the country at different schools, but my relationship with Debbie was always in the back of my mind. As I began considering law schools in other parts of the country, I wasn't sure what would happen with us. Debbie had already accepted a job teaching school in Denver, so she needed to remain there. It was up to me, basically, whether we would stay together or not.

At that time, Debbie and I were infatuated with one another. Ours was a relationship of compromise and support, one that was very healthy. At that point, we had bright futures ahead of us and dreams of being an ideal lawyer–school teacher couple.

It seemed very possible. Denver was my world of dreams. Every day I lived there I discovered something new. More and more, it seemed as though I had been there before, in another life. To this day, I am still coming to terms with my spiritual beliefs, but there have been few times in my life when I felt such strong, powerful instances of déjà vu that it really makes me wonder whether I had a past life in Denver.

It seemed that Michael Burg and Debbie White's future was in Denver, and we could make our dreams come true there. But I had to decide whether that was the best place for me to pursue my dream of becoming a lawyer, and not just any lawyer—one that could make a difference in the world.

CHAPTER 8

CLEARING THE BAR

Clarence Darrow was the ultimate lawyer. At thirteen, I read *Clarence Darrow for the Defense* by Irving Stone, a book that inspired me to want to become a lawyer. That book led to a profound sense of respect and admiration for the way one man risked everything and set aside his own life to defend the downtrodden.

I was riveted by Darrow's work. In the 1925 Scopes "Monkey" trial, he defended the right of a teacher to teach human evolution in violation of a Tennessee law. In the Leopold–Loeb trial, he defended two University of Chicago students who had murdered a fellow student with the egotistical endeavor to commit "the perfect crime." At the end of their trial, when the two boys were essentially condemned to life in prison, Darrow gave what is said to have been the best speech of his career, in which he criticized the use of capital punishment in the criminal justice system.

Darrow was a powerful orator. He had a unique way of engaging the judge and the jury, and guiding them through a finely crafted argument while also entertaining them. The way he created a map with words caused something in me to light up. He inspired me to want to follow in his footsteps, to be both a persuasive and a moral person, and to help others in the most significant way possible.

What struck me was that Darrow always fought for the rights of individuals. In addition to the Leopold–Loeb case and the Scopes trial, I read about *Debs vs. the United States*, in which he defended Eugene Debs' right to speak out against World War I, despite laws on the books that forbade him from doing so.

In these cases, Darrow had an unflinching track record, fighting for issues that mattered to me, and that I thought should matter to everyone. In the Leopold–Loeb case, he fought against the death penalty. In the Debs case, it was for free speech. And in the Scopes case, it was for the right to teach evolution in a public school.

Ironically, the debate over evolution versus the Bible continues to rage to this day. We certainly chuckle at the fact that doubters of science continue to exist as they did in the late 1800s. We have taken a few giant steps as mankind since then, but we still have plenty of stragglers.

After reading Irving Stone's book on Darrow and watching *Perry Mason* on TV, it occurred to me that I could become a lawyer. Even more, I *wanted* to become a lawyer. I wasn't entirely sure exactly what lawyers did other than provide theatrics in a courtroom, but I decided early on that that was the career I wanted to aim for. I was also hit by something that seemed obvious. Darrow once said, "The only real lawyers are trial lawyers, and trial lawyers try cases to juries." Clearly, if I ever wanted to be a *real* lawyer, according to Darrow, I would need to be a trial lawyer. I held on to these thoughts through college. After four years were up at the University of Denver, it was time to start making moves on the future I had been dreaming of since middle school. I had scored well on my LSAT exam, so I decided to aim high for law school. I applied to Georgetown, George Washington, Yale, Stanford, and my beloved University of Denver. I didn't get in everywhere, but I was admitted to my top choice at the time—Georgetown.

At the same time, I was committed to my relationship with Debbie White. I wondered, though, if it might be time to move on from Denver for the opportunities that would be offered to me in the nation's capital.

Seeking a learned opinion on my move East, I called 10th Circuit Court of Appeals Judge William Doyle, hoping to talk to him about law schools. I suppose it was a rather gutsy move, but I just picked up the phone and called him. I knew Doyle had gone to Georgetown, and I wanted to talk. To my surprise, he agreed to meet with me. As we sat down for lunch, Judge Doyle looked at me and pointedly asked if I wanted to be a government lawyer. I said that no, I wanted to be a trial lawyer. After all, Darrow had informed me that that was the only kind of real lawyer.

The judge deadpanned: "Then why would you want to go to Georgetown in Washington, DC? And by the way, where do you want to live after that?" It took just one meeting with Judge Doyle for me to realize that I did not want to leave Denver. The city was in my blood. I knew already that I could build a life there, and it seemed like a perfect place to raise a family. I easily gave Judge Doyle the answer to his second question, which led to me fully contemplating the first question.

I left the lunch meeting with a clearly defined path ahead of me. I would attend the University of Denver law school, move in with Debbie, and from there we would build a life together. This wasn't a compromise; personally or professionally there was simply no reason to do otherwise. I was setting my own path.

Law school itself was not nearly as difficult as I thought it would be. I actually did pretty well, considering I had to put up with some colorful professors along the way. One of my professors was named Thompson Marsh. He was straight out of the movie *Paper Chase*. Like John Houseman's Professor Kingsfield, Marsh was dictatorial and unrelenting. He would make his students stand up in class and ask us questions as if he were cross-examining us. He might ask, "What's the Black Letter Law?" Or he would pick a case and say, "What are the facts being relied on? What's the decision being made?"

Marsh had no tolerance for grade-grubbing ciphers. To him, no question was too hard, and we were expected to know everything. He wanted to see if we were truly comprehending and grappling with the material the way he thought real law students should. He insisted that we underline in our textbooks, using black, red, or green ink depending on the type of material.

The syllabus said that Thompson Marsh taught property law, but in that class we learned very little about property law, other than that the shape of property was an inverted pyramid that went all the way down to the center of the earth. By the way, that was a question on his final exam. In his class, I learned how to learn the law.

I also had the privilege of taking Conflicts of Law with an adjunct professor of the law school named Joe Branney, who was one of the finest personal injury lawyers in the country. Throughout law school, I was a solid B student, but Conflicts of Law was different. The class was difficult and also confusing.

I took that class with Branney in the final semester of my final year of law school. Because I was clerking at the firm of Ireland Stapleton Pryor & Holmes at the time, I needed all the credits I could pull together to graduate on schedule. I became concerned that my entire GPA could be derailed by Branney's class.

Just before grades were due to be posted, I received a phone call from Professor Branney. I picked up the phone and listened to him announce his name as if he were appearing in court. He then asked if I was "present."

I had a sinking feeling and started to sweat. As I pressed the phone to my ear, I could already hear the words I was dreading: *Sorry to report, Michael, but you've unfortunately failed my class.* I thought back to when I was studying for the exam with some other students, and how different all of my notes had been from theirs. I was sure that my answers on the multiple choice questions, as well as the essays, were drastically different from everyone else's. But had they been all wrong?

My heart pounded and I cleared my throat. "Yes, this is Michael Burg, sir," I said.

"Is this Lucky Burg?" he said, lightening his tone.

Immediately, I breathed a sigh of relief. I thought that I must have just passed by one point or something absurdly close like that. Why else would he be calling me lucky?

"Well, this is Mike Burg," I said, unsure of where he was going.

"I have to ask you a question then, Mr. Mike Burg," Professor Branney continued. "I read your test, and either you're the smartest person I've ever had of all the students I've ever taught, or you're the luckiest."

My heart pounded on. "Let me assure you, Professor Branney, I am the luckiest."

"I'm not so sure about that, Mr. Burg," he said. "I've read your paper and it's the finest exam I've read in all of my years of teaching. And you will be getting the A and the AmJur Award." The AmJur Award, or American Jurisprudence Award, is given to the student in class who gets the A-1, or highest grade.

I couldn't believe it. One of the best trial lawyers in the state of Colorado had just told me that my exam was the finest he had ever read and that I was receiving the highest award given in a law school class. I thanked Professor Branney profusely. The triumph was incredibly affirming. I was on top of the world.

When I hung up, I knew in my gut that someday I would be a trial lawyer—and a great one at that.

I was still clerking for Ireland Stapleton. I felt that I could stick with them for the long haul, climb my way up in the ranks, and establish myself at that firm and therefore in Denver's legal circles.

I had decided to start working both for the experience and the extra money. My parents had been very generous. They had paid for my education and for most of my expenses. But I was growing up, and it was time to start supporting myself. I had worked a little on and off through college, but in law school I wanted to commit myself to something a little more serious than the local college bar.

Things went well for a while at Ireland Stapleton. I worked alongside the son of the former mayor Ben Stapleton, who was a senior partner. I was confident that I could stay there and make a career with this very prominent firm. After all, this was the path I had set for myself when I stayed in Denver.

My mentor was Bob Hawley, a Harvard graduate who had tutored me in school. He had a pleasant face, with a full head of hair fraying along the sides. He was a generous man, and he treated me with respect.

One day he invited me to lunch with "a surprise guest." When I arrived at the table, I saw that he was sitting next to an older gentleman with a stern face, squarish, thin-framed glasses, and half a head of dark hair. I did a double take. It was Associate Justice Byron White of the U.S. Supreme Court, former halfback for the Colorado Buffaloes, and All-American player. I was speechless.

During lunch, I sat in awe and listened to these two great lawyers talk. I must have seemed like a quiet, awkward student to Justice White, but it was only because I was so awestruck. At one point, Justice White asked me what I wanted to do. I proudly told him that I wanted to try cases and be a trial lawyer. He wished me luck.

Unfortunately, my stint at Ireland, Stapleton turned out to be much shorter than I had anticipated. After a year of clerking, the partners had a meeting to determine whether or not to extend me a job offer. Bob Hawley called me into his office to deliver the news of the partners' vote. He said that I would be working with him and Gretchen VanderWerf, another lawyer, doing environmental law. But there was a snag.

The head of their trial team was a man named Ken Starr. (No, not the special prosecutor against President Clinton, but a different yet difficult Ken Starr all his own.) This Ken Starr was a Harvard graduate who thought himself to be the smartest trial lawyer in the world. Hawley explained to me that if I wanted to work there, I would have to work with Ken Starr. Problem was, Starr had already told me that he would never let me try cases, and that I would be carrying his briefcase for him for the next five years, which didn't appeal to me much.

I decided that I would look elsewhere. I knew that I wanted to be a trial lawyer, and I reasoned that I needed to work at a firm where I could get into the courtroom sooner rather than later. The courtroom was where the action was; that was where I wanted to be.

After talking to a few other law firms in Denver, I received an offer from Atler, Zall & Haligman. They recruited me and another aspiring lawyer named Theodore Gelt, who worked in the tax department. Apparently, I impressed him with my work and demeanor, and he recommended me to the other partners when they were looking for a trial lawyer.

The firm offered me a job with a starting salary of $11,200 a year. This was big money for me at the time, so I accepted the offer on the spot. It was very exciting. I had a job at a major Denver firm—with decent pay. This was my first "big boy" job. Now all I had to do was pass the Colorado bar exam, and I would be all set to work and try cases.

I studied extremely hard. I skipped nights out with my friends and stayed in with Debbie while she graded papers and assignments. Debbie and I had established a good rhythm. With my new job and her continuing as a teacher, I felt we had a solid foundation under us. By then, I had already proposed to her, and we had made plans to be married by both a priest and a rabbi in Stamford, Connecticut, where Debbie grew up.

Being Jewish was not an issue with her parents, though it did provide for a few awkward moments. As we were planning the wedding, Debbie's mother wanted to know if our kids would wear "beanies" when they grew up. I had to explain to her, gently, that they weren't beanies; they were called yarmulkes.

We were not long married, and I had taken the bar exam. Debbie and I were holding our breath, to see if I had passed—thereby firing the starting pistol on our future. The exam was very difficult. The tests were written in blue composition books and my handwriting was still terrible, that same seventh-grade, chicken-scratch handwriting that Mrs. Douglas had railed against. I understood that I would lose points if my handwriting was illegible. I attempted to write as quickly and clearly as possible, but because of the time constraints, I feared that much of what I wrote might not have been entirely legible.

I waited on pins and needles for the results. I had my job. I was newly married. I was ready to try cases. My life was set to begin. I just need a passing grade on the Colorado bar exam.

On a blustery day in October 1975, the letter finally arrived in our mailbox. It was almost like receiving college decision letters. I opened the door to the mailbox and pulled out a thin, white envelope in my hands, unsure of whether the lightness even had a connotation one way or the other. Hands trembling, I tore open the envelope. I had failed the bar exam and I had failed it by one-tenth of a point. *One-tenth.*

How could I have failed? How could I have come so close and failed? I was absolutely despondent, and contemplated the consequences. This meant that I now had to tell everyone—Debbie, my parents, and, most important, the partners at Atler, Zall & Haligman—that I had failed the bar exam. Surely, this would be the end of my brand-new dream job. I felt as though my life and my future plans were crumbling away at the center.

My parents could tell how upset I was. They made a trip to Colorado from Chicago and took Debbie and me on a little getaway to Aspen to try to calm me down and reassure me.

With a heavy, worried heart, I delivered the bad news to the partners at Atler, Zall & Haligman. To my relief, they decided to let me stay on. But the catch was, they were going to start looking for someone else to hire, just in case I didn't pass the bar the next time. They told me, very seriously, that I had failed to meet their requirements and that they were on the edge of a precipice, deciding whether or not they would keep me on.

I appealed to have them keep me without any caveats, as I had only failed the exam by one-tenth of a point. Surely, I would pass next time. Of course, they denied the appeal and mandated that I had better pass the second time. I was so frustrated by the bar exam grading system that I asked to meet with Justice Groves, who was a Colorado Supreme Court Justice at the time. I presented him with my narrow failing grade.

Justice Groves seemed somewhat sympathetic that the margin of failure was so slight. But he explained to me that if they had let me pass short just a tenth of a point, that would create a slippery slope. What about the people who had failed by two-tenths? What was the real difference? What he said made sense, in honor of fairness, but I still found it infuriating.

To this day, I think the bar exam is a pretty ridiculous way of gauging a lawyer's worth and preparedness. It has nothing to do with whether or not you can practice law and be a competent lawyer. It is a trick test, designed to trip you up.

The great Gerry Spence, a nationally known trial attorney from Wyoming who had a huge case against *Penthouse*, and who has authored a number of books on how to be a trial attorney, and Federal Judge Sherman Finesilver, one of the finest judges I have ever met—a *federal judge*, for crying out loud—failed the bar the first time. There is no longer any shame for me to tell people that I failed the bar, especially now that I have become well-established nationally, and my opinion on that ridiculous test is respected. But back then, nobody cared what I thought.

I never went around trying to hide that I had failed. Obviously, when I was younger and the failure was fresh, I did not introduce myself to everyone saying, "Hi, I'm Michael S. Burg, bar failure." But I certainly never denied it if it came up.

A few years ago, I was actually approached to be a bar grader. That was the fastest and most emphatic "No" I ever gave in my life. I continue to believe that the bar is the most ridiculous exam in the world.

In 2013, I had to take an ethics test, a similar exam to the bar, to be admitted to try cases in Arizona. As I was reading the questions, I was thinking to myself, who cares? The questions were things like, "Is X a mandatory conflict? Is Y a permissive conflict?" The bottom line is, no lawyer has all those terms memorized. When you are a lawyer working on a case, you look it up. For the record, I passed the test and am admitted in the Arizona courts, but in my opinion, those kinds of tests do not measure anything meaningful.

Unfortunately, at the time, failing the bar was a setback on my budding law career. Staying on at the firm meant taking a pay cut to clerk level. Not having the extra money I had been expecting proved difficult for my home life because we were already living on a very tight budget.

Debbie and I lived in a small, inexpensive apartment. I did everything I could to save money, which for me meant eating at Burger King almost every day. Debbie and I talked about buying a house, but of course, neither of us had the money for that kind of investment. We discussed borrowing money from our parents, especially Debbie's.

After we were married, her father retired, at a relatively early age, and moved to Pinehurst, North Carolina, to play golf. He never worked again after age sixty-two. Her family was well connected. They were related to the Henry family—as in the Founding Father Patrick Henry. Debbie's grandmother, who was still alive at the time, told me that her husband, Debbie's grandfather, had been a dentist in Cambridge and had gambled a lot of their money away. He had also become good friends with the Kennedys and Fitzgeralds. They had lived in a small, wealthy community in Cambridge, and happened to be neighbors with the right people.

I knew that if I asked my parents, they would lend us money. But when I proposed the idea to Debbie, she was less than enthused. I told her I would only ask my parents if she would get half from her parents. She never asked her parents and I said, "I do not want to ask my parents. We'll be indebted to them forever, even after we pay the money back, and that's too high a price to pay."

I then proposed that she ask her parents. "They won't do it," she said.

We decided to hold off asking anyone and to try to make the money on our own. In addition to clerking at the law firm, I managed to pick up another job teaching business law at Metro State College, as well as teaching a class at Colorado Women's College.

Through the mid-to-late 1970s I was teaching pretty much every night and so I was able to supplement my income. Coupled with Debbie's teaching salary, we managed to cobble enough money together so that we could buy a small house.

Even though I had failed the bar once, I was certainly not about to give up. Alongside all of my jobs, I was studying even harder than before. I was determined to pass this time. To me, failure was not an option.

It was torture taking the bar exam a second time. I was confident that I knew the material already. It didn't hurt my ego too much to have failed the first time, because from talking to many other people in law, I understood that the bar exam had very little to do with a person's ability.

My determination paid off. I passed the second time. I finally had the green light to start my career. My salary jumped back up to a lawyer's level. Debbie and I knew that we could afford to start a family, and we began to figure out how and where and when. It was a very exciting time in our marriage. All the necessary ingredients for our future seemed to be coming together.

CHAPTER 9

"ROW, ROW, ROW YOUR BOAT
GENTLY"—TO THE COURT

I walked into the courtroom to try my first case. It was my court-room debut as a lawyer, and it was exhilarating. I felt like a basket-ball player starting in his first NBA game. I knew these rooms from TV shows and movies, but to be there, in person, to start a trial that I was involved in was something else. It was a moment that I had waited for a long time.

I took in the row of benches that made up the gallery, a place for friends, family, and spectators to sit and watch the trial. I moved along the aisle and approached the long rail dividing the room. I paused at the bar, and looked beyond it to the two plain wide coun-sel tables, then off to the right to the jury box, and finally the bench itself with witness stands on either side.

The bench was intimidating. Elevated and made of rich, shiny wood, the bench stood nobly and proudly before me. The great seal of the state of Colorado was mounted on the wall behind it, flanked by two American flags.

I hovered at the bar, an ironic place for me to pause. I remem-bered failing the bar exam, and all the extra time and effort I had to put in to earn my right to become a lawyer. With great relish, I unlatched the knee-high door that separated the public half of the courtroom from the private, elite half where the lawyers took center stage to argue cases. What a feeling to pass the bar—and now to cross *this* bar—and to step into my new world, the world in which I knew I belonged.

Here was the case: a new homeowner had filed a claim against our client, a real estate company by the name of Van Schaack at the time, alleging they were aware that the house they bought had water damage but had failed to tell them about it. Our key witness was one of the sellers. The husband said he knew of no water damage that had occurred prior to the time of the sale. He and his wife had divorced, and so his former wife was going to testify.

I arrived on the day of the trial and met with Jack Silver, a lawyer with Atler, Zall & Haligman. He had been the original lawyer on the case, and I had been assigned to work with him. Jack gave me a firm handshake and prepped me for the case. He talked softly to me as we walked through the main entry hall of the courthouse.

"This case is probably going to be a loser," he began, "so I think our best bet is to try to discredit the witnesses. The evidence clearly shows that there was water damage, and the realtor either knew or should have known about it. You'll be cross-examining a witness or two, so get excited, Bud."

His voice dripped with good-natured sarcasm, but he didn't have to tell me twice. I really was excited, and more than ready. But I was hoping we'd be able to pull a win out, somehow.

Once the trial was underway, the wife spoke about the severity of the water damage. She said that at one point, she and her husband went down to check out the basement and couldn't even reach the bottom few steps because of how much water there was.

"I mean, it was just terrible," the woman said. "There was so much water that to get around the basement my husband and I hopped in a plastic basin that was actually *floating* around, and we could actually *sit* in it. We sang, 'Row, Row, Row Your Boat, Gently Down the Stream' because it was just so ridiculous that it was a perfect time to sing it."

She explained how they had called the emergency department and had the water situation corrected, but that the damage was never fully repaired. She insisted that they had, without a doubt, let the realtor know prior to the point of sale, contradicting her ex-husband's statement.

In my cross-examination, I asked this woman numerous questions concerning the basin that she claimed to have floated in during her "Row, Row, Row Your Boat" story.

"Were you actually sitting in it as the basin was floating?" I asked. "Because your husband looks like a heavy guy." I paused to let my question sink in, as everyone had seen her 250-pound husband. "How in the world would it continue to float?"

A few chuckles came from the gallery. But the lady stuck by her story, claiming that she and her husband were sitting, or at least kneeling, in the basin while they sang the song in the midst of their basement flood.

I glanced over to the bench to see how far I could go with my line of questioning. I noticed that the judge appeared to be sleeping, which struck me as funny. This was a "trial to the court," which meant the judge, not a jury, was going to make a decision. Testimony made it clear that the realtor, lies or not, knew or should have known about the water damage and should have disclosed that to the buyer.

As the trial was coming to a close, with just a few more minutes before closing arguments, Jack Silver leaned over to me and whispered in my ear.

"Hey, Mike, I've got to leave court a little early for a call," he said. "You're going to do the closing argument."

"What?" I mumbled. I glanced over at the judge again, who still appeared to be sleeping.

I was not at all prepared to do the closing. It appeared to me that Jack was making up excuses to leave because he didn't want to hang around to hear the verdict. He clearly thought we were going to lose. He ignored my quizzical response, gathered his papers, and ducked calmly out of the courtroom, leaving me on my own.

Well, I wanted to be a trial lawyer, so here I was. When the judge appeared to look in my general direction, I knew it was time for me to stand up and sing. I rose, looked him straight in the eye, and said, with a pounding heart, "Judge, there has been no credible evidence in this case. It doesn't make any sense that anyone would be singing 'Row, Row, Row Your Boat' while their house was being damaged. That's all, your honor."

And with that, I sat down, feeling my face burning a bright red. I felt like a fool, trying to sabotage someone who was clearly telling the truth, but that's what I was there to do.

The plaintiff's attorney rose and eloquently argued that there was evidence of water damage from the fact that repair records existed, but also because the sellers had openly indicated that there had been water damage. There were clearly visible lines and marks along the walls, but it was a very old house and it was hard to know if the marks were the result of water damage.

At this point, the entire room was in the plaintiff's favor, as of course, they should have been. Even I knew from the start that we weren't walking out with a victory in this case.

At the end of the trial, the judge finally seemed to wake up. He decided that he would issue his opinion from the bench. He looked out with his bright blue eyes sunk into the folds of his wrinkled face, across the room from the plaintiff to the witnesses for the defense to me. And then he spoke in a tone of judicial wisdom.

"Over the course of this two-day trial, it is my opinion that there has been no evidence at all that there were any signs of water damage, which the realtor knew or should have known about," he proclaimed.

There was a moment of perplexed silence in the court. Nobody, especially me, had expected this outcome. For a second I thought it was some kind of joke, but that was it. Case closed.

The gavel rang out in the courtroom. I sat there, dumbstruck. Somehow, I had won my first case. I was pretty sure that my closing had nothing to do with it, and that the only reason we had won was because the judge had slept through all the evidence.

However, as time has gone by and I've thought back to my first victory after all these years, I stand by one thing: *nobody* whose house is being damaged by water is going to be so casual about it that they would sing nursery rhymes—plastic basin boat or not—in the face of thousands of dollars of damage repairs to come. So not only did I get my first win, but also, the judge ultimately got it right.

I was bitten by the bug in my first trial. From that trial forward, my favorite part of the process of being a trial attorney has been walking into a courtroom and trying cases. This is why I signed up for the career in the first place.

The courtroom is the lawyer's "playing field," as it were. It is our baseball diamond, our football stadium, our basketball court. It is the place where all the fruits of our labor come to life. Once a lawyer enters the courtroom, there is no turning back. If the lawyer doesn't know his or her stuff, the client is being done a tremendous disservice, and, so in some instances, is the law itself.

I have come a long way since that first case. I have faced some two hundred juries. But my process is the same every time. When I walk into a courtroom to face a newly seated jury, I find a way to consolidate an entire case and explain it to them in the time allotted by the judge—generally just a few minutes.

It might be a case I have worked on for years. It might be a case with hundreds of thousands, even millions, of pages of documents, and I might have spent countless hours poring over those documents to pick out all the critical details of the case. I might have met with dozens of witnesses, taken hours of deposition testimony, and digested an unending series of papers, memos, letters, and records on the case.

Yet there I stand, facing men and women who know *nothing* about a single fact of the case. Most of them, in fact, know nothing at all about the process of a trial to begin with. I have to use my allotted minutes carefully and try to take all the years and all the volumes of documents and all the testimony and find a way to make them understand in a half hour what has taken me an inordinate amount of time to wrap my head around. This is not for the faint of heart, nor is it a task I take lightly.

The jurors I face are likely not very happy to be sitting in what are probably uncomfortable chairs, in a small courtroom. Some of them are too hot, some are too cold. Most have been removed from their own lives for a period of days or even weeks, so that they can perform their civic duty by sitting on a jury. All of them are uncomfortable to some degree.

My job is not to make them pay attention and learn all that I've learned, or to teach them the relevant case law, or to enlighten them about how much time I've spent learning all the things I could never make them understand in half an hour. My job is to make them want to do the right thing. My job is to make them understand that a person's future is in their hands, and that they have at their disposal one of the most precious rights we have: the right to a trial by a jury of our peers.

When I approach the jury, I explain the way they should look at all the evidence that is about to be presented to them. I have to take myself a little bit out of where I am most comfortable, too: as a seasoned trial attorney with a lot of knowledge, facing jurors who have little to no knowledge about our legal system, the trial system, courtroom etiquette, or the court's rules and regulations. Many people don't understand that individual courts even have their own sets of rules and regulations. Every court must adhere not only to the rules of evidence and the rules of civil procedure, but there are also "local" rules. These are rules that every judge sets for his or her own courtroom and if you don't follow them, your entire case can be affected.

Judges, in their long, black robes, sitting behind a high bench, can be very intimidating, and so can the uniformed marshals and deputies armed with guns.

I have to remind myself that the jury is not where I am in terms of understanding the case or the process, and I have to take some giant steps backward to find an entry point where I can allow them to come into the case so that I can begin to explain the facts in a way that they can understand.

The lawyer's job is to draw a picture for the jury, which is a lot like putting together a jigsaw puzzle. I can do that only by giving the jury individual pieces, one at a time, to construct a picture, just like the picture on the cover of a puzzle box. As evidence is introduced, I assemble it for the jury like the pieces of a puzzle.

I have learned that a jury must hear all the evidence before they can piece together the facts of a case and realize what the finished puzzle is supposed to look like—or at least what I want it to look like. My job is to lead them there, piece by piece, until they can clearly see the same picture that I've been looking at for months, or even years.

The most interesting aspect of the evidence, however, is that the pieces are never quite that easy to assemble in light of all the component parts of a case. There are witnesses, reports, records, medical issues, permanent and temporary issues, job-loss or wage-loss issues, emotional issues, and psychological issues that the client is dealing with.

Often what happens is that I construct an issue, piece by piece, and then assemble the smaller pieces into a larger piece. Once the larger pieces have been established, I can begin to put those pieces together to further define the more complete picture. This process can also be described as removing layers and layers of film, one layer at a time. Though definition and detail start to emerge after only a few layers have been peeled back, the overall image is not fully visible until the very last layer of film has been peeled away.

From that very first trial in the basement flood case, I realized that I needed to make certain the jury did not draw conclusions about the case too quickly. I needed to show them the small pieces, some of which might seem insignificant, and then convince them they added up to the larger picture. I approach the assembly of my life and career in a similar way.

CHAPTER 10

SO A LAWYER WALKS
INTO A COMEDY CLUB

I have always felt that the best lawyers were the ones who had other creative outlets. I know some lawyers who paint to clear their heads, while others have taken up gardening. Sports are a big outlet to blow off steam and can be creative—though I don't include golf in this category because it's so frustrating. For me, I took this idea in a slightly different direction and tried my hand at stand-up comedy in the early '80s.

I don't know exactly why I was interested. Partly, I just wanted to try it, to see how far crazy Mike Burg could take it. My wife, Debbie, thought I was losing my marbles. I thought I was pretty funny—maybe wrongly so. I would guess all comedians, be it a guy on amateur night or Jerry Seinfeld, believe that to some degree. Though I can get quite caught up with myself sometimes, I honestly believed I could get up on stage and make people laugh. And I wanted to try. I wanted to know what it felt like to be on stage and make a room full of people laugh.

Strangely, I was never the funny one growing up or in school. From grade school through law school, I was fairly serious. But I loved to laugh, and I knew it would be so great and rewarding to give that to other people, too—provided I could.

I had always admired comedians. My affinity for stand-up was solidified from my very first trip to Las Vegas. Every time after that when I visited the city, I would seek out a comedy show. That was part of the fun of being in Vegas for me. Over the years, I saw Don Rickles, Bob Newhart, Sam Kinison, Johnny Carson, Milton Berle, Howie Mandel, Joan Rivers, Rodney Dangerfield, and Sinbad (who I played basketball against in Denver), among others. I left every show feeling uplifted and happy to be alive.

In my daily life, I was always noticing offbeat things and coming up with little jokes to tell to anyone who would listen, at the office, at home, or at a party. One day I finally just said to myself, why not? I'm going to try it—which tends to be my motto.

I went to the Comedy Works club in downtown Denver that had an amateur night. You auditioned the day before and if they liked you, you were up. The performers were given two minutes at the microphone to impress the audience. To use comedy parlance, some people killed, others died.

On this particular Tuesday, the room wasn't packed. I worked out my two minutes on the stage, and then I spoke to the maestro, Matt Berry, who gave me the go-ahead.

I stepped up onto the elevated stage. A spotlight was shining directly into my eyes. I could barely see anyone in the audience. A tall stool was set up just in front of the microphone, in case the performer wanted to sit down. I moved the stool off to the side. Then I went right up to the microphone and stared out past the blinding lights into the darkened space. I could make out the faint outlines of faces and see the bar at the front of the room by the door.

Silence fell over the room. All I could hear was the clinking of ice cubes. Everyone was waiting for me to make them laugh. My heart was pounding and my legs felt weak. For a moment, standing up there in front of a half-empty room of about eighty people, I wondered if I was making a mistake. What if I flopped? What if no one laughed? What if I wasn't funny after all, and I became known as the unfunny lawyer?

The adrenaline boosted my energy and my confidence and helped me push those thoughts aside. I forced myself to open my mouth and began spewing the first bit that came into my head.

"You guys ever notice those bumper stickers that everyone in Colorado's been into lately? The native stickers?" I paused and waited for the audience to nod or shake their heads. I saw enough nods to keep going.

"Everyone's going on about this native business. Native, native, native. Everyone is *so obsessed* with bragging about being a Colorado local! Sheesh, guys, let's not be prejudiced against people from other states, right? People can come on vacation and appreciate the beauty of our gorgeous state, can't they? Plus, if you're not a native, what are you? A tourist? Nah, not according to the guy at this Italian place I go to. Let me tell you, guys, I went to that restaurant the other day and asked for a table. The host asks me, smoking or nonsmoking? I say nonsmoking. And then, get this, he asks me, native or alien?"

I paused and wrinkled my face in an "I didn't understand" gesture for the audience.

"I say, 'Native or alien? What?' And he says, 'Yeah, native or alien?' Now as much as I feel like a native, I've got to admit, I was born in Chicago, so I own up to it and tell him, 'Alien, I guess.' So he leads me to the alien section, and there I am, drinking my beer with a guy with antennas and a big third eye on his forehead!"

The audience laughed! Hallelujah! It might not have been rolling in the aisles, grab your gut laughter, but they laughed. That sound gave me life. It made me feel alive, invigorated, and completely powerful. I thrived off that feeling and delivered a few bits—all of which received welcome guffaws and chuckles.

After the show, the maestro found me and told me that I was great. He asked me if I would like to do regular Tuesdays. "But you'd need five minutes of material," he added. Yes. Easy. I took it.

Over the next few weeks, I developed several little bits that got a decent number of laughs—at least, laughs enough to keep me coming back. Obviously, it was not a paying gig. But the validation from the audience was payment enough.

I had bits about everything. The natives and aliens bit was popular, and I had a few other big winners. One was about condoms, always a favorite with the young bachelor crowd. I would comment on one-size-fits-all condoms—but if they came in sizes for men's ego, they should be in large, X-large, 2XL, and Super Super Large. Of course, all men would ask for the Super Super Large, even if it slid right off. And, oh, I'd say, don't even get me started on lubricant. I used to call it whale spit, which the audience seemed to get a good kick out of. Maybe the half-price beer helped.

Another fun one was about Mr. Rogers. I would come out in a little cardigan and do the entire "Would you be my, would you be my, would you be my friend?" bit. And then I would talk about how I didn't know if I'd let Mr. Rogers be friends with my kids.

I also liked to mess with the audience sometimes, like I had seen the comedians do in the big leagues in Vegas. I would hop down off the stage and pick on people, play with them, because I was quick on my feet and could come up with some slapping insults on the spot. All of my bits were original, timely, and decently well-liked.

One of the other Tuesday night performers was a then-unknown Denver local named Roseanne Barr, who later starred in the runaway success sitcom *Roseanne*. At the time, she was an up-and-coming comedian, not even a headliner.

Offstage, I could see the difference between her and some of the other regular comedians. She was very driven, but also nasty. She would appear at the club, do her housewife routine, composed basically of jokes about sitting home with her fat, lazy husband, and leave. The entire feeling she conveyed to other comedians was, "Get out of my way."

I only did regular Tuesdays for a few months before I quit. I had to stop because it was really hard to do. It was too hard to research my trial cases adequately, write new material for Tuesdays, and then entertain.

Doing stand-up was fun, but it was also challenging. It taught me a lot, both about how to deal with other people and how to conduct myself in the courtroom.

I remember my first regular night. I was doing great, people were laughing at the jokes, and I felt like I had the audience in the palm of my hand, so to speak. But then I came back the next week, told some of the same jokes, same timing, same intonations, and everything, and yet the audience just looked at me with that blank, scrutinizing, unsatisfied look, which seemed to say, "All right, let's hear something funny."

What is tougher than the blank stares are the hecklers, those obnoxious drunk guys who just yell at you all night. "Come on, funny guy, make me laugh!"

It was really nerve-wracking for me to take the stage in front of a crowd after that. I would be so nervous sometimes that I would throw up before I went on stage. That's how bad the nerves got.

I would get the jitters on stage because it was me—just me. It wasn't Mike Burg the lawyer, fighting for something or someone. With stand-up it was all me, just plain old Mike Burg, up there practically naked, just trying to make people laugh.

On my second regular Tuesday, there was a loud heckler, and he really got under my skin. In Vegas or anywhere else, when there were hecklers, they would always drive me crazy, even as an audience member. I was always so impressed with the way professional comedians could handle them.

This particular heckler was destroying my act. Every time I would start talking, he would scream. Because it was a Tuesday night and the place wasn't packed, there was not much anyone could do.

After being harassed by the heckler, I left the stage, dejected. Maestro Matt Berry tapped me on the shoulder.

"Don't worry about it," Matt said. "I'll show you how to take care of hecklers."

From the wings I watched Matt strut out on stage. He put his hands on his hips and addressed the audience in a serious tone.

"You know, I hate hecklers," he said, without a trace of a joke in his voice. "People are up here trying to do their damn job."

He was scanning the audience. He went on about how hard it was to get up on stage, about how much guts it takes. As he spoke, he grew angrier and angrier, to the point that he was red in the face.

"I can't stand hecklers! You, sir!" he yelled as he jumped off the stage into the audience. "You're a bastard, a drunk bastard!"

He walked right up to the guy that had been giving me a hard time, a balding guy in the second row, drink in hand. When Matt was about two steps away from him, he whipped out what looked like a real gun and held it up to the guy's head.

"You motherfucker, I'm going to blow your fucking brains out!" Matt shrieked.

The room fell silent. Honestly, everyone was scared.

The heckler threw his hands up and started yelling, "No! No! No!"

After an extremely long, extremely tense moment, Matt let the gun drop to his side. "That's what we do to hecklers in this place," he said.

Matt slapped the guy on the back and shook his hand. Everybody laughed along and clapped, but you could tell how scared shitless the heckler had actually been.

When Matt passed me, he winked. Matt was a pioneer in the Denver comedy scene in the 1980s, and he taught me a great deal. In addition to being the MC, he was a comedian in his own right. He would perform little skits between each act. He truly was the king of icebreakers, the silly little bits that loosen up the crowd.

My favorite of his icebreakers was one that he did on an unbearably hot summer day. It must have been 102 degrees in Denver. People walked into the bar dripping sweat, shirts plastered to their skin. As they were soaking up the air conditioning, Matt walked onto the stage dressed in boots, gloves, snow pants, a muffler, and a flap hat. He looked around, and said, "Is it hot in here, or is it just me?" And of course, on a scorcher of a day like that, he got a big laugh.

Matt ended up hitting it big as a comedy writer. He moved to Los Angeles to write for *Roseanne* in the mid-1990s. He went on to write for *Married with Children*, Ellen DeGeneres' sitcom, *Ellen*, and eventually the monster hit *Desperate Housewives*.

Not for a second do I believe that could have been me.

I learned that in comedy sometimes you have to go for it, no matter how ridiculous you feel. There are elements of performing stand-up that translate to trial law. An icebreaker makes the audience or the jury relax and feel comfortable. In the middle, you need the guts of the show or the case. Finally, you need a strong finish to leave everyone feeling great, be they audience members or the jury.

The biggest crossover between comedy and being a trial attorney is communication. In stand-up, you have a live audience that you need to make like you. You need to gauge their reaction and adjust your presentation accordingly.

Comedy is so much about timing, too, about bringing the audience to the edge of their seats, about leading them to expect one thing and then slamming them with something else, something funny as hell.

Timing is also a key component to law. There are times when I give a closing argument that I know exactly what I am going to say, but I will pause for dramatic effect to work on the judge and jury—not to manipulate them, but to most persuasively convince them. A good stand-up comedian pauses often and pretends to search for words, to make the audience wait. In trial, a lawyer can do the same thing. In both cases, the goal is to build suspense.

The fact is, much of trial law is acting. The argument is 100 percent real, but sometimes the emotions and the delivery of the facts need to be emphasized in a way the jury can understand, if only to hold the interest of the judge and jury.

People in court don't want lawyers to be perfect all the time. I have seen some amazing orators in court who garnered applause but didn't win. In those cases, they were not communicating effectively with the jury. If a lawyer cannot forge that connection with the people he is trying to convince, then he or she doesn't stand a chance.

I never go for the applause. I go for the engagement with my audience. And I have developed a reputation that precedes me on that front. One time I had an arbitrator tell me that she was excited for my case because she had been sitting through the most boring cases the past few days.

"Well, this one won't be boring," I told her with a gleam in my eye. "I promise you that." After I was finished, I didn't see her applaud, but I hope she agreed.

CHAPTER 11

FORCED OUT ON MY OWN

I did not become a lawyer to be rich, but I thought that I would earn a nice living. In my first job as a law clerk, I worked alongside lawyers who drove nice cars and lived in mansions like the ones I remembered in Wilmette, near where I grew up. I somehow felt that the profession would take care of me at every level.

Having passed the bar in 1976, my salary at Atler, Zall & Haligman had been returned to "lawyer levels," but when I received my first paycheck, I thought that there had been a mistake. The amount on the check was even less than what I had been receiving as a clerk. I was planning to start a family and had been expecting bigger paychecks, not smaller ones. I needed someone to explain why. My salary had dropped by a couple of hundred dollars.

In a huff, but trying to stay levelheaded and be a professional, I knocked on one partner's door after the next to see if I could speak with them. I tried to talk to Ron Zall, who disinterestedly told me paychecks weren't his department. He suggested that I take up the matter with Ed Haligman.

I didn't really know Haligman. He was the managing partner, but I did not report to him, either directly or indirectly. Instead, I went to Larry Atler, who was my biggest supporter at the firm.

But even he demurred. He said there was nothing he could do, and explained that Haligman was really the guy I needed to talk to.

Over the next three days, I tried and tried to meet with Haligman, but he was somehow always busy or absent every time I stopped by his office. Three days later, I happened to spot him walking across the office lobby in front of me. As Haligman passed, I lightly tapped him on the shoulder and said, "Excuse me, Mr. Haligman, could I talk to you about something?"

Haligman stopped in his steps and glared up at me. He was short, only five feet two, balding, wore glasses, and had a long, pointy nose. He looked at me with great animosity, and said, as if I were a pile of trash that had miraculously grown arms, legs, and a mouth, "I do not have time to talk to you right now. I'll speak to you some other time."

He held my gaze for a beat longer than he should have, and in that moment I sensed that I had gained an enemy. I wasn't quite sure what it was that I had done to make this man so very angry, but I knew it meant trouble for me. Certainly, any salary appeal was going to be even more difficult now.

I went home that night and told my wife about the strange encounter. She was reluctant to give me any advice. I told her that I hoped to be able to clear up the salary issue in the next day or two. The next day was a Saturday. As I was running some errands in downtown Denver, I bumped into Larry Atler. He said to me, "What happened yesterday with Ed Haligman?"

"What do you mean?" I asked.

"Haligman told all of the partners that you pushed him," Larry said hesitantly.

"I what?"

"You pushed him. Didn't you?" Larry asked.

"I never pushed him," I said firmly. I then tried to defend myself, indignant at the wrongful accusation.

I explained to Larry what had happened. He listened but seemed removed from what I was telling him.

"I swear," I told Larry, almost pleading, "I never pushed him. I would never do that."

He told me that the firm was having a partners' meeting at 9 A.M. on Monday and that I needed to be there to explain my side of the story. "Otherwise, you'll probably lose your job."

For the life of me, I could not figure out what was going on, or what was being said, or why it was even being said at all. I didn't understand how Haligman could claim that I had used any force on him.

On Monday morning, I was summoned to the main boardroom. The partners were sitting around a long wooden conference table, and all of them were looking at me. Haligman stood up. He spoke emphatically to the room about how I had pushed him, how that was unacceptable behavior, and how he wanted me fired—immediately.

I spoke up. "I never pushed you," I said, as levelly and calmly as possible. "I *tapped you* on the shoulder, did I not, Mr. Haligman? I just tapped you. All I wanted to do was to talk to you to clear up a point about my salary. Just a tap."

There was silence in the boardroom. Suddenly, I felt I was on trial—and for a crime I hadn't committed. I looked around the table. I had to defend myself.

"Ron, I came to your office to talk to you about the salary issues, and you directed me to Mr. Haligman," I said, looking at Ron Zall. Then I looked at Larry Atler. "Larry, I told you the same thing and you also directed me to Mr. Haligman."

I turned my attention to the pouting, beady-eyed man sitting at the head of the table. I began to cross-examine him. I was not going down without a fight.

"Mr. Haligman," I began, "tell me where I pushed you?"

He made no move to reply.

"You can't tell me where I pushed you, because I didn't push you. Isn't that right, Mr. Haligman?"

No one spoke. The lights of the boardroom flickered above us as the silence stretched on. Haligman finally piped up with some weak, defensive remark. The more I questioned him, the more defensive he became. In the end, he conceded my point. "Well, maybe you did only tap me," he said. "But you tapped me very hard."

That was it. I was asked to leave the room. I returned to my office. To keep myself occupied, I did some paperwork, but really I sat there wondering how long it would take them to determine that Haligman was a stubborn fool and that I was innocent.

Two hours later Larry Atler came into my office. "Michael, the news is good and bad," he said.

"Give it to me," I said, leaning back in my chair.

"The firm's going to keep you," he said, his voice trailing off.

My chest swelled. That's right—it is, I thought, because not only am I in the right, but I also got Haligman to admit that I had only tapped him.

Larry continued. "At least, temporarily," he said. "But Ed will make your life here a living hell. He will do everything in his power to destroy you and your career, so I think it would be in your best interest to leave. You ought to get out of here and find another job. We're giving you sixty days."

I felt like a bus had just hit me. How could this be? I was the good guy here, and yet *I* was the one being fired? Or, at least, encouraged to quit? It left the worst taste in my mouth.

"I am sorry," Larry said, before leaving my office, which was soon to be somebody else's office. I put my coat on, left all the papers scattered across my desk, and went home.

I told Debbie what had happened. We were both in a state of mild shock. But the truth was, I didn't have time to sit around and be mad or sad about it; I had to get back to work. I had sixty days to find a new job.

I sent out my résumé to all of the other firms in Denver, from top to bottom. I was thorough and made sure I did not miss a single one. After the résumés were sent, I waited a week and then started calling to follow up and see if I anyone would consider me for an interview. I was trying to be proactive and enthusiastic, but nobody was interested. Not one firm.

A few days later, I called Sheldon Friedman, a partner at Isaacson, Rosenbaum, Spiegelman & Friedman, whom I knew. I asked why they wouldn't give me a chance. He told me that Ed Haligman had put the word out to every firm in Denver that I had pushed him, and that I would never get an interview with any firm in this town. He promptly hung up.

I was absolutely beside myself. I had no idea what to do. I was persona non grata in the Denver legal world. I had no job and no clients.

As I tried to figure out what do, I needed to face reality. Debbie and I had no nest egg. Yet another wrench had been thrown into our dream of starting a family. We would have to live off Debbie's teaching salary, which was barely enough to get by.

It wasn't long before I began to grow scared, and even desperate. I wanted to be a trial lawyer so badly, and I really didn't want to have to leave Denver to do it. I racked my brain for any possible connections that I had yet to reach out to. Finally, after about a week, I came up with a last-ditch plan, my last hope.

I phoned Jack Silver, the lawyer who had brought me in on the "Row, Row, Row Your Boat" case, and asked if there was any possible way I could do something with him again. Jack had gone out on his own after the trial to be his own boss.

"Sure," Jack said, his voice coming across the line distracted but amiable. "Come over to the office tomorrow. I'll find some work for you."

I showed up to his office, at 4155 East Jewell Street, at 8 A.M. the next morning dressed in a sharp suit. I was shocked at how extremely underwhelming his office space was. The offices at 4155 consisted of a bunch of lawyers who shared the same space. The landlord was Jerry Dunn, a lawyer in his own right who apparently liked other lawyers, so he gave them a deal. What choice did I have? I began working with Jack, doing research and collection work on cases that Jack and the building owner, Jerry Dunn, brought to other firms.

My parents were aware of my current state of semi-employment, how shaky it was, and how I was essentially out on my own. My dad flew to Denver to visit me shortly after I agreed to begin working with Jack. He bought me a gift to help keep me motivated.

It was a desk—a plain, simple wood desk. But more important to me than the piece of furniture itself were my father's words of advice that came with it.

My father said: "Michael, I have three things I want you to understand. One, the harder you work, the luckier you get. Two, when you start this business and go try to build it, don't chase the money. Be the best you can possibly be, whatever you do. If you're the best, the money will follow. And third, we're here to help you in any way we can, even though financially we're not in much of a position to help you anymore."

That short, choppy, but very clear speech of my father's embedded itself in my brain. Those words lived on forever. They became a touchstone for who I wanted to be and I returned to them often. It meant so much to me then to have my father's support, and to know that he and my mother believed in me.

The advice reminded me of the days when I was a kid. When my father would come home from grueling days at Gold Seal, he would say aimlessly into his beer can, "If you thought today was tough, just wait till tomorrow." Then he would look up with a smile and either ruffle my hair or kiss my mother's cheek.

Sharing an office and a secretary with Jack Silver led us to get to know each other well. He even talked to me about us becoming partners and forming our own firm, Silver and Burg. That sounded fine to me.

After I had worked there for sixty days, I started to feel more comfortable that I could survive in this situation, out on my own, away from a big firm. One day, Jack knocked at my door. He leaned in my office, in his cool, dry, Jack Silver way.

"I have some good news and some bad news," he said, hardly waiting for me to motion him in.

"Why don't we go with the good news first," I said.

"The good news is," Jack said, leaning against the door frame, "I just formed a partnership with Bob Jaros."

"Great," I said. "So what's the bad news?"

"The bad news is that I can't take you with me," he said. With that, he spun out of the office and closed the door behind him.

A beat of silence passed in my empty office. As what Jack said sank in, I felt a surge of emotions rise within me: anger, frustration, anxiety, and then sadness, and a touch of hopelessness.

I stared down at my desk. I had no clients. I had no money. I had no way to survive. The rudeness and the abruptness of Jack's dismissal burned hot in my chest. I was scared. What if this was it? Jack had seemed to be my very last hope.

Not ten minutes later, however, there was another knock at my door. Into my office walked a very tall, handsome man with a businessman's demeanor—someone I had never seen before. He was even taller than I was.

"Hello," he said. "I'm Jerry Dunn, landlord and lawyer."

He took one look at me and saw how emotional I was. I had tears in my eyes. It was the first time I had ever met Jerry. This was not the ideal first impression I wanted to make, but I tried to keep myself together. I had heard he did some legal work for Mountain Real Estate Development. "Jerry, hi," I managed. "Nice to meet you."

Jerry was concerned with my mood. "Man, you look like you're ready to jump out the window," he said.

I couldn't even make eye contact with him. "I don't know what I'm going to do," I said. "I can barely pay my rent."

He cleared his throat. "Look. Don't worry about it. I will help you. How much can you pay for a secretary?"

"Uh, nothing," I laughed. "I have no clients. I have no money."

"Like I said, don't worry about it." His voice had softened, just a fraction. "I'll get you some clients."

Jerry told me the cases that Jack had been working on were actually his collection cases and asked me if I was willing to do collection work. I told him I was willing to do whatever it took. He told me that he would cover half the cost of my secretary for the first ninety days until I got on my feet while he was getting me some work, which he did.

I agreed. I took the only path I had left to survive in this career: I became a collection attorney.

My first outside client was the manager at the Burger King. I still went there for my daily fifty-nine cent Whopper. I had made sure that the manager of the Burger King knew I was a lawyer, which was about to pay off. He brought me my first collection case, and though it wasn't much of a case, I appreciated him coming to me.

To drum up work, I also contacted some of my old connections from Denver, one of whom was Dale Coplan. Dale was a lawyer who had been a friend of mine when I was an undergraduate, and he had gone on to work for an electric company before starting up on his own. Dale forwarded me a few cases that didn't produce much income but still helped out nonetheless.

Between Jerry and Dale, I cobbled together enough cases to keep me going through those dry days. I never forgot what people like Jerry Dunn and Dale Coplan did for me. They helped me when I was in a time of dire need, and they believed in me, which was what I needed most.

Today at Burg Simpson Eldredge Hersh & Jardine, Dale Coplan is of counsel (legalese for a consultant) to our firm and has been for twenty-five years. An of counsel attorney acts as an advisor to a firm but is not employed by the firm. Though Dale pulls his own weight, giving him a home is my way of paying him back. Jerry Dunn is also of counsel and has access to a free office in our firm for the rest of his life.

My first two years of practicing law made an indelible mark on me and on my career. I can't say that I held a grudge against Ed

Haligman, though I certainly wouldn't have gone out of my way to help anyone connected to him.

However, helping those who helped me when I was down is what it is all about in the legal world, and indeed the greater business world. There are some people that come along and have your back when you least expect it. They help you out on your journey, and when the time is right, you give back to them for all they have done.

Many years later I ran into Haligman. I walked across the room and shook his hand. I thanked him for what he had done for my career. He had no idea who I was. From the look on his face, he seemed to be congratulating himself for mentoring me. In an ironic way, I guess he had.

CHAPTER 12

FLYING SOLO

Being a solo legal practitioner is one of the hardest things anyone can do. It is downright Sisyphean. From 1976 through about 1980, I worked as a solo practitioner. I was the lawyer, the administrator, the bookkeeper, the researcher, and the law clerk—I was *it*. A one-man show. A guy with a desk and a phone. I had to take every last piece of business I could get my hands on. But as a solo, I learned to be a jack-of-all-trades—and I mastered a few things along the way.

Every day I came into work hoping the phone would ring. My hands would be sweating, knowing that even if the phone did ring, it would more likely than not be someone referring me a case or looking to hire me to represent them for some cockamamie problem. I worried that they might ask me questions that I would have no idea how to answer, which meant long hours of researching issues that I knew nothing about. It was extremely daunting, and, quite frankly, it was depressing.

I didn't know how I would ever become proficient as a trial attorney. I had no mentor. I had no help. Unfortunately, I had lots of tormentors—lawyers on the other sides of my cases. I quickly learned that was the way it went.

When you are a solo practitioner, lawyers from big firms torment you, try to get inside your head, both before and during trial, saying,

"You don't know what you're doing" or "You can't handle this case." In deposition and court, they object to every question you ask and every piece of evidence you bring in, merely in the hopes of rattling your cage.

Unfortunately for my tormentors, their taunting only toughened me up and put a bigger chip on my shoulder. In many ways, I felt like I was back in Chicago, taking on the Ridge Runner gang that tormented the Jews. But in the beginning of my legal career, just like in my youth, I was definitely nervous and let them get to me more than I should have done.

Nevertheless, I swallowed my fears and insecurities and went to work on everything Jerry Dunn could get me. They were mainly collection cases, but I also wrote up some simple wills and handled divorce cases. The wills were easy, but they were merely paperwork and didn't involve going to court. Eventually, because I still had my eye on being a trial lawyer, I leaned toward taking divorces and collection cases, knowing those were the ones that would get me into court.

Collection work, which at the time was most of my work, has always been known as some of the worst work in the legal world, or any other world for that matter. Basically, it meant going after poor people who had borrowed money to buy a leather couch or a TV/VCR combo and could not make the payments. Oftentimes, this was because they were being charged 25 percent interest.

When these people couldn't pay back the money they owed, I had to go after them. First, I would secure a judgment against them. Next, the collection company would seize the collateral to try to collect the debt. After the company had their collateral back, there still remained a "deficiency" judgment.

Long story short, the collection agencies would go in and take back the couch or the TV or whatever the consumer purchased with borrowed money, but the people still owed a thousand bucks or more.

The entire process was predatory. It was not very fulfilling work, and it made me feel lousy to play a part in taking things away from poor people. But at that time, it was my only choice. It allowed me to pay *part* of my bills, along with the money from my teaching jobs. The pay from collection work was on contingency, set at a 30 percent cut of what was recovered, at most. But the numbers were very low. Even then, sometimes the people were so poor and desperate that the company could not recover enough money and, therefore, would cheat me out of my fee.

To be fair, Jerry Dunn had warned me about this aspect of being a solo practitioner. He told me that it was important to get the money from the client up front, because many clients would not pay when the services were completed. Though I was naive about that initially, I learned the lesson very quickly.

Here's how it would happen: a business would come in needing legal help. I would inform them of the cost up front, and after the work was done and the bill was out, I would never hear from them again. Some people would go from young new lawyer to young new lawyer to take advantage of them, have them work their cases, and then never pay the bills.

That lesson was a hard one to swallow because in truth, I was a big softy. If people had problems, I wanted to help them, even if I knew how unlikely it was that they would be able to pay the creditor.

Today, that seems like a distant memory. But back then, it was the way I did things, and small collection cases were the only work I could find. I also needed all the advice I could get.

When I was just getting started with collection work, Jerry took me out to a business lunch with one of his friends, Bob Dial, the collection manager of Kwal Paints. I was collecting for Kwal, a process that basically involved threatening people who had not paid their paint bills.

Bob gave me some of the best advice on collection work and practicing law I ever received: "Don't spend your whole time trying not to make a mistake, because if you do, then all you're really doing is creating nothing. You're just covering your ass. You're only going to get paid if you collect the money, so don't try to give me excuses. Do something, and move the ball forward."

It was advice that paid off. I took what Bob Dial said to heart and decided that even though collection work was not my ideal job, I was still going to give it my all.

I called and met with every bank and every finance company I could. I told them they should let me do their collection work because I would do whatever was necessary to succeed. Not only would I do the work, I would do it better than the guys they had and I would do it for cheaper.

My main sales tactic was honesty. I told them that even if the job only paid $1,000 or $2,000, it didn't matter. I needed the money so badly that I would be extremely happy to represent them.

My pitch worked most of the time, and I was able to develop relationships with other creditors. In addition to Kwal Paints, I worked for HFC Associates, Jefferson Bank and Trust, and Metro Bank, to name a few. Over the course of doing collection work, I even came to know Marvin Davis, the owner of Metro Bank, who later took over 20th Century Fox, though I never had the gumption to call him when I later tried my hand at acting.

Another beneficial element of my collection work was that I got to spend lots of time in court. Each case was similar, and invariably the defendants would ask for a jury trial. The case would be set for between a half- and one-day jury trial, generally in county court.

During this time, I was trying cases three to five times a week, and I cannot think of one collection case that I lost. It was a great way to get into "trial" and get testimony. I must have tried somewhere between seventy-five and a hundred jury trials, without losing a single one. To be fair, I'm not sure that anyone would have lost those cases, as long as the bank had the promissory note and the signature of the defendant, but it still felt good to be on such a winning streak.

One thing that amazed me was how many people would fight back on a promissory note that they had signed. However, in many situations, they really had no choice. They were in a tight financial spot, and I often felt for them. It was never fun threatening people, but I had to do it.

Dreary as it was, collection work had a few highlights.

One of my bigger-dollar collection cases was for Jefferson Bank and Trust. The amount owed was $6,000 or $7,000, and I was to receive a 30 percent cut, which was a lot of money for me.

The defendant was a guy named Gary Morris. I sued him, and he called me to tell me he was having a real hard time. He said that he wasn't trying to renege and would pay the debt when he could.

"But, Gary," I had to say, "I can't do anything for you. You are delinquent."

He told me he was working on a career, and that he was just barely making ends meet—just like me, I thought, with my law practice in the day and three night jobs.

I indulged him. "What's your career?" I asked.

"I'm a singer," he said. "Aspiring, anyway."

I felt for him, but there wasn't anything I could do. The bank wanted their money. He told me he had no savings, he was renting a house, he had no assets, but one day, he promised that he would pay back the bank.

Fast forward two years or so. Gary Morris called me—not vice versa. He told me that he had landed a role on Broadway in *Pirates of Penzance*. "I've got your money, including the interest, where should I send it?" It was crazy. I was so happy for him.

In another offbeat case, I was collecting for a small business that leased out heavy equipment, such as front-end loaders to excavation and construction jobs. The debt owed was about $40,000, which was a high-dollar case compared to others at the time; however, I was on an hourly rate of $75 because the company would not agree to contingency.

The case went to federal court in front of Judge Richard Matsch, the judge who later heard evidence in the Oklahoma City bombing case, the brutal, domestic terrorism case that stemmed from the bombing of a federal building that killed 168 people. Judge Matsch is a no-nonsense judge. He meant business. He is known as one of the toughest judges there is. He is also one of the finest federal judges in the country. It was my first case in front of him, so I needed to be prepared and ready to go.

The night before the trial I got a call from the lawyer on the other side, Wendell Dunn. He was young and inexperienced, whereas I had been practicing for six years. Over the phone, he said to me, "You know we're just going to give you a confession of judgment," which simply means that the other side agrees that we should win.

He was trying to convince me that I had the case in the bag so I would back off, but I refused to take the bait. "Well, that's nice, but I know Judge Matsch and he's a fair judge," I replied. "I'm going to be there at nine o'clock sharp, and I hope you will be, too. You can tell the judge whatever you want to tell him then, because this trial is happening."

The next morning I showed up right on time and scanned the room for Wendell Dunn. He was nowhere to be seen. The atmosphere was tense. Judge Matsch was there, of course, sitting gruffly and sternly in his black robe, with his handlebar mustache neatly combed over his top lip and his eyes sharp behind his oversized square glasses.

He barked out to me, "Have you heard from Mr. Dunn?"

I approach the bench. "I did receive a call from him last night, Judge."

"Yes," Judge Matsch gruffed behind his mustache. "He left a message for me, too, and I left a message back for him telling him that if he was not here by nine o'clock I was going to send the federal marshal to put him in prison." He paused. "So I assume that Mr. Dunn will be here shortly." There was not even a hint of a joke on his face.

Sure enough, Wendell Dunn showed up minutes later. But it was apparent that he had no witnesses. I had my witnesses lined up and my case fully prepared, as the trial would likely only last one day.

"Where are your witnesses, Mr. Dunn?" Judge Matsch asked.

Young Wendell Dunn said, "I want to give opposing counsel a judgment."

"But we're at trial now, Mr. Dunn," Judge Matsch slowly asserted. "As such, we are going to have a trial."

I put on my case, walking the judge through all my evidence and arguments. The crux of the case was that the equipment was returned to the company in a damaged condition; therefore, they could not lease the equipment out to other customers for six months until it had been repaired.

As I was conducting my closing argument, Dunn jumped to his feet and said, "Your honor, I don't think it's fair that they took the equipment back and they still have the right to get more money."

Judge Matsch put his hand up before I could say anything. He then looked at Dunn like he was a first-year law student. "Mr. Dunn, is this similar to a criminal defendant throwing himself on the mercy of the court?"

What a cheap plea for grace, I thought. But this guy thought he was doing something smart, because he had that conniving, hopeful glimmer in his eye.

"Yes, your honor," Wendell said emphatically. "I would say it's very much like that."

Judge Matsch took a beat before he said, slowly and sternly, like a king taking pleasure in decreeing a death sentence, "Motion for mercy denied." I will never forget the voice of Judge Matsch as he delivered that line.

Judge Matsch slammed the book on Dunn and his client. He gave us a judgment for the full amount we asked for and awarded us interest as well. As he issued his verdict, I was looking at Judge Matsch. In the middle of his pronouncement, he motioned to me with the slightest of nods, which meant the world to me coming from a judge of his caliber.

I knew that the life and pay scale of a solo practitioner was not what Debbie had bargained for. Working at 4155 was a totally different experience from working at the huge, merged firm where I had been. There were just three secretaries, and only about seven or eight lawyers working in the space.

Money was tight. Between my jobs teaching at Metro State and my small case work, I was making just enough money to pay my overhead and bring home a few bags of groceries. Debbie and I were doing all right personally, mostly because we had started a family that had two young men in it, our sons, Scott and Stephen. But finances were a major issue. Debbie was a public school teacher and I was a low-wage earning solo, a combination that caused us to spiral into debt.

Debbie struggled to accept the new shape our life was taking. It was hard work living from paycheck to paycheck. Even though I was doing everything I could, she wanted me to try to find a nine-to-five job working for a big firm. She thought that it would be a better, easier way to make money rather than juggling all of my smaller jobs.

But the problem was, who would hire me? As a result of being blackballed by Haligman, I remained persona non grata in the Denver corporate legal community.

Our relationship took a turn around this time. Our conversations often escalated into talk about our old dreams. She would always remind me of my fleeting aspirations to be a U.S. senator, or a millionaire, and then remind me of where I stood now.

But I was not ready to give up on myself. Now that I had made the move to be out on my own and try to start practicing independent of a big firm, I wasn't about to drop that so quickly. So even though Debbie and I had our differences, we stayed together. I kept at my work in the ad hoc legal offices at 4155, hopeful that things would soon turn my way. I felt that I just needed a big, interesting case to give me my big break and open everyone's eyes to my talents—my own personal Leopold and Loeb case.

CHAPTER 13

A MATTER OF PRINCIPLE

My first big case after Atler, Zall & Haligman fired me came from an unlikely place. One afternoon, I was at my favorite Burger King, waiting by the pickup window for the kitchen to finish grilling my Whopper. The manager, who I knew because I ate lunch there every day to save money, popped out from behind the counter. He was well aware of my plight. He told me that he had a major case for me, a sure-fire winner. Never mind that he was the manager of Burger King and would have no way of knowing what a case was worth, I was immediately interested.

Here are the details of the case: show dog/beloved family pet is left in a kennel while the owners go on vacation. Dog becomes bored, sad, lonely, what have you, and gnaws on some of the metal bars on his cage. Dog proceeds to suffer a slow, painful death by internal bleeding from the metal chips he swallowed.

This dog was no ordinary dog. It was a beautiful specimen—a purebred German shepherd—the spitting image of Rin Tin Tin. He had papers and had been a champion in several dog shows. But above and beyond that, the owners regarded and treated the dog, Fritz, as a member of their family. They had a "puppy book" for him, like a baby book, but instead of pictures of baby's first steps, it had Fritz's first feeding time, Fritz's first chew toy, and so on. These people loved Fritz like a child.

When I heard the pitch from the Burger King manager, I had my doubts about the case as a piece of business. It sounded like a loser to me. How can a person, even one who runs a kennel, control what a dog does? And, after all, it was the owners' choice to leave the dog in a kennel with metal bars on the cage. Nevertheless, I agreed to meet them and see what they had to say.

The owners, Lisa and David Willfork, told me the story in detail. They showed me the "puppy book" and also the paperwork from the boarding kennel where Fritz had died. After I heard them out, I explained that they had signed a release, as well as a limitation of liability of $500 with regard to damages that could be assessed. However, the willful conduct and the failure of the kennel to take proper care of the dog might allow us to circumvent the release and the limitation of liability.

Even though this case would be my first major jury trial, I told my clients that I could not take it on a straight contingency. I was excited about trying a case in front of a jury, but I could not afford to do it without some guarantee, as it would take time away from the bread-and-butter collection work. I asked that they pay me $500, plus 20 percent of whatever I recovered for them.

"Just to be clear," I reminded them, "the $500 may be more than we recover. Are you still okay with that?"

At this point, Lisa Willfork raised her chin and gave me an affirmative nod. "The money isn't the issue," she asserted. "We're doing this because it's a matter of principle."

Even though I was a young and inexperienced lawyer, hearing those words uttered—"a matter of principle"—caused a red flag to immediately wave in my head. Nevertheless, I took the case. I needed the work.

Lisa and David Willfork agreed to pay me the $500. I agreed to fight to recover damages, despite the fact that they wanted to fight on principle. We set up the trial dates, and I delved into the research and worked up my case.

The trial judge was set to be Judge Michael Vellano, a very affable gentleman who suspected correctly that I was a novice at trying cases in front of a jury. He called a pretrial conference to meet with both me and my opposing counsel, Leo Gemas, who represented the kennel.

"Are we really going to try this dog case? It can't be settled?" Judge Vellano asked.

Both of us said that it could not be settled. Both our clients felt that the case needed to be tried. I explained that my clients were unwilling to accept any amount of money, even if the kennel was willing to pay, because they believed Fritz deserved his day in court.

The judge seemed almost on the brink of laughter, thinking about the fact that we were about to go through a court trial on behalf of a dog, but he held back his skepticism. He set the trial for two-and-a-half days.

The morning of the trial, Leo Gemas requested to talk to Judge Vellano. He had a new defense that he wanted to put in the case. After spending literally the past two months working on my case, I was slightly bewildered and did not know what to expect. Judge Vellano called me into his chambers, too.

"So, what do you have to say, Mr. Gemas?" Judge Vellano inquired.

"Judge, the kennel recently informed me that they found a note," Gemas said, sounding dead serious. The judge and I were equally perplexed. A note from a dog? Judge Vellano furrowed his eyebrows. "What do you mean, a note?" he asked.

"According to the kennel," Gemas deadpanned, "they found a suicide note. Fritz had really been suffering, apparently. They said the note was found by the poodle in the next cage."

We all had a hearty laugh over that one. Sometimes humor comes in very handy in court, and that was really one of the perfect times to crack a joke.

Judge Vellano gave Gemas a good-hearted slap on the shoulder and said, "All right, boys, let's pull ourselves together. We've got a case to try." The three of us were chuckling as we left the chamber for the courtroom.

As I sat down besides Lisa Willfork at the plaintiff's table, she asked, "What's so funny?"

Of course, I didn't think she would appreciate the comment. "Uh, the judge just made a joke," I said. "It would have been impolite not to laugh." Sometimes ignorance really is bliss, or at least tactful.

My first real jury trial began. I have to admit, I did not know what I was doing. It was my first time ever picking members from a jury pool. When it came time for me to use my first peremptory challenge, I stood up and asked that one of the members be removed from the jury.

In Colorado, the peremptory challenge in civil cases is supposed to be done silently by passing a paper back and forth to strike jurors, but I was an amateur and was not privy to that knowledge.

Judge Vellano interrupted me after I stood up and announced my challenge. He informed me that in his courtroom—and, in fact, in the state of Colorado—challenges to jurors were not done verbally. They were done by paper. Embarrassed, I redid the challenge by passing a piece of paper to the bailiff, who in turn passed it to the judge. Several chuckles could be heard in the courtroom.

During the trial, I presented evidence of how the family had diligently cared for Fritz and how much he had meant to them. Lisa Willfork took the stand and echoed everything I had said. Then I pulled out my secret weapon: the puppy book.

But just as I approached the witness with puppy book in hand, Gemas rose to object. Judge Vellano shook his head at me. "Oh no," he said. "That book is not coming in."

That was a setback for me. Much of my argument was going to ride on the client's emotional attachment to the dog, as well as the merits of the dog itself, which were all displayed in the book. I sat down, somewhat bewildered with the decision.

Under Colorado law, the question being examined was how much the dog was worth. To my clients, Fritz was worth a lot more than the few thousand they had dropped to buy him as a puppy. He was a member of their family, as well as a respected show dog of fine breeding. I had to show the judge and the jury, somehow, that this dog was worth more than a normal pet, and that the kennel had mistreated the valuable and much-loved member of their family while the Willforks were away.

It came time for my closing argument, and my first time ever addressing the jury. I picked up the phone book that I had brought to the courthouse. My tie felt tight against my throat, and sweat beaded at my hairline. I took a deep breath, flipped open the phone book to a page on which the kennel had an advertisement, and began to read aloud.

"Let us love your dog while you're away," I read. I repeated it, slowly, emphatically, as I stood before the jury.

I ripped the ad from the phone book and held it up for the jury to see, mostly for dramatic effect.

"Let me ask you," I said. "Did this kennel love Fritz while the Willforks were away?"

I paused, making eye contact with the stern faces of the jurors. I noticed one woman with her eyes trained down who refused to look at me as I addressed the jury. I had been told that that was a bad sign, but at this point my argument was underway, and there was no going back. Aside from her, the other members seemed focused.

"Did they love Fritz?" I repeated, before answering for them: "No! No, they did not love Fritz, and, in fact, they killed him. They killed him because they didn't pay attention to him, attention that should have been paid to an animal, a *life*, left in their care."

My voice echoed through the room, and I hoped that the jury would see it the way I saw it, and the way the Willforks saw it.

"Thank you," I concluded, and returned to my seat.

It turns out that the jury did see it my way. They awarded my client over $10,000 for the value of the dog. I was ecstatic (for the monetary award), and so were my clients (for justice being done).

After the judge excused the jury, I spotted the one woman from the jury who would not look at me during my closing speech. She was a tiny little woman with a sprig of dark hair who was wearing a red blazer. I approached her and said, "Excuse me, ma'am, why didn't you look at me during my closing argument? I noticed that you kept your eyes down."

She examined me for a moment and then let out a little laugh. "I thought I might start crying if I looked at you," she admitted. "That poor dog, that poor dog suffered so much."

After the verdict, the judge reduced the judgment to the maximum $500 amount allowed under terms of the contract with the kennel, but I had won my first jury trial. Despite working fifty hours on a real dog of a case, that was a day I would remember forever.

It was only my first case, but I learned a couple of valuable lessons.

The first was immediate: a good lawyer must be very careful about juries. There is no way to know what they are thinking or what they will decide. A lawyer can try to read expressions, but that's like reading tea leaves.

I also later learned that jurors generally do not tell lawyers the truth at the end of a case. In my later cases where I was awarded large verdicts, I have heard them tell the other side how much they loved *their* lawyers, as well as their clients, despite that fact that they awarded millions of dollars in punitive damages against them.

The final lesson was larger in scope. Over my four decades in practice, I have learned that when a client comes in and says they want to fight on principle, a lawyer should be very careful about taking the case. Lawsuits are decisions that are based on business, legality, and ethics. The decisions are not based on matters of principle. While principles can be involved, and while it's important for all lawyers to stand up for principles, a case should never be solely about principle.

The principle a client wants to fight for may be compelling, and the bigger the case, the more determined they can be, especially when it comes to sizable, multimillion-dollar cases, like the ones that I currently work on. But you never want the cure to be worse than the illness. In other words, if a case is going to cost $100,000 to win what would be at most a $50,000 award, coupled with the risk of losing, then it does not make sense to take it to trial. That said, my firm does pro bono work, meaning cases in pursuit of the public good; for those cases, we sometimes try them for free without recouping our costs.

Recently, I took on two contingency cases, both of which I lost, and both of which I knew I would lose. Still, I felt I had to take them. I knew the chances of winning either case were very slim, but I felt ethically motivated to at least try.

In the first case, the client was a paraplegic young man, and in the second, the client was dying. In both cases, I thought these people had been cheated. Many other lawyers had already turned them down. I took their cases because I thought there was a chance I could win for them. Because I lost them, they cost our firm money. On the paraplegic case, the firm lost over $100,000 in costs. As a rule of thumb, I try to avoid cases where the cure is worse than the illness, but sometimes being human gets the better of me.

It troubles me that most people cannot afford to hire a truly good lawyer to represent them on a small claim. Clients remind me that I am supposed to be fighting for justice and that I am supposed to be the kind of lawyer who changes lives for the better. I agree. Unfortunately my firm, and other firms, have to turn down lots of smaller cases. Money is often a deciding factor. Decent lawyers are trying to make a living and support their families and keep their firms afloat. If taking a case means losing money, it can be hard to justify that trade-off, even if it means doing something truly good for someone else.

Another issue for my firm is that we take cases to try them. We do not mess around, cut corners, or accept cases in hopes of settling them quickly. We hire the best experts we can find and put in all the hours necessary, which for some cases can be hundreds, maybe even thousands, of hours of research and diligent work. The amount of time my firm would put in on a $50,000 case is probably not a lot less than we would put in on a $5 million case, because there is only one way to do it and that's the right way.

My firm has never figured out how to take car accident whiplash cases and make money on them. Many firms skip the lawyer and use case managers to settle these cases as quickly as possible to save time, regardless of the amount. But that is just not the way my partners and I want to practice law.

Perhaps our attitude is misplaced or even elitist. But to me, that method of handling cases is not practicing law at the level it should be practiced. It represents a flaw in the system, as I am the first to acknowledge, but for me, my way makes sense. It *is* tough turning down cases. I always feel bad when a prospective client cannot afford my work, but unfortunately, that is how I make my living and keep my firm going.

However, I still do take the occasional small case, usually for people I know or for friends of friends. If someone can convince me that I should be fighting for him because his cause is truly just, then I will consider it. But many people are just looking to squeeze some extra money out of a company and are hoping to use my firm's reputation to help them.

I am most motivated by justice and by wrongdoing, and I will always want to fight for the little guy, but unfortunately, we do not live in a vacuum. The necessities of the real world apply. This does not always allow for my generosity, no matter how much I may want to fight for a client—even if my client is a purebred German shepherd that died a tragic and unnecessary death.

CHAPTER 14

BLOODIED BUT STILL FIGHTING

One of my hallmarks as a lawyer is that I never quit, *ever*. Our firm has the same determination. We have worked on cases for as long as eight years as we sought justice on behalf of clients. Years ago, I tried a case that cemented my reputation as a lawyer who can push through just about anything during trial.

The case came to me through Jeff Kraus, a client and friend of mine. Jeff had been successful at real estate development and a lot of other things, but his main business at that time was working with Sun West, a company that was building and managing senior housing. He had recently been named chief financial officer (CFO), and was helping them expand.

One Sunday while watching football, Jeff told me that he thought something was fishy. He told me that his checks seemed a little short. He suspected that the CEO was skimming money off Sun West's real estate deals. I asked him if he had approached the accountant, David Ickovic, a mutual friend of ours. He said that he had been reluctant because things were going so well. He didn't want to upset the proverbial apple cart.

I looked him right in the eye. "Look," I said, quoting the great lawyer Louis Nizer, "if you can imagine they did it, they did it—and worse."

I've always used that philosophy when looking at cases, because experience has shown me that it is true every time. I suggested to Jeff that if he was not receiving fair compensation, it was likely just the tip of the iceberg of financial malfeasance.

Though Jeff was reluctant, he agreed to meet with David. The three of us began poring over all the books that he had. Sure enough, we discovered that they were cheating him out of his percentage of ownership. David put forth a plan to find out what was going on.

We hired a forensic accountant named Sheri Betzer to examine the books. Sheri, who looks like your seventh-grade teacher, is a polite and cordial lady, but she had worked for the IRS and knew how to investigate fraud. After examining the books, she wrote a report that laid out the scam.

Sun West owned more than one hundred assisted living facilities around the country. Each one was a separate limited liability company (LLC) with different investors. A small slice of each LLC was being diverted into the personal bank account of John Harder, the CEO of Sun West. I told Jeff that due to these irregularities he needed to resign immediately as CFO. The possibility existed that he was being set up to take the fall. He agreed.

Next we filed a case in federal court in Portland, Oregon, where the company was based. Judge Mossman, a fairly recent George W. Bush appointee, was assigned to the case. Sun West hired the blue chip Portland firm of Perkins Coie to defend the company and CEO John Harder. They denied all of our charges.

We had information that showed that not only was Harder diverting the money to his own account, but he also was taking money from the LLCs that were doing well and moving the funds over to the LLCs that were not doing well. Basically, he had established a personal slush fund using company funds. The proof was all there in the books and records—not surprisingly, he had two sets of books.

We asked for a preliminary injunction to show that there was a likelihood we would win the case, and that to maintain the status quo of Sun West through trial, the judge should appoint a receiver to run the company. Judge Mossman ordered a three-day mini-trial on the issue.

I put on our case. We brought Jeff in to testify, as well as Sheri Betzer, the forensic accountant. I showed video clips of the depositions I had taken of Harder and a couple of his henchmen to show what a thuggish operation Harder was running. I took this position because we were also suing them under the Racketeer Influenced and Corrupt Organizations act (RICO), the federal law that provides for extended criminal penalties and a civil cause of action for acts performed as part of an ongoing criminal organization.

In one deposition, a guy who looked like an NFL lineman testified. I asked him if he was "the muscle."

"What do you mean?" he said.

"You're the tough guy, and you're here to protect Harder, aren't you?"

"Yeah, man, I'm here to protect Harder. Why?" he said.

Day three of our mini-trial was closing arguments. I was very confident we would win the motion. But as I rose to do my closing argument, to deliver the knockout punch as it were, blood started spewing from my nose.

I don't know if it was going from the dry climate of Colorado to the wet climate of Portland, but I do know that my beautiful white shirt and sky blue tie were drenched in blood. I pinched my nose to stop the bleeding. There were gasps in the courtroom.

Judge Mossman asked me if I wanted a continuance for my closing until tomorrow. "I've got little kids. I've seen blood before," he said.

"Judge," I said, "I've bloodied witnesses on the stand, but this is the first time I've ever bled in court."

The judge chuckled. I told him that I just needed a brief bathroom break. I hustled into the men's room, squeezing my nose all the way. I jammed some Kleenex up my nostril and returned to the courtroom.

"Your Honor, I'm ready to go with the closing," I declared.

For the next forty-five minutes, I railed away at Sun West and CEO John Harder. I went back through the forensic evidence of the fraud. What I didn't realize is that the tail of the Kleenex was hanging from my nose, blowing back and forth with every breath I took. I finished my closing. The judge thanked me, and I sat down.

"I'm going to rule on this case," Judge Mossman said. He then ticked off three areas on which he was basing his ruling. "Number one," he said, staring down the CEO, "Mr. Harder, I've been a judge for a while now and you're the least believable person I've ever seen on the stand." Ouch.

The judge then said he found that we were likely going to win on the merits, and that we had met all of the burden of proof to get the injunction. However, he said he was concerned about giving control of a huge multimillion-dollar business to a third party. He didn't believe that there was immediate, irreparable harm, meaning that the company would not be put out of business if a third party was not appointed, so he did not grant the motion for preliminary injunction and the appointment of a receiver.

It didn't matter. Within the next week, having heard the judge declare that Harder was the least believable person he'd ever seen, the other side settled the case. As a result of the case, in 2012, in a fifty-six-count indictment, John Harder was indicted by a federal grand jury for defrauding more than one thousand investors out of $130 million. He was charged with a host of crimes, including money laundering and wire fraud. In 2014, he was sentenced to a prison term of not less than ten years.

Before Harder went to prison, Kelly Rudd, a lawyer from Portland who had moved to Wyoming, asked if he could come to Denver and meet with me about teaming up on some cases. When he walked into my office, he told me that he already knew me. I couldn't place his face, so I asked him how.

"Remember the Sun West case in Portland where you had the bloody nose?" he asked.

I laughed, turning bright red with embarrassment. I asked how he knew the story.

He had been clerking for a judge in Portland, when Judge Mossman told all the clerks in town to come to my closing in the mini-trial. He was impressed with me in the courtroom, he said. Of course, they got more than they bargained for once my nose started bleeding all over my suit.

"We were all in the gallery watching you with the bloody nose," Rudd said. "And we were all laughing because every time you said a word, the bloody Kleenex was going up and down, up and down." Yes, I agreed, that was embarrassing.

"That's not the point," he said. "After it was over, Judge Mossman had us come to his chambers. He said, 'I want you to remember what you saw out there. That's what real lawyers do.' He said they don't quit; they don't let anything deter them from what they're doing."

It was a nice compliment. But the best part of the case was that while I may have ruined a brand-new shirt and tie, John Harder went to prison, where he belonged.

The "We Don't Quit" philosophy also extends to our firm pushing for years on cases and constantly working the angles until we prevail. A case in point was an insurance action where we represented a developer/lender who lent money on a run-down property in Michigan to a developer.

I tried the case with my law partner David TeSelle, one of the shareholders who heads our commercial litigation group. I often team up with David in commercial cases because of his ability to understand the most technical aspects of these cases and translate them into simple language that a jury can understand.

The property was an apartment building that the developer wanted to convert into an assisted living facility. Our client had loaned money to the developer. After the developer failed to pay our client, he took back the building and took out a $3 million insurance policy on the property and building from James River Insurance Company. From the outset, James River raised the premiums because of the poor condition of the building. Though there was nothing structurally wrong, the building had several code violations, such as broken windows and doors that didn't work.

Less than ninety days after our client took out the policy, vandals burned down the building. Our client filed an insurance claim. James River came back and admitted that our client had insurance, but insisted that the building wasn't worth anything. In fact, they claimed that the building was worth less than zero; therefore, they reasoned that they didn't have to pay. They backed that up with a report from an appraiser who had no expertise in that area.

From our standpoint, even if that were true, it had nothing to do with the insurance. Our client had paid for $3 million of insurance; hence, James River was required to pay the claim. James River refused, so we took the case to trial in federal court in Colorado.

We hired an insurance expert named Kent Miller, one of the best bad-faith lawyers in the country. Kent wrote the book on bad-faith insurance claims. Actually, he wrote several books; definitive tomes on the subject. I stacked them up next to him on the witness stand. For some reason, the James River lawyers didn't see what was coming.

"What are all those books?" I asked him.

"Those are books I've written on insurance," he replied. "A few of them anyway."

We had the jury's attention.

"Aside from testifying for insurance companies, you have been quoted by the Colorado Supreme Court in its decisions, have you not?" I asked.

"Yes, I have," he replied.

"And also by federal judges in their opinions?" I asked.

"Yes, frequently," he said.

"So you've testified in hundreds of cases on behalf of insurance companies and against them," I said.

"I have," he said.

"And what do you think about this case?"

"I think this is the worst case of bad faith I have ever seen," he said. "Ever."

That was a knockout blow. The jury returned a $2.9 million verdict in our favor, plus $2.3 million in punitive damages, for a total of $5.2 million. (James River had already paid a $100,000 "salvage fee.") The jury also found that James River had acted in bad faith.

We assumed they would pay our client. Instead, they appealed based on the fact that our client had testified about the value of the building. They claimed under Colorado law that the owner could not testify as an expert about the value of his own building. We believed that he wasn't an expert; he was just testifying about buying insurance.

The 10th Circuit Court of Appeals agreed with James River and ordered a new trial on damages. The court left the bad-faith claim in the case, which had been the basis of the punitive damage award. What constituted bad faith was taking our client's premiums and not ever offering anything for the value of the building. So we had to retry the case on damages alone.

James River hired new lawyers for the appeal. The problem for us was this: Judge Christine Arguello had previously been a law partner at that firm. The chumminess between defense counsel and judge surfaced in our first hearing. One of the lawyers kept calling the judge Christine and rubbing it in my face that he was friends with her.

We had a hearing to determine what kind of evidence could come in. Our position was that in order for the court, or the jury, to determine how much damage there was, they had to hear about the conduct. The defense's position was that the case was only about the value of the building, which meant that if they had their way, we would lose out on punitive as well as regular damages.

At the start of the hearing, I told the judge that I needed to talk to her about something that had been troubling me throughout the case. I asked her if I should discuss this before or after the hearing. Afterward, she said.

After the hearing, I told the judge that I was uncomfortable with defense counsel calling her by her first name. The judge replied that she was known as Christine when she had worked at the firm.

"It's more than that," I said. "You never told us that defense counsel was your boss, so basically what he says to you is going to have greater weight. I have great respect for you, Judge, but I'm really concerned about that."

The judge was displeased and became defensive. "If you think I can't be fair, then you need to tell me and I'll recuse myself," she snapped.

Over the next few minutes, she repeated herself three times. The third time, the defense lawyer jumped up and said that she couldn't recuse herself because there was no grounds. The judge instructed us to file a brief stating the grounds on which she should recuse herself. We reviewed the case law and found that we did not have grounds to ask for her recusal. But that wasn't the end of it.

We obtained the transcript from the hearing where she had volunteered three times to recuse herself. Then, we filed an unprecedented motion asking the judge to do what she had promised to do on the record—recuse herself because we felt she might not be fair with us.

In response, the judge wrote a scathing order about how we were "judge shopping." But in the end, she did the right thing. She recused herself.

We weren't done yet. We then filed a new case against James River on different grounds. We found a Colorado statute that said that you have a bad-faith claim against a company if they don't do what they are supposed to, and if they delay or deny payments. In that event, a penalty of two to three times can be imposed. So we sued, saying that because the jury had already found James River in bad faith under common law, and the company had not yet offered us a settlement, the company was violating state law as well.

Now we had two cases running side by side, the retrial of damages on the first case, and the new case. We wanted the second case, the statutory claim, to go first because James River had failed to pay our client on the bad-faith claim stemming from the jury verdict, as the law required.

In the pretrial hearing on the second case, Judge Schaefer asked why we needed two cases. Shouldn't he consolidate them into one? As magistrate judge, he was responsible for handling many such issues prior to the start of a trial.

"The word in the courthouse is that you guys are judge shopping," he said.

"That may be the word, but that's not what we do," I said. "We are filing under our client's right to be compensated."

The judge declared that there would only be one set of depositions for both cases and that all notices for one case would serve for both cases. The defense promptly started filing notices in the first case and refusing to combine the notices with the second case, as the judge had ordered. Judge Jackson, the judge on the first case, who had replaced Christine Arguello, issued an order asking why the defense wasn't cross-noticing. The defense team responded that they were different cases.

When Judge Schaefer heard that the defense was ignoring his order, he called us all into court. He told us that Judge Blackburn, the trial judge assigned to the second case, had set a date for the case on his docket two months ahead of the retrial date for the first case.

Basically, it was game over. James River ended up settling with us. They knew we would win the second case and that would have a ripple effect to the retrial. We had made a gutsy move, calling out the judge and then filing the second case, but it had worked.

It was really satisfying when the James River attorney had to come to my office to deliver the settlement check. Not because the check was a large number, which it was. But because of the look on his face, one of defeat, anger, and bewilderment that they had been so outflanked. Metaphorical blood had been shed. We had fought the big insurance company and the system, laid it all on the line, never given up, and found a way to prevail. There's nothing more satisfying—*nothing*.

CHAPTER 15

READY FOR MY CLOSE-UP

Times were tough in my early years as a solo practitioner, and I was willing to try anything to make a better living—including another career.

After Debbie gave birth to our first son, Scott, in 1978, she took maternity leave to be with the baby, and I became the sole breadwinner for our family. Quite frankly, the pressure that fell on me to support us was extreme. For the first two years of Scott's life, Debbie pushed me to go back to working for a large firm—any firm.

But with the Haligman incident casting a shadow over my reputation, I doubted that I would be able to find work at any of the big firms in Denver. Every time I put out feelers, they were met with doubts or silence. I was doing the best I could bouncing around between collection cases and my teaching jobs. Even with all of my jobs, the money was barely enough for us to get by. I knew that I needed to figure out another way to supplement my income.

There were two ways that I could see doing that. The first was to pick up more teaching jobs at night schools, which made sense for me as a lawyer. I also enjoyed the work. The subject matter was not very complex, and from my prior experience and my years of education, I found it easy to teach.

I was a popular teacher. I had a reputation for being dramatic in the way I taught, which made it more enjoyable for students to listen to me. Compared to many of the other older, more traditional lecturers, I was definitely different—young, exuberant, enthusiastic, and yes, at times showy. Because I was a hit with the students, I became a hit with the faculty and the administration and was promoted to an adjunct professor at Metro State. I still enjoy teaching. Today, I am an adjunct professor at the University of Denver Sturm College of Law, teaching classes in mass torts and trial tactics.

But as hard as I was working, the bills were piling up. I found that my credit cards were maxed out. I knew that I needed to start thinking outside the box. This led me to arrive at a new way to generate income.

With all my successful dramatics both in the classroom and in court, I decided that it was time to pursue drama more seriously. It was time to start acting—and not just in little side-street productions for the community theater. My next step would be real screen acting.

In high school, I had never been much of an actor, but that was because I was unsure of myself and struggling to figure out my strengths and weaknesses and who I really was as a person. I loved to work elements of dramatic flair into my lectures at Metro and elsewhere. In the court cases I had been involved with so far, I enjoyed having everyone's attention. I took pleasure in crafting my arguments and leading my listeners along.

I did not harbor any illusion that I was particularly handsome or talented, but I did believe that I had potential. The movie stars of the day were Robert Redford and Paul Newman. I knew I didn't quite look like them, but I also knew that I wasn't unattractive. And man, was I a fan of their movies. Robert Redford in *The Way We Were* blew me away.

The moment I came up with the idea of becoming an actor, I felt swept away by some crazy energy. I honestly believed that I could do it, and I really wanted to try. And maybe there was some deep-seated, subconscious motivation to try to extricate myself from the field of law, which at the time really wasn't going very well. I was working relentlessly, giving law my all, but making virtually no headway, at least not financially. At some level, escaping law to become an actor was definitely a little bit of a fantasy. I was under a lot of stress. But I figured that if I kept up all my other work there was no reason why I couldn't explore acting, or at least television, on the side.

I heard that the Channel 9 Local News was looking for a backup sportscaster, which served as my catalyst to begin my career in acting. I applied for the job and was called in for an interview. But the producer conducting the interview took one look at me and declared: "We're not hiring you. What are you doing here, guy? You're a lawyer. You're not going to want to do this long term. You'll have two weeks of fun and then decide you're sick of it."

Though that opportunity died on the spot, the excitement of the interview fueled my fire. I decided that I wasn't about to give up on this so easily. Debbie was not excited about the idea, but said I should give it a try. I had to pursue it. I had no acting experience, so I thought it might be smart to take some acting classes. I started looking into acting schools in the area.

Lonnie Grant had a well-known acting and modeling studio. Even though I had virtually no money to spend on acting classes, she and I worked out a payment plan deal, and she agreed to allow me into her acting and modeling classes.

Although I didn't take many acting classes, I enjoyed them. Memorizing lines was easy for me. I had decent stage presence and the ability to forge connections with my fellow actors quickly and easily. In acting, I learned that so much relies on those connections with other people. Overall, I found that I had a natural aptitude for acting and that more than anything, *it was fun.*

In one of the acting classes I took, I had a coach named Kathy Christopher. She looked like Bo Derek in *10*, but I thought she was egotistical and full of herself. Something about the way she walked around the room and directed the students rubbed me the wrong way. In short, I really didn't care for her.

As an acting coach, she was tough, and she did make me better. But her attitude bothered me—perhaps because hers was similar to mine in the sense that she could completely focus and had no fear in her primary craft. Or perhaps her confidence threatened me. I couldn't quite pinpoint the rub.

She wasn't confident without justification. Kathy had been in every Hollywood production that had rolled through town. *The Duchess and the Dirtwater Fox, How the West Was Won, Snow Beast,* and a starring role in *Beasts*. She also did TV, from *The Dick Van Dyke Mysteries* to the *Perry Mason* remakes, as either a district attorney, a judge, or a witness. She was one of the top actors in Denver. She was also vice president of the Screen Actors Guild (SAG) of Colorado and was on the national SAG board.

Eventually I began getting work. One job resulted in an acting job with Kathy. I was one of two finalists to play a husband in a commercial for Kansas State Bank and Trust. Kathy had already been cast as the wife.

She was involved in choosing the role of the husband. I read the script with her, and so did a comedian. Whether it was Kathy's choice or the director's, I got the role.

Neither of us was thrilled to be working together, but we sucked it up and got on with it. The commercial was downright goofy. Kathy and I played husband and wife twenty-dollar bills. We wore green leotards and Styrofoam twenty-dollar-bill costumes. The concept was that we were coming from the bank and she was bringing home our interest, little five-dollar-bill kids.

We shot several takes that went fairly well. But on one take, there were technical difficulties on the set. The camera crane kept creaking, and the director became irate. All of this stressed Kathy out to the point that she began forgetting her lines—for take after take after take.

At this point, I still thought she was "hot stuff," so I reaped a measure of petty satisfaction that she was messing up and that I was doing well. I thought, "Well, well, well, Ms. Actress who has done all these movies and TV shows can't even remember her lines for this little commercial."

I leaned over to her and said, "Hey, do you want me to just write the lines on my chest so you can read them?"

It was a mean thing to say, and she stared daggers at me. We were both frustrated from doing the same take over and over. I had been saying my lines—thanks to my photographic memory—but she just could not get hers right. It didn't help that we were shooting three commercials back to back, and there were a lot of lines to remember and to keep track of. Nevertheless, by the end of the day, she thought I was the biggest ass there ever was.

Even though Kathy and I did not start off well, we later became friends after I was named to the local board for the Screen Actors Guild of Colorado. Interestingly, she had asked the board to invite me to join, reasoning that a lawyer might be of some help. Because Kathy was the vice president of the board, we ended up spending much more time together. As I got to know her better, I found out that I had judged her wrongly. She turned out to be a very nice person, very smart, and yes, very kind.

As a result of having to spend time with one another on the SAG board, the bad feelings between Kathy and me diminished. As I saw her interact with others more, I realized that if she ever came off as arrogant or egotistical, it was a result of insecurity, a bluff of bravado to boost her confidence.

One day, out of the blue, she approached me and said, "I have a question for you."

I took one look at her posture and said, "You're getting a divorce."

She crossed her arms and threw her weight onto one hip. "How did you know?"

"Well, you haven't talked to me much, and I'm a lawyer, so I assume that's what you want to talk to me about. Am I right?"

I laughed, and she laughed too. I was right. From then on things were much friendlier between us. Many years later, we were married and I have no doubt that Kathy was my "muse" who believed in me and helped me to become successful.

I came to know Lonnie Grant very well. She was a gorgeous young woman, but there was no physical relationship between us, despite how rocky my relationship with Debbie had become by this point. But Lonnie and I did click and got along very well.

As she worked with me in acting classes, she saw what my skills were and helped me hone them. One day, after an especially tough class where I just could not seem to get our improv skit to go anywhere, Lonnie and I decided to unwind afterward over drinks.

Lonnie told me that she thought I had the guts and the personality to become a working actor. "I think if you persist you could really go somewhere with this," she said.

Wow! It meant so much to hear that from someone, especially early on. My confidence was unwavering, and maybe foolhardy, but Lonnie's input only bolstered it.

Lonnie had modeling connections. As a result of working with her, I landed a few modeling jobs and also did commercials with the Steve Vannoy Agency in Denver. I was told that I did not have the build to be a fashion model, yet I did have a friendly, boy-next-door face that was perfect for commercials.

I played the ordinary guy, the average Joe, the husband, the neighbor, and the hopeful homeowner. Through these silly commercials, I managed to make some money. I earned between $300 and

$500 a job, a significant amount for me at the time. My biggest payday came from playing a hockey coach in a Canadian tire commercial, which won Commercial of the Year in Canada.

Through Lonnie, I also met John Husband, another local director who did commercials and industrial films. Lonnie set me up with him and we had lunch one day to discuss how to go forward in film and TV. The key, I realized, was to get my SAG card.

John agreed to help me. He cast me in a role in an industrial film, the kind of films shown in the workplace to teach employees either how to do their jobs or about interpersonal relations. In this film, I played an uptight executive. The film taught about different types of executive personalities; I played the jerk.

By playing a part in this industrial film, I was able to get my SAG card, which meant that I was the real deal. I couldn't wait to move my acting career forward.

I went to JF Images, the biggest agency in Denver, to meet with Jo Farrell about representing me as my agent. The only way she would agree to take me on is if I bought $2,000 worth of classes. Well, I definitely could not afford and would not spend $2,000 on classes that I didn't feel I needed.

In order to actually be in the stable of actors JF Images pulled from, I would also be required go through an audition process. JF Images sent a number of their actors out to Los Angeles for jobs, so I knew that if I sucked it up, paid the money, took the classes, and made the audition, it could very well be worth my while. But $2,000 was a lot of money for me at the time. I just couldn't bring myself to do it.

I decided to circle back after trying JF Images and remain with the Vannoy Talent Agency. Steve was gracious, but his issue was that I had very little acting experience on my résumé. Without some credits, it would be hard for him to book me work.

Just when it seemed like I was hitting another dead end, things took an interesting, Hollywood-like turn.

CHAPTER 16

HOLLYWOOD CALLING...

D enver was fertile ground for film and television production in the late 1970s and early 1980s. Colorado had one of the first film commissions outside of Hollywood, and it attracted plenty of stars and attention. *The Dick Van Dyke Mysteries*, *Perry Mason* remakes, and the TV series *Father Dowling* were all shot locally. Because there was so much activity, *The Hollywood Reporter* decided to publish a special Colorado edition.

The magazine's reps came to town and began pushing ads to local actors who were hoping to be noticed. For $250, an actor could buy a tiny 2 × 3-inch ad with a picture of his or her face along with agent information .

At that point, my résumé was pretty bare. I had been in one industrial film. There were many professional working actors in town who had all been working together since they were in junior high, but nobody knew me.

Lonnie Grant had an in with the Colorado correspondent for *The Hollywood Reporter* and he was able to snag me an invitation to a promotional party in Hollywood for Colorado actors. I was thrilled at the prospect of going to Los Angeles, the movie capital of the world.

The correspondent for *The Hollywood Reporter* said he wanted the party to be a big deal, a fancy shebang to fire up Hollywood about

Colorado. The party was being held at an estate in West Hollywood up in the hills. A lightbulb went on. I had an amazing angle.

One of my (few) legal clients at the time was a real estate developer who was also working on plane options. For a $50,000 deposit, he could tie up an option to buy a Cessna that was not yet built. There was no "escalator" clause in the contract, meaning that if the plane increased in value to $400,000 while it was being built and delivered, he could sell his position in that plane.

Because I had been doing his legal work, he decided that instead of paying me by the hour, he would give me 5 percent of his take. Not only was that a potential financial windfall for me, he also gave me access to the delivered planes to try them out.

I reasoned that the Colorado contingent needed a way to get to Hollywood, and I just happened to have access to a luxurious private plane. I hatched an idea that would both help Lonnie and really help my acting career. I volunteered to give the Colorado contingent a ride to LA on a private jet in exchange for a full-page ad in *The Hollywood Reporter*.

The deal worked. My client agreed to let me use the plane for a "test run" to LA, and *The Hollywood Reporter* correspondent brokered a full-page ad in the magazine. In the ad, it listed me as "the hottest discovery in Colorado," which pleased me quite a bit.

However, I realized, with the ad lined up, that it probably would not be worth much if I didn't also have an agent to help me negotiate with any interested Hollywood people.

I went back to Jo Farrell, my first choice, with news of the full-page ad and asked if she would be my agent. I told her it would be a great deal for her, too, as her name would be on the ad. For whatever reason, Jo turned me down.

I then went to Steve Vannoy. He jumped at the opportunity. It was a great deal for both of us—I had an agent, and he now represented "the hottest discovery in Colorado." The results were pretty amazing.

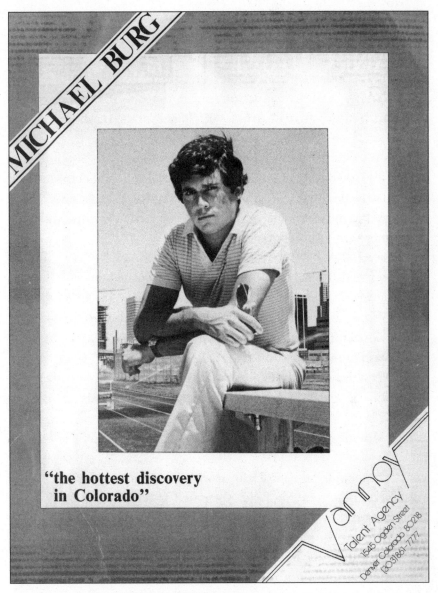

MICHAEL BURG

"the hottest discovery in Colorado"

Vannoy
Talent Agency
1545 Ogden Street
Denver Colorado 80218
(303)861-7777

The self-proclaimed "Hottest Discovery in Colorado"

The ad ran in the *Reporter*. I took my handful of guests on the plane. We flew to Hollywood and had a great time at the party and living it up on the West Coast.

California was beautiful. I loved the warm, balmy weather, the relaxed, windswept, sun-bleached vibes of Santa Monica and Venice Beach. The houses in the Hollywood Hills were beautiful and unique, lodged into the sides of canyon walls. The desert air reminded me of Denver, and, of course, there were beaches, a geographical feature that Colorado tragically lacks. In short, I loved California.

We partied at the nicest houses in the valley, ate at some chic restaurants in Beverly Hills, and explored Hollywood clubs. Seeing the stars on the Walk of Fame was a really humbling and exciting moment for me. I wondered if someday my handprints would be down there with all the greats.

The ad also generated more interest in me in Denver. All of a sudden, I had several jobs lined up. I shot commercials for Boycott Safeway, which were organized by a union whose thinking was very much in line with my liberal political views. I also did ads for Channel 7, Marriott Hotels, and Medina Homes, to name a few.

It wasn't long before Jo Farrell called. She saw that I was a success and asked me to become a client. As that had been my goal all along, I said yes—especially because she agreed to waive the classes and the fees. With Jo, I had access to all of Colorado's top agents, including Annie Maloney, who was very well connected in Hollywood at the time.

I was feeling on top of the world. I had acting and modeling gigs lined up, and my popularity seemed to be growing. I still practiced law on the side and taught night classes at the colleges, but at this particular moment in my life, I had my sights set on becoming an actor. I still cared very much about law, still loved the law and wanted to practice, but suddenly my acting career was looking like it would take off. I had bright, rose-colored dreams of becoming the next Robert Redford. All I needed was a big break. Amazingly, I got one.

My big break came in 1980 through Annie Maloney. Apparently Joyce Selznick, a casting director with ABC in Los Angeles, had seen my ad in *The Hollywood Reporter* and wanted me to come out to LA for an audition for a TV remake of the movie *Breaking Away*.

Breaking Away tells the story of four recent high school graduates living in Bloomington, Indiana, who face off with the privileged college students at Indiana University over issues of socioeconomic class and ambition. The story focuses on the four "townies," one of whom I was auditioning for the role of, and their aimless, unmotivated summer days after graduation.

Though I was excited about the attention, the first thing that occurred to me was that I was a thirty-year-old man reading the part of an eighteen-year-old. I was skeptical about how well that would work out. I did not look eighteen.

Nonetheless, they had liked my picture in the ad, and they wanted me to come to LA. I decided to use the opportunity as a chance to give myself the real shot in LA that I deserved. In a way, it seemed as if my days as a lawyer might be coming to an end and that my calling would be acting.

I arrived in LA and rented a tiny bungalow on Roxbury Avenue in Beverly Hills on a week-by-week basis. It was a cramped space with a tiny kitchenette, a bathroom that was more like a tiled broom closet, and an adjoining balcony barely big enough for two to stand on shoulder to shoulder. Still, it was good enough for me. All I really did there was sleep and cook myself the occasional meal.

The day came for my *Breaking Away* audition. I prepped myself well. I combed and gelled my hair, put on my coolest, hippest outfit in honor of the young part I was auditioning for. I wasn't quite sure what to expect, especially since I had not been given a script to work with ahead of time. I had my portfolio neatly organized and tucked under my arm, ready to hand it over to anyone who requested it.

I rolled up to ABC Studios in Century City, where the auditions were being held. After checking in with the receptionist, I was directed to a large, bare room for the reading.

It was intimidating. I walked into the cavernous room where three people sat calmly in their chairs, silently examining me. As I approached them, I took my portfolio from under my arm and opened my mouth to say, "Hi there, I'm Michael Burg, here for the *Breaking Away* audition."

But before I could even get a single word out, the tiny, older woman sitting in the middle chair announced in a surprisingly strong voice, "You're too old. Thank you for your interest."

And that was it! I was too old. I was shocked that I didn't even get to read a single line before they turned me down. But, after all, I was a thirty-year-old auditioning for the part of a teenager.

I stopped in my tracks, shrugged, spun on my heel, and headed back toward the receptionist's office. I was a little irked because I had been excited about a real Hollywood audition, but I didn't let myself get discouraged.

⧁◊⧂

I was thrilled to be in LA, living in Beverly Hills, developing contacts, and making connections. I had meetings and appointments lined up. I was also spending time with a friend of mine from law school, Larry Raful, who had become the dean of the University of Southern California's law school.

One of my favorite hangouts was at the actor Carroll O'Connor's bar, The Ginger Man. It was a dark pub and a fun place to grab a drink, and grab drinks I did with casting directors, writers, small-time directors, two-bit Sammy Glicks, you name it. It was an ideal place to network, and I enjoyed it immensely. I loved working the room and talking to people.

Everyone kept talking about William Morris, the venerable talent agency. But I had no contacts at that agency, and nobody seemed able to give me any numbers or names. Finally, somebody's assistant to an assistant casting director suggested that I should just go down there and see if someone would meet with me. That was what I ended up doing.

I arrived and took a seat in the William Morris reception area. As I was sitting there plotting what to say, I heard the receptionist say into the phone, "I'm sorry, sir, Mr. Jones is in Paris. Can I take a message?"

Aha! A name. I've got something to work with here.

When the receptionist turned her attention to me and asked me who I was there to see, I told her that I had an appointment with Mr. Jones. She asked my name and told me that, unfortunately, Mr. Jones was in Paris.

I feigned ignorance. I told her that I had flown in from Denver for this appointment. The receptionist looked flustered. She apologized and told me to sit tight for a moment while she checked if someone else could speak to me.

The next thing I knew, a guy walked out to greet me. He was wearing a dark suit and shiny loafers. By the look on his face, I suspected that he thought I was a bullshit artist, but he invited me back to his office.

I passed him my portfolio over the table. He looked over my stuff and said to me, "You know, we only have so many types in Hollywood."

"Types?" I asked.

"Yeah, you're kind of like a Jimmy Farentino type," he said. "You guys look a bit alike, dark eyes, dark hair. You'd probably get cast for the same roles. So if you're working"—he paused to steeple his fingers together over the desk—"what is Jimmy gonna do?"

"Uh," I drawled, "I don't know. I don't care what Jimmy does."

So that was a dead end, too. But he at least indulged me and talked to me for a half hour. It turned out he represented Jimmy, so I was somewhat buoyed that he felt I was threatening his client's livelihood. In the end it was "Thanks, but no thanks," but I vowed to press on.

Between business meetings, or should I say, attempted business meetings, I was also having some fun. I went out to nearby Roxbury Park and found a pickup basketball game with Elliott Gould and Jon Voight. Gould was known for such classics as *A Bridge Too Far* and *MASH*, and Voight had just done *The Champ* and *Coming Home*. But they were there to play basketball, not talk acting.

Every Sunday morning, a group of us would play the roughest pickup game, elbows flying, shoves all around, bulldozer drives to the basket. We all loved it. Who says actors aren't tough? It was just the kind of de-stressing game all of us needed.

I was also fielding regular phone calls from my parents. Most of them went the same way. "Michael, have you lost your mind?" my mother would say. "What are you doing out there? You have a family. You've got work and a life in Denver."

But they were both more concerned than angry. I always gave it to them straight, exactly as I saw it.

"Mom," I said more than once, "I don't know if the law is really going to work out for me. I'm trying. You know I tried so hard. I'm doing the best I can with it, but I don't know. Law in Denver is very hard right now."

She was always conciliatory. "Nothing's perfect," she chided gently over the phone. "You want everything to be perfect; you want everything in life to be the best of everything. But what you don't understand is that you have to take the good with the bad."

Of course, she had a valid point. Maybe I was being idealistic, somewhat selfish and self-absorbed, and even immature. But I wanted my life to look a certain way, and I wanted to be able to look back on my life and feel proud and accomplished, and trying to forge an acting career would help me feel that way later. I just had to keep trying and give it my all.

Though my parents didn't provide me with any kind of financial support while I was in LA, they made two trips out to keep an eye on me. I had the feeling that they would always think of me as Crazy Mike Burg for the stunts I had pulled, but it was fun having them out in LA. We went out to dinners and shows. If one of my sons had a midlife crisis and decided to pick up and move across the country, I would probably be out there checking in on him, too.

Obviously, I needed an agent to have any hope of solidifying my professional career there. A couple of friends from Denver now living in LA helped me set up meetings with some agents. I also met a few casting directors. Through these contacts, I was able to get on the studio lots of 20th Century Fox and MGM.

While on the Fox lot, I bumped into a casting agent I had met in passing at a bar. Seeing a familiar face, we stopped to chat and catch up. After a few minutes of light conversation, the guy said he could probably find some roles for me. I was interested, very interested— until he placed a hand on my shoulder in a slightly unprofessional way. I realized, oh my God, this guy was making a pass at me!

"Thank you, really, but no thank you," I said to him. "I'm not interested in that."

I beat a path out of there as quickly and politely as I could. I couldn't help but chuckle. It was truly eye opening. I had never been hit on by a man. It was an LA experience through and through.

Another agent I met through a friend invited me to meet him for an early drink at a bar around 5:30 P.M. This agent, who had slicked-back hair but honest eyes, leaned back in his chair, drink in hand, and began firing questions at me.

"How many years did it take you to be where you are as a lawyer?" he asked.

"Well, four years of college, three years of law school, and I've practiced for a while, so we're talking about ten years, more or less," I answered. As the words came out of my mouth, I realized, *Damn, that's a long time to work at something, just to give up on it.*

The agent put his drink down on the cherry wood of the bar and turned to face me directly. "You will work in this town," he said. "I don't know how successful you'll be, but you will find work.

I'm almost sure of that. You've got guts, determination, brainpower. You've got what it takes."

Just as I began feeling really good, buzzing on my drink and the praise of this agent, he hit me with a heavy dose of reality.

"But," he went on, "here's the real question. You've got a wife and two little kids. Are you willing to spend another ten years, just like you did to become a lawyer, washing cars, waiting tables, doing what it takes to become a working actor and make a decent living in this town? Could you be a star? Maybe. Who knows? But you'll have to work long and hard for it. And that's what you need to think about."

He paused. "I'd sign you," he said, causing my heart to momentarily soar, "but only if you give me the commitment that you're willing to do what it takes, for however long, and that you *will* become a star."

I looked him in the eye for a long moment. He was serious. A dazzling future of red carpet premieres and fashionable tuxedos twinkled in my mind's eye, then vanished. I realized I was overlooking all of the dead-end, shit jobs that I would have to work before I could ever get anywhere near the red carpet.

The agent explained to me what becoming a successful working actor at my age meant. There would be years of struggle, years of rejection, and years of baby steps, going essentially nowhere. Only 5 percent of all actors in SAG have constant work. He told me to take a moment to really look inside myself and see if I was willing to do whatever it would take to make it as a working actor.

While I was confident in my appearance, acting abilities, and determination, the talk with this agent had a profound effect on me. It took me two days to make up my mind. The agent had delivered reality to me. I wasn't about to slave ten more years when I had already established myself in law, regardless of the headaches I faced in my legal career. As much as I enjoyed acting and LA, I decided that I would return to my original plan.

At the end of the week, when the lease was up on my Roxbury bungalow, I flew back to Denver with a renewed concentration and determination to become the best trial lawyer I could be. I vowed not to forget my time in LA and my dalliance with acting, but rather to apply what I had learned in the courtroom and integrate my acting skills with the practice of law. I was reasonably certain that that would make me a better lawyer.

CHAPTER 17

RETURN TO REALITY

M y life was changed after I had explored acting and lived in Los Angeles. I had explored a passion and found a niche in my world for it without being reckless and derailing my life. However, in returning to Denver from LA, I embraced two very important things.

The first was that I could give my all to law and still dabble in theatrics. The second was that my wife Debbie and I could not stay together. The financial pressure, as well as my up and leaving for LA, had done bad things to us and to our relationship. Part of the reason I had been able to move out to LA for that period was because Debbie and I were on the rocks. It seemed like we were heading for a legal separation. Certainly, we loved our kids very much, but our relationship dynamic had been forever altered.

The deterioration of our marriage was sad and frustrating. For my part, I had begun to feel the marriage wasn't working. I felt Debbie and I were moving in different directions, but I also felt she could not be flexible about the way my life had changed and would continue to change. Things had begun to turn sour when my big-firm, corporate law career got off-track with the Haligman incident. From then on, Debbie had continued to push me to return to a big firm, working from nine to five, and being the big-time lawyer I had told her I would become. But what she didn't understand was that the path to becoming your best self is not always the one you hope it will be, or even the one you plan it to be. Sometimes life throws you for a loop.

While I was able to flex and bend with the changes, to roll with the punches, Debbie was not. Though she demonstrated admirable patience with my struggles, she clung to an original, idealized plan that could not be executed. In the end, what happened was not her fault. We were just under too much pressure to survive.

I had encouraged Debbie to go back to work as a teacher, but she felt it was more important to be at home with the kids, which left all of the financial responsibility to me. It was a big burden, and I was not able to handle it. Finally, one day, it just did not seem workable. I came home and said, "Maybe we ought to separate."

When Debbie replied, "How about today?" I was a little hurt, but also relieved. She'd had enough, too. It was over. Debbie and I separated in 1984, and eventually divorced in early 1986.

As tough as things became between Debbie and me, we continued to focus on our children as they grew up. Our two sons, Scott and Stephen, became incredible men. Scott was born on Halloween, but there's absolutely nothing scary about him. He earned his degree from the University of Colorado and was on the football team there after earning a scholarship his first year at the Colorado School of Mines.

Scott says that he remembers me telling him to make a lot of money. As much as that may have been a result of the financial troubles Debbie and I had spilling over into his life, he always had expensive taste. Whenever we went out to dinner, he always ordered steak. Either way, that was the direction he was headed.

While working toward a master's degree in finance from the University of Denver, my alma mater, he started an independent pricing system to value hard-to-price assets on a monthly basis for hedge funds. After graduating, he moved to Connecticut, where he worked for Pursuit Partners, a hedge fund that dealt in mortgage-backed securities.

Eventually he moved back to Colorado and became a partner in Deer Park, a very successful hedge fund in Steamboat Springs. When he started at the firm in 2010, it had $34 million under management; it now oversees well over $1 billion. Scott is now married to my beautiful daughter-in-law, Sarah, and they have given us two wonderful grandsons, Emmett Michael Burg and Isaac James Burg.

My younger son, Stephen, was born on Lincoln's birthday. I wanted so badly to name him Abraham Lincoln Burg, but Debbie would have nothing to do with that. Instead, we named him Stephen Jonathan Burg, a fine name, but not on the level of my first choice. Stephen went to Columbine High School and, unfortunately, was enrolled there at the time of the 1999 shooting that made national news, in which two students murdered twelve other students and one teacher. Stephen was eighteen at the time. The experience was understandably traumatic and changed his life. It was heartbreaking, actually. He did not want to leave the house or go back to school, let alone go off to college.

He took some time to recover from the trauma and eventually went to the University of Wyoming, where he became a great student and an All-American rugby player who took part in the national championship game. Stephen later went to University of Denver College of Law, where he earned his JD. Fortunately for me, and for our law firm, he joined the firm and is now a shareholder at Burg Simpson. He is on his way to becoming a successful trial attorney in his own right. He is married to my beautiful daughter-in-law, Amy, and they have two children, Maximus Alexander Burg and Madeline Penelope Burg. To this day, Debbie remains an integral part of her sons' lives and the lives of her grandchildren. She recently remarried and moved to Florida.

Stephen, me, and my brother Peter

When Debbie and I separated in 1984, I moved out so she could stay in the house with the kids. The separation opened up room for new romantic encounters, and for new ways of seeing people, namely my one-time acting coach Kathy Christopher. Kathy and I were working together on the SAG board. I helped her finalize her divorce while I was going through my own separation. Suddenly, it all felt very synchronized, like the planets were aligning and everything was falling into place.

I remember we were out to drinks one night with a group of SAG people. It was a dimly lit bar, and we were all laughing and having a good time. I happened to look over at Kathy, across the table from me, engaged in some kind of conversation about the pros and cons of romantic comedic acting, when it hit me. I thought to myself, *Wow, she has beautiful eyes. I never noticed.*

We soon started going out and dated for over three years. Our relationship went a little bit like a cheesy romantic comedy, a *When Harry*

Met Sally, because when we had first met years before, we really did not like each other. And then we became friends. Only years later, in 1989, three years after Debbie and I were divorced, would we marry.

With that, my family increased. Reese is Kathy's oldest son. He is a commander in the U.S. Navy. He has two master's degrees and is working on cyber security for both the navy and the IRS. He has given us a beautiful granddaughter, Sydney, who has the same name as my dad. Kathy's daughter, Samantha, has been a shining light in my life. She has both a bachelor's and a nursing degree, and works at Burg Simpson as a nurse–paralegal.

Kathy has truly helped me in so many ways. She patiently listens to my closing arguments as I practice them over and over to get her "juror" opinion.

After I rededicated myself to the law, things slowly started to happen. The firm soon got a huge boost when my brother Peter called and told me he wanted to join my small firm. I thought he was kidding. "Are you crazy?" I said. "Why would you come in with me?"

Peter and I have been friends since he was five years old. As little kids, we would hang around together, even though I was five years older. My mother would constantly tell me, "You take Peter with you." We would go to ball games, we would play together, and we would have fun together.

Peter decided to attend law school, and on a visit to me in Denver, he chose the Sturm College of Law at the University of Denver. After graduating, he had his choice of firms. He was recruited aggressively by many of the blue chip firms. In 1980, he went to work at Wood, Ris & Hames, a well-established insurance defense firm. Four years later, they were offering him a partnership that he was contemplating turning down to join me.

So aside from the fact that Peter and I had always been close, I knew that it would be stimulating having him around. I knew that he was a smart lawyer and had valuable experience in insurance defense work that could attract clients.

I gave it to him straight. "Peter, if you're coming out here because you think you're going to make money, then you're making the wrong decision," I said. "Stay there. Build security. Have a life. Be the lawyer you think you can be, and be successful."

Then I offered a caveat. "On the other hand, if you want to come here to have more fun, even though we're going to be struggling, then that's the reason to do it," I said.

By the next day, he had talked to his then-girlfriend and future wife, Sandy. He told me that he had made up his mind that he was going to join me. At the time, I had an associate, Dave Aspinwall, who had gone to school with Peter, and Scott Eldredge. They were excited about his joining the firm.

When Peter left Wood, Ris & Hames and told them his plans, a number of the partners said he was making an awful mistake. They told him that he would be the only *real* lawyer in our firm. He relayed that information to me and I tucked it away, knowing again that it's not how many times you get knocked down, but how many times you get up. The disrespect that they were showing me was something I would remember for the rest of my life, and it made me continue to fight to be the best I could be.

So a turning point in my career, as well as for the law firm, was Peter Burg joining us in early 1984. Not only did Peter leave Wood, Ris & Hames, but to his surprise and mine, a number of insurance companies, including Transamerica Insurance, Northwestern National, and American Family, thought so highly of Peter that they decided to give us some of their work. All of a sudden, from a struggling, small plaintiff shop, we became an insurance defense firm. In the meantime, we continued to develop our commercial and litigation practice, as well as our personal injury practice.

The Fabulous Kangaroo brothers had just jumped into the legal business.

Just before we started the insurance defense work, which quite honestly became our bread and butter, a call came in from a law school classmate of mine, Bob Preeo, who was with a large Denver firm. He had a client whose case had been turned down by two or three major law firms in Denver, all of whom had begged off. Now, no one wanted to touch the case, because the other firms had dropped it.

"Nobody else will take this case," Bob said. "But if you want it, you can have it."

The client was Dave Wilkin and a company called American Airport Development Company, based in Denver. Wilkin and his company had built airplane hangars at a private airport in Erie, Colorado. At the time, there was a tax advantage for building the hangars and leasing them out to small planes. To calculate the tax advantage, he had hired the elite law firm of Ballard Spahr in Philadelphia. He then sold tax-free industrial revenue bonds based on the tax advantages given to him by Ballard Spahr. But in the process, Ballard Spahr had dropped the ball and failed to provide the tax opinion in a timely fashion, causing the deal to collapse and Wilkin to lose several million dollars. The case centered on whether or not Ballard Spahr had committed malpractice in the process.

Ballard Spahr was represented by one of the top trial lawyers in Colorado, William Steele, from the firm of White & Steele. Steele's reputation preceded him, both with lawyers and judges. I had gotten to know him through my brother Peter and his defense firm. Steele was defending the case with a young associate, Mike O'Donnell. (Since that time, Mike and I have grown to be good friends. Today, he is one of the top defense trial lawyers in the country.)

I wasn't sure that the complex case was something I could handle, but I certainly thought it was interesting—and either potentially lucrative or a nightmare waiting to happen. I decided to take over the case and sue Ballard Spahr, one of the most prominent firms on the East Coast, as well as the First National Bank in Denver, the bank backing the transaction, on behalf of the Airport Development Company. The Ballard Spahr partner assigned to keep an eye on me was Oliver Biddle. What a perfect name for a Philadelphia lawyer. Mr. Biddle was related to the Mayflower Biddle family.

Over the next three- to three-and-a-half years, I worked tirelessly on the case. I did everything I could to try to keep the case alive and bring it to trial. I ran up debt and mortgaged my house.

I took the depositions of the lawyers who had handled the bonds. The first series of depositions were held in my small office in Denver; the second in Philadelphia.

When Biddle came to my office, we held the depositions in a cramped conference room that was the size of a small office. Biddle arrived in the morning. To be hospitable, I greeted him with three boxes of donuts. However, when I went to Philadelphia for three days of depositions at their wood-paneled Center City offices, they had nothing in the conference room, save for oil paintings of equestrians.

After the first day, I turned to Biddle and said, "Here you are this big lawyer with this big firm. I gave you a whole plate of donuts and you don't have the courtesy of giving me any donuts when I come all the way to Philadelphia."

The next morning when I arrived for the second day of depositions, there must have been fifty donuts piled up on a huge serving plate on the table. He looked at me and said, "Do you have enough donuts now, sir?" Indeed, I did.

I admit I was obnoxious then. I don't attribute it to my acting, or to my confidence (or lack thereof). I just was. At some level, I thought that would help me. The lawyers defending Ballard Spahr were doing everything they could to throw me off my game, disrupting my rhythm with objections and constantly letting me know that everything I asked would be reviewed by the judge.

I had finally had enough while taking the deposition of the defendant bank's president. I was being browbeaten, and my cockiness surfaced. In an effort to get even and get them off my back, I did something that to this day embarrasses me.

I lit up a cigar to create a haze. It was all theatrics; I didn't even smoke cigars. Every time the bank officer gave answers that were vague or overwrought, I blew smoke in his face. I would pause and say, "So . . . (exhale) . . . are you telling me . . . (exhale) . . . that you did not know . . . (exhale) . . ."

This went on for half an hour. The situation evolved into such a smoke-filled haze that his lawyer scolded me. "Would you stop blowing smoke in my client's face!"

I feigned ignorance. "Oh, I'm sorry (exhale)," I said. "I didn't know it bothered him."

But in those depositions in Philadelphia, I found the smoking gun of ineptitude on which the case would turn. It happened when I asked one of the lead lawyers at Ballard Spahr when they had received the information on which they issued the tax opinion. The lawyer told me that the documents had been delivered to him six to eight months before the tax ruling needed to be issued. When he looked for the documents to give the opinion, the documents had "disappeared." In the interim, the rules had changed to the point where my client never would have gone through with the deal. Therefore, the delay resulted in negligence.

I knew I was in good shape, though not as good as I thought. Bill Steele, who had flown to Philadelphia for the depositions, was on my flight back to Denver. Steele, of course, was sitting in first class. He came back to my seat somewhere in the back of the plane and asked if he could speak to me. He motioned me forward.

I walked to the front of the plane. I took the empty seat next to him. He told me that I had done a tremendous job in this case and that he saw that I could be a great lawyer. His subtext was that I had landed a knockout blow to his side, though, being a cagey veteran, he didn't say as much.

I was floored by his compliment. The case was an amazing experience for me. At that point, I was still unsure I could ever do a thorough job on a complex case or become a good lawyer, as I had just dropped acting and redevoted myself to law. It was gratifying to

have one of the finest defense lawyers tell me what a wonderful job
I had done.

Within the next ninety days, we settled the case. I was able to pay
my bills, pay off my personal debt and the firm's debt, and put a little
money aside. Though the settlement is confidential, that case changed
everything; without it, we probably would have gone out of business.
With Peter joining the firm in 1984 and the cash flow we received
from the insurance defense cases, we became a viable law firm.

Things eventually changed with regard to insurance defense work.
While we were continuing to build the insurance practice, we understood that the rates and profit margins were very slim—each case
was monitored very carefully by the insurance companies. But
everything was about to change dramatically.

I was invited to San Francisco for a meeting with the company
formerly known as TransAmerica Insurance, now TIG. The chair
of the Wall Street firm that acquired TIG/TransAmerica entered
the dining room. He took the podium and asked us to look around.
He said that they had cut over half their panel counsel from each
city. It was important that we understood we were the lucky ones.
We were the ones left, and our cases were going to increase; however,
there was a price for that increase.

He made it clear that we were no longer in a partnership with
the company. His bean counters would be watching us like hawks
and they expected our rates to be minimized. Second, they were also
going to institute an auditing process, in which they would scrutinize
every one of our bills. Going forward, all depositions would have to
be approved before they could be taken. The company would not
allow us to do what we felt we needed to in taking depositions and
making sure that their insureds were completely protected.

Third, our rates would be cut and there would be delays in
receiving payment. The company clearly wanted to cut our fees to

the bare minimum. If we did not like this arrangement, there were plenty of other firms waiting to take our spot.

Then he looked over the crowd of more than one hundred lawyers and said, "Yep. You're the lucky ones. Oh, by the way, I'm wheels up soon. My private jet is heading back to New York, so I can't stay. Enjoy your lunch. We'll see you soon."

We had paid our own way. As I flew back from the meeting, I knew that everything was changing, and changing in a hurry in our defense practice.

Back at the office, I gathered my partners, Peter Burg, David Hersh, Kerry Jardine, Scott Eldredge, Holly Kammerer, and David TeSelle, and told them that we needed to get out of the insurance business. I told them that the chair of the firm that had acquired TIG had made it clear that all lawyers were the same to them, and that they would do anything they could to make sure that we were no longer making a profit.

Our firm had been a huge beneficiary of insurance defense work, but we would clearly have to move on. That work had given us a financial base from which to operate. But now we would have to start winning good old-fashioned, nitty-gritty trial cases on behalf of people who had been wronged by insurance companies and giant corporations.

CHAPTER 18

BLAZING MAD

People who steal drive me crazy. Corporations that steal drive me even crazier. Two of my clients, Ted Hellen and John Yanni Stavropoulos, developed an idea for pet insurance called Household Pet in the late '80s. They then entered a joint venture partnership with a large, billion-dollar insurance company, the Orion Group, to underwrite the idea. The problem was, Orion appeared to have stolen their pet insurance concept and marketed it without giving them credit or compensation.

Ted and John were very likable entrepreneurs. John, in fact, was also one of the finest chefs of Greek cuisine I have ever met. He had a restaurant called Yanni's that had the best lamb chops in the city. They had trouble finding a firm willing to take the case on a contingency basis. Myself, Scott Eldredge, and my brother Peter, our insurance specialist, all agreed that we should handle it.

After taking on the case, my team and I traveled around the country in search of documents showing that Orion had decided to cut Household Pet from their joint venture partnership and then restart it as their own product. It was clear to me that Orion had made the agreement in bad faith. Not only was the joint venture partnership made in bad faith, but it also seemed to me that there appeared to be questionable aspects to the handling and paying of claims.

Peter and I took several depositions together, but I decided that when we got to Orion, I wanted to do something a bit more over the top than usual. The day before the depositions in Hartford, Connecticut, I asked Peter to drive up to Orion's building and let me out of the car.

"What are you doing?" he asked, as I slammed the door shut.

I straightened out my suit and marched up to the stone edifice. Like a madman, I screamed obscenities at the deaf walls of Orion's headquarters. My brother thought I was totally crazy, as did anyone else who might have happened to overhear my little show. But for me, it was my way of getting psyched up and ready to go. Sometimes you've just gotta let loose.

The following day, we showed up to take Orion's depositions. My edge had not worn off. From the moment I dressed that morning, I could feel that I was in one of my moods—a little more aggressive and indignant than my usual calm, collected lawyerly self.

When Peter and I checked in at the front desk in the lobby, the security guards told us that we had to wear badges. To quote a line in Mel Brooks' *Blazing Saddles* that was misappropriated from *The Treasure of the Sierra Madre*, I said, "Badges! We do not need no stinkin' badges."

Orion's lawyer, Phil Cardi, and his team were just leaving the lobby and none of them were wearing badges. I wasn't sure if they were trying to gain a psychological advantage by making us feel like kindergartners at the zoo, but I was not going to wear a badge unless they wore badges. Not that day, no way.

"Why do I have to wear a badge when the Orion lawyers aren't wearing badges?" I said. "Honestly, we're going to win this case, and when we do, this company is going to be owned by us."

The security guards gave each other a "This-guy-is-crazy" look and then turned their attention back to me. They didn't know what to say. It was probably smart of them not to provoke me further. After a minute or so of this standoff, one of the guards motioned us through to the elevators.

Peter and I headed into the conference room. Phil Cardi and Orion's general counsel were seated at the table with a few other lawyers.

"You know," I said to general counsel, "Cardi here is sending you down a very dangerous road."

General counsel gave me a blank look. I was trying to rile them. I felt like pushing their buttons was the thing to do—maybe not the smart thing, but at the time it felt like a way to gain an advantage.

"A road," I went on, "that's going to lead to a very large verdict entered against Orion."

"Hey, excuse me, don't talk to the general counsel," Cardi said to me, lifting a hand in my direction.

I laughed. "I'll talk to whoever I want, thanks," I shot back.

Cardi then stood up a bit too fast. All of a sudden, the tension in the room increased. Tempers were running high. There was a beat of incredible suspense. Cardi moved quickly in my direction and threw me up against a wall.

Man, I was instantly carried back to my childhood days in Wilmette, to when I was bullied by the big guys, my back against the wall and nowhere to go but forward.

With one hand pinning me against the wall and the other curled into a fist and pulled back, Cardi was clearly ready to punch me. But I wasn't backing down.

"Get your damn hands off of me!" I said. "I'm going to shove this case right up your ass."

At this point my brother Peter intervened. Peter pulled Cardi off of me before I could get at him. He grabbed my arm and led me outside the conference room to the hallway. Ever the rational one, Peter talked me down from my state of aggression. After I had calmed down sufficiently, he looked me in the eye and told me that I needed to be a professional and smooth things over with Cardi.

While it pained me to do so, with the most pleasant face I could manage, I went back in the conference room and walked straight up to Cardi. I took a deep breath. "Phil," I said, "let's just forget about all this and move on. Fresh start."

I held my hand out to him. He examined my hand and then me, with a look of pure disgust and disdain. My hand hung in the air, unshaken.

"Put it away," Cardi said.

He shook his head sharply before walking away, refusing my peace offering. The bastard. He only fueled my fire to win the case and kick the crap out of him afterward. I did not see Cardi again until the first day of trial.

We returned the following day for more depositions. When we checked in at the front desk, one of the ladies who had heard the exchange about the badges and my declaration that we were going to buy the place leaned over to me. In a whisper, she said, "I hope you win because we really want to move to Colorado."

The next day, the depositions were moved to a hotel to keep us out of the firm's offices.

The case was going to hinge on my finding a first-rate expert to testify on the bad faith issues. I had just the man in mind: Gene Hames, who had been a partner at Wood, Ris & Hames, the firm where Peter had worked prior to joining our firm.

Initially, I decided to seek out Gene to have him look over the case to determine whether or not he thought that Orion had, in fact, acted in bad faith. Gene had been the lead defense lawyer for the insurance industry for just about every bad-faith case that had taken place in the state of Colorado, so he certainly knew what to look for. He had never handled a plaintiff's case and had never represented a plaintiff. Moreover, he was also retired.

I met with Gene. I told him that I did not want him to testify. I merely asked him if he would look over the case and render an opinion. At first, he was reluctant. He had dedicated his life to representing insurance companies. Though he agreed, Gene told me unequivocally that he would never testify against an insurance company.

After Gene reviewed the file, he told me very plainly that in his opinion our opponents had committed bad faith, both in their joint venture agreement with Household Pets and our clients, as well as in their failure to pay claims as they were coming in from pet owners. Bad faith on two accounts, not just one.

I made my move. "Well, I know you said you would never testify, and that you're retired, but would you consider testifying?" I said. "You'd be a great expert."

If Gene, the dean of defense lawyers, believed it to be a bad-faith case, it obviously had to be one of the worst bad-faith cases ever. I thought maybe he would be motivated by just how egregious the situation was.

"I already said I would not testify against an insurance company," he said calmly, "but let me review the facts on my own."

Two weeks later, we had another meeting. He had spent hours looking over the facts, files, and circumstances, as I expected he would. This was not a guy who gave short shrift to anything. We sat down at the table together, and after a few minutes of small talk, he looked me in the eye. I could see that he was angry.

"You know what, Michael," he said. "I *will* testify in this case. I don't believe insurance companies should ever act this way." We had found our expert.

Much to Phil Cardi's dismay, the case was going to trial. Cardi had been pretty sure that it would not reach that point, but his clients were not willing to settle. And so to court we went.

This was a case I really wanted to win, not only because the insurance company had acted so poorly, but also because Cardi had been such a jerk to me. Although it's not my normal modus operandi, this time I could not refrain, I wanted to get back at him.

We had sued Orion, as well as certain employees, for conspiracy. Because it is very difficult to prove a conspiracy, such a claim carries a distinct advantage: it is exempt from the hearsay rule. This meant it was permissible for us to work in hearsay evidence and this would be very helpful to our case.

Before the trial, we made a strategy shift. Ted Hellen's deposition took five days to complete. At that time, there were no time limitations on depositions. Orion's lawyers asked him every question imaginable, multiple times, in an effort to wear him down. Ted held his own against them. While his answers were not inconsistent, it was difficult for him to keep all of his answers straight. We switched him out for his partner, Yanni Stavropoulos.

Yanni was a gregarious, likable, and honest man. Instead of Ted, who was clearly drained from the badgering during his deposition, and had made some statements that could be easily discredited, we decided Yanni would be our new main witness to tell the story of how Orion had failed to live up to its obligations.

When the trial began in front of Judge William Meyer, I discovered that Cardi had brought in reinforcements. Lord, Bissel & Brooks had joined forces with Cardi and showed up with a platoon of lawyers in red-striped ties and several computers that needed to be set up in the courtroom.

It was quite a spectacle. The firm's paralegals and lawyers seemed to fly erratically around the courtroom trying to figure out how or why they were going to cross-examine our new witness. It looked to me like they were going to pull out all the stops to try to convince the jury that they had done nothing wrong.

The first witness we put on the stand was an Orion vice president. He testified that Orion was very careful indeed with their joint ventures. They owed a duty to its shareholders to make sure that every joint venture they entered into would be successful, he explained; they entered into joint ventures less than 1 to 2 percent of the time. The pet insurance business was very risky and would have failed, he said.

But while he claimed caution and insisted that they only did joint ventures with projects they felt confident would be successful, I pulled statements from their public offering memorandums, as well as their quarterly reports to shareholders, to contradict what he was saying. They *knew* that pet insurance would be very successful. Orion's defense appeared to be based on the vice president's assertion that the company thought it would not work, but I had a memo that showed otherwise. They specifically mentioned pet insurance in their quarterly shareholder report and how successful it would be without my clients as partners.

When I moved to introduce the smoking gun memo, my opponents immediately objected to the memo as hearsay. I stood up, blazing with excitement, and looked at Judge Meyer. "Judge, if you remember, we have a conspiracy claim on our hands here, and therefore there should be an exception to the hearsay rule," I argued.

Judge Meyer looked sternly at us. "Mr. Burg, approach the bench, please."

I walked up to the bench and stared up expectantly at him.

"Mr. Burg, I know you have a conspiracy claim but I must ask you, are you going to be able to prove it?" he asked. "Because if you do not prove a conspiracy claim by the end of your case, I'm going to declare a mistrial and assess all the costs against you for the cost of this trial. And then, as you know, we'll have to retry the case. So having clearly stated all that to you, let me ask you again, Mr. Burg, are you going to prove a conspiracy?"

I held Judge Meyer's gaze. I was confident that I could land the conspiracy claim. "Yes, we are, Your Honor." I knew I was heading into shaky territory.

"Very well," he said. "Objection overruled."

From there, our case took flight. The Lord, Bissell & Brooks lawyers, all three of them, seemed discombobulated. Each of the lawyers Cardi had brought in were clicking around on their computers. The paralegals were running back and forth with documents. It looked to me like they were desperately trying to figure out how their case could be salvaged.

Shortly after the judge ruled on my smoking gun memo, I called a key witness to the stand. She was one of the assistant general counsels for the Orion Group. Her dark, curly hair and tight expression gave her the appearance of having a strong façade—but we would see about that.

I brought out the smoking gun document that showed indisputable evidence of their conspiracy. She had authored the very document I held in my hand. I asked her about the document, and she launched into some wild tale about it. What was most significant was that her explanation was completely different from what she had said in her deposition.

In her deposition, she had specifically stated that she had no recollection of the document. Over and over, she had repeated the line that her lawyers had clearly fed her: "I have no present recollection of the document or its contents."

But at trial, all of a sudden, magically, she *did* remember the document. And she had a lengthy story to go along with it. This was a glaring inconsistency, and I played it to the hilt. As I began to impeach her with her deposition, two or three of the Lord, Bissel & Brooks lawyers leaped up and objected. I smiled and said to the judge, "Only one lawyer can object to this witness, whoever is taking the witness." I knew the rules of the room. Judge Meyer overruled the objection, but they soon objected again. The judge asked Cardi to approach the bench.

"What's the problem here, Mr. Cardi?" Judge Meyer asked.

Cardi's explanation was laughable—something about how her not having a recollection then, but having one now, did not call for impeachment.

"Judge," I responded to Cardi's ridiculous claim, "her answer that she had no recollection then but that now she does, under penalty of perjury, is *certainly* impeachable."

The judge agreed with me, as I expected, and allowed the cross-examination to continue. Cardi huffed back to his table. His case was falling apart.

I pressed on. I asked the witness what research she had done, what she had used to create a recollection, and whether or not she had gone back and amended her answers to the deposition.

She told me she had done no new research or investigating with regard to the document. Her explanation was that she had woken up in the middle of the night and had a recollection of it. In the middle of the night, really! Her testimony was completely unbelievable, so I let it lie there in open court for the jury to contemplate.

When the closing arguments were finished and the jury had retired to the jury room, the alternate juror was excused. Now that deliberations had begun, the alternate was not needed. Once the alternate went out into the hall, the defense lawyers corralled her and asked how she would have voted with regard to the verdict on this case.

"For the defense," she said without hesitation. "I would have voted for the defense. There's not sufficient evidence otherwise." That was not good news for me to hear.

After hearing that the alternate was voting his way, Cardi waltzed up to me. With a toothy, smarmy grin, he said, "I can't wait to get the verdict from the jury and assess costs against you and your client."

It was dirty lawyer talk. He was trying to get in my head and mess with me. Even though I knew Cardi was being a jerk, after hearing the alternate's judgment, my confidence was dented. Suddenly, things weren't looking great for us.

But as time passed and the jury failed to return from their deliberations, hope crept back in. The longer the jury was out, I reasoned, the more closely they were examining the case.

The jury deliberated for more than five hours. When they came back, one of the jurors looked me right in the eye. That made me feel very positive about the verdict to come. Generally, if the jury isn't going to side with you, they won't look at you at all.

The verdict came back in our favor. The jury awarded a $3.2 million judgment, plus $1.4 million in punitive damages for a total of $4.6 million, plus interest. Our clients were jubilant, as were we.

I resisted saying anything to Cardi, but I did go over and shake hands with his team of lawyers, as a demonstration of civility. When I got to Cardi, I reached my hand out. Once again, he refused my handshake and spun away, muttering to himself, "We'll appeal this crazy verdict." And they did.

On behalf of Orion, Cardi and his team of somewhat computer-savvy lawyers appealed the verdict to the Colorado Court of Appeals. The Court of Appeals affirmed the verdict. After hearing the oral arguments to determine if there were grounds for appeal, the Colorado Supreme Court denied certification, thereby affirming the judgment.

The day we received the court's order, I called Cardi, who amazingly took my call. "Where is my check?" I asked. "If you don't deliver it soon, we're going to have to garnish the policies of Orion Group. Business is business."

"You're an asshole," his voice snapped through the line before he slammed the phone down.

I couldn't help but chuckle. In the twenty-five years since that case, I have not seen Phil Cardi, but I certainly look forward to trying another case against him if I get the opportunity. I'll open things with the offer of a conciliatory handshake.

The pet insurance case was an important one for our firm because it gave us a real boost; in short, it kept us afloat. We received a large sum from the award and a great deal of prestige from that victory, both of which go a long way in the world of law firms.

Before the pet insurance case, we were struggling to keep our heads above water. We did not have any reserves or a strong cash flow, both within the firm and in my personal bank account.

I actually had court reporters after me all the time, putting me on COD. One reporter, Sherry Richardson, would give me extended payments until I could settle my cases. We owed her a lot of money, which we eventually paid. Today, I still use her professional services because I will never forget the confidence she had in us and what she did for me. In fact, for years while she had her own company, we were her biggest-paying client.

CHAPTER 19

WINNING CASES

Everyone I meet, be it in a bar, on a plane, or at a dinner party, always asks me about my favorite cases. They don't care about the dogged research that goes into each case, the examination of legal precedents, or complicated pretrial maneuvering. They want to know which ones were the most theatrical, the most John Grisham–like, the ones with boldface names. They want stories from the front lines, and I have several.

In my career, I have worked on some amazing cases—from representing the Little Rascals to All-Star athletes—but there are a handful of cases that will always stand out in my mind as some of my favorites, or at least the most memorable. They are my go-to stories when I am at events and have a small audience to entertain.

A favorite is one that I call "The Super Bowl Case." In actuality, it was *Bundy vs. Colorado National Bank*. The case occurred in the late 1980s. My client was Bob Bundy, a car dealer, and he was suing the bank that backed his business dealings, Colorado National Bank (CNB).

Bundy, who owned a successful Denver dealership, was on the board of directors of the CNB, giving him knowledge of the bank's inner workings. The CNB financed the cars he bought and held in inventory, and he would repay the bank when the cars were sold.

Once a month, a CNB representative would come to his car lot and count the cars to make sure the bank was being duly paid on cars sold. This was not the type of business conducted on trust.

When Bundy grew older and started looking at retirement, he decided that it was time to sell the dealership and the stock he held in it so that he could up and move to sunny Palm Springs and play golf all day. Bundy sold to Herb Neufeld, another old-time car guy. Neufeld was also a big gambler with a slick look who "walked the walk and talked the talk," to use a cliché that fit him well.

In the sale, Neufeld purchased stock from Bundy over a long period of time. As part of the deal, Neufeld also gained access to Bundy's $500,000 line of credit from CNB, which was supposed to be used to purchase cars that would be displayed at the dealership lot to be sold.

During this time, Neufeld made a big bet on the Denver Broncos to win the 1988 Super Bowl over the Washington Redskins. The Broncos lost, and Neufeld used the dealership's $500,000 line of credit to cover the bet. Problem was, he needed that line to buy cars. The solution: he had the bank raise his line of credit to $1 million— half of which covered the bad bet, and the other half of which was used to finance the cars.

After the line was increased, the CNB stopped coming to the dealership for the monthly count. However, when the bank finally did count the cars, it realized that Neufeld had been selling cars without informing them—all to cover the half million dollars he had lost on the Broncos.

The CNB took swift action. It shut down the dealership for breach of contract, and set up a liquidation of all the assets of the dealership, from the existing inventory of cars to the desks and the soda machines, to cover the $1 million it had loaned Neufeld. The fire sale cleaned the place out of everything that was worth anything.

The problem was, Neufeld still owed Bob Bundy $300,000 from his buyout agreement. Bundy went to CNB and proposed that he and the bank split the money from the liquidation. The bank balked. Because Bundy was a bank insider, CNB's position was that his money came last—or after the bank recovered the full amount it was owed.

Bundy objected. He tried to work out a deal with them, proposing a 3-to-1 or 4-to-1 split ratio. The bank refused. Bundy came to us looking for a law firm that would take his case against the bank on a contingency basis.

When I met Bundy, my impression was that he was a nice older man who had worked hard all his life and then retired, thinking he was in the clear financially. He just wanted what was rightly his. I told Peter that I had my doubts winning the case, even though Bundy was in the right. The deck seemed stacked against him. The bank was in first position, and the fact that Bundy was on the board of the bank created a conflict of interest that would be hard to overcome.

But Peter kept saying we should try it, so we took the case. Despite the fact that the case was on contingency, Bundy was a high-profile client for us in 1988, and the Super Bowl gambling aspect of the case was sure to grab Denver headlines. We reasoned that in the end he would see around $150,000 if the case settled, and therefore we could lose money. So the case would basically be about publicity for us.

As soon as we filed Bundy's lawsuit against CNB, Herb Neufeld ran for the hills—literally and figuratively. He returned all of the stock from the deal to Bundy and moved to Montana. After this happened, the bank went to Neufeld and made a deal with him that allowed the bank to challenge whether or not he still had the stock, or if he had truly given it back to Bundy.

In essence, the bank was trying to get Neufeld to say he had all the stock, and therefore as the owner, he could kill the lawsuit. This underhanded tactic failed.

In researching the case, we hired an expert to analyze the books and determine what the true value of the dealership would have been. The expert concluded that after the bank paid itself back, if it had gotten the actual value of the assets of the dealership it sold, there would have been at least another $1 million that should have gone to Bob Bundy. The case went to trial.

In a pretrial hearing that Peter handled, it was determined that Bundy did, in fact, own the stock. We then went forward with the case on the basis that the bank—which had ignored the inventory that it had loaned against—had ultimately used Herb Neufeld to dismantle the dealership. It turned out that other car dealers had come in and ripped off the bank rep, getting used cars for significantly less than their value and buying parts at a deep discount.

During the trial, CNB's lawyers were very aggressive. During Bundy's testimony, one of the bank's lawyers questioned why Bundy was even fighting this case because he had plenty of money. "Go back to Palm Springs," the lawyer snidely concluded after a long, disheartening rant against Bob. They also objected to nearly every piece of evidence we brought in. For two days, there was an echo in the courtroom of "Objection! Objection! Objection!"

At one point, Bundy claimed to have never been in court before, and said it was the first time in his whole life that he had been in front of a judge and jury. But during the other side's closing, they brought in and laid out a huge stack of files on their defense table.

"Never been in court? What about all these Bob Bundy Motors cases we dug up?" the lawyer said. He rattled off a long list of cases where Bob Bundy Motors had sued people for refusing to pay their bills. In my rebuttal closing, I was determined to redeem Bundy.

"Ya know what," I said, "if this case is about who has filed the most lawsuits, the Colorado National Bank wins. It has filed lawsuits against hundreds of thousands of people. Bob Bundy never said his company never sued anyone; he said *he* had never been in court before."

Of course, one of the bank's lawyers jumped up with an objection. Screaming at the top of his lungs, he said: "I object! I OBJECT! This is improper! I object!"

The judge told the other lawyer, "This is the closing argument, sit down and shut up," though in more judicial terms, and motioned for me to continue.

Here is where I used some of my acting skills. After the spectacle the other lawyer had made, I took my time. I waited for the courtroom to quiet down and for the jury to return its attention to me. I wanted to create suspense. Finally, I looked up at the jury, taking a few steps toward them. I surveyed every single face in the box as I began to speak.

"Every time we speak the truth in this trial, this man"—I gestured back to the other lawyer—"this man jumps up and objects. But he will not be in the jury room with you when you find the truth."

I was laughing to myself on the inside because I knew how badly he wanted to object again, but now he could not because it would only affirm my point.

The jury was out for two-and-a-half days. I had made it clear during the trial that I needed my client to be awarded a verdict over $1 million or he would not see a single dime because he owed the bank the $1 million. The jury heard this. They returned a verdict in our favor that came out to more than $2 million—a great win for us.

One of the largest verdicts I have ever received on a single event case turned out to be one of my greatest defeats. I tried the case with Holly Kammerer and my son Stephen. It was Stephen's first trial and, in fact, the only case I have tried with him.

Going into trial, it is critical to put together the right team of lawyers. If you have two very aggressive lawyers paired together, you can end up putting yourself in a bad position with the judge and jury right from the start. This is why I have tried more cases with Holly than any other lawyer in the firm. She is a great partner for me because while I am very aggressive, she is the opposite. She's attractive, has a good smile, and takes a softer but no less effective approach to cross-examination than do I.

The case involved a man named Von Phathong who had come to the United States from Cambodia at age nine. He arrived in Louisiana, speaking no English. He went to work at age ten cleaning toilets at the school. He knew that if he wanted to be successful in America, he would have to work his tail off. Because he had never received much of an education, his English wasn't great, though his work ethic was first rate.

Phathong went to work for a number of oil and gas companies for very meager wages. He was a roughneck, the term for a guy who sets up the rigs. One morning around 4 A.M., he was working a rig in thirty-below weather. The roughnecks on his rig were trying to change the piping from three-quarter inch to five-eighths inch, but they couldn't get the pipes to connect.

They woke up the onsite supervisor, who told them to drive to another job site and find a new pipe. Phathong and the roughnecks made the trip but the new pipe wouldn't fit properly. The foreman and the driller were becoming anxious about the lost time. They made a snap decision to force the pipes together. Phathong was told to hold the pipe with tongs while they made the connection.

Things went horribly wrong. The top drive, the part that pushes the old pipe into the new one, spun around and threw Phathong against the wall, crushing him against the oil rig. He was sure he was dying. He couldn't breathe. They rushed him to the hospital.

Phathong lived, but he was seriously injured. He had broken bones in his back, and there were fractures in several discs. Many of the injuries could have been prevented, but the company had not provided him with the proper safety gear.

At the exact time all this was transpiring, the entire company was being sold. The deal was signed at 9 A.M. that morning, five hours after Phathong's injury, but it was retroactively dated to midnight. Therefore, Phathong had technically been working for the new owners. This meant that the former owners were not responsible for his injury because they did not own the company at the time he was hurt.

Phathong applied for workers' compensation through the former company, but they rejected his claim, saying they were not his employers. He then applied through the new owners, who agreed to pay his workers comp.

We sued the previous company in federal court for gross negligence in not providing proper safety gear because they had denied his workers comp claim. The judge ruled in our favor: they were not the employers, because they didn't own any derricks or rigs, but they still maintained an obligation for their workers' safety. That was the basis for our suit.

The trial was perfect teamwork. Holly did the opening to soften the jury. I did the direct examination of our client and of the roughnecks who witnessed the accident. Holly questioned Mrs. Phathong on direct examination, having her detail what their lives were like, and their dreams and aspirations that were now dead. Stephen handled the medical doctor, and I did the closing.

The jury returned a great verdict and awarded Mr. Phathong $4.4 million from the previous company for negligence, for not having the safety equipment, and for making him perform unsafe acts. Victory was ours, as the defendants had never offered us any money to settle—until the inevitable appeal.

The 10th Circuit Court of Appeals changed the facts! The court said that even though the former owner had sold the equipment the night before, they were still the employer. This meant that Phathong could not sue for negligence. The court reasoned that all the company would have to do to avoid liability is buy equipment and hire employees back to go drilling for gas.

This was ridiculous. I couldn't believe the ruling, as it flew in the face of logic, common sense, and, I believe, even the law. In forty years of practicing law, I had never had that happen.

I had to make the hardest phone call I have ever had to make, to Von Phathong, to tell him that he was not getting $4.4 million. He was getting nothing. Mr. Phathong and his wife cried when I told them. Then he regrouped and thanked us for everything we had done. To this day, I can still hear his wife sobbing in the background.

Personally, I believe the appellate court judges made that ruling because they do not like seeing plaintiffs win large verdicts against corporations. One of the judges was appointed by President George W. Bush, and his appointments were very much pro big business. But rather than pout, a ruling like that only makes me want to take the next case—and win it big.

Like so many kids over the generations, I grew up watching *Our Gang* on TV. The show, which was made in the mid-1930s and repeated for years, focused on the adventures (and misadventures) of a group of poor neighborhood kids known as "The Little Rascals": Spanky, Alfalfa, Buckwheat, Porky, Darla, The Woim, and Froggy. The friendly gang often found themselves at odds with bullies, like Butch, rich kids, and overbearing adults—not unlike my youth growing up as a Jew in the Chicago suburbs.

One day in the mid-'80s, my law partner Scott Eldredge and I were sitting in his office when he got a call from a recent acquaintance he had made, a man named Gordon Lee. They had met through mutual friends. But he wasn't just any Gordon Lee—he was Gordon "Porky" Lee, the adorable, chubby Little Rascal known for wearing overalls and being jovial to a fault.

Gordon told us that he had been traveling in Europe and mentioned that throughout his trip he had seen cartoons in which his character, Porky, was rendered. He thought it was pretty awful that the Little Rascals series and movies were being played around the world without him receiving any compensation. Additionally, Hanna-Barbera, which at one time owned the rights, had created a cartoon, and the character of Porky was drawn in his likeness. He asked if there was anything we could do to allow him to collect what he felt was just compensation.

Scott and I met with Lee and agreed to take his case, and we worked feverishly on it. We felt that we could get what Lee was due, but it was also important to involve not just him but all of the Little Rascals, or at least as many of them as possible.

With Lee's help, we arranged meetings with several of the actors who had played characters on the show. The actor who had played Alfalfa was dead, but we were able to meet with the actors who had played Spanky, Butch, and The Woim. A concern we expressed to everyone was whether or not Hanna-Barbera and TV distributor King World, which had purchased the rights from Hanna-Barbera, had the legal right to use the Little Rascals' likenesses in these spinoff cartoons.

At one point, we rounded up the remaining Little Rascals gang for a meeting. It was as if they were back to being kids on the show. The dynamic was the same. George McFarland, who played Spanky, was still trying to be the leader, telling everyone what was best and that they all should follow his lead. It was fun to see them all together again, bickering and laughing, exactly how I imagined they used to be when the cameras weren't rolling.

Syd Kibrick, who played The Woim, could not make the meeting, so Scott and I went to his house to see him separately. He was a very successful real estate developer. He lived in Beverly Hills on a wide boulevard with skyscraping palm trees.

We rang the doorbell. The woman who answered the door informed us that she was Mr. Kibrick's personal assistant and that he was not at home at the moment. She led us to a living room that was decorated with huge pieces of art. On the wall across from us was a giant painting of a dock on a lake. A boat bobbed in the water.

While interesting to look at, the artwork was, shall we say, rough. With nothing else to do, Scott and I sat there examining this painting. We noticed a cloud in the painting that turned out to be not just a cloud but some kind of written inscription. I went for a closer look. The cloud read, "It's your turn now, Minnie, to weep in vain." Scott and I looked at each other.

"Wow," I said, trying to hold in a laugh.

"What do you suppose that means?" Scott said.

I could tell by his expression that we were equally amused and confused. We spent some time trying to figure out what that could have meant. Eventually, we chalked it up to the strange paintings that you might find in the houses of former child actors.

It turned out Kibrick would not be back from Palm Springs any time soon due to a business delay, so we didn't end up meeting with him that day. But every now and then, Scott and I will walk around the firm's office saying, "It's your turn now, Minnie, to weep in vain."

After some time spent meeting with the actors and working out the logistical issues, we went to work on the case. The first issue was the original contracts with our clients, who had signed them as children. We began to look through the contracts that had been excavated from our clients' filing cabinets, which we had received in discovery. The contracts were very detailed, and even though they were signed in the 1930s, they covered television and animation rights.

But there was something very odd about the contracts. We noticed that all the contracts were signed with "X"s. One of the issues was whether or not those Xs truly bound them, even after they became adults, because at the time they signed the deals, they were all minors.

The critical issue was the legality of the transfer of the contracts. Did King World have the rights to use the Little Rascals' likenesses in the cartoon? King World had purchased the rights from Hanna-Barbera. However, Hanna-Barbera was not the original owner. It had purchased the rights from Hal Roach Studios.

In the mid-'80s, Scott and I went to California and took some of the most interesting depositions either of us had ever taken. The first was from a former lawyer involved in the transfer of rights. To put it mildly, she was a California flower child, with long flowing hair and a permanently serene expression on her face.

Through her testimony we discovered that the rights were transferred through quit claims, legal documents that transferred the rights, which was legitimate. However, through further research we suspected that there might have been a glitch in the title somewhere along the line, thus rendering one of the transfers of rights improper. We suspected that at the time the transfer occurred, they did not have the official rights to use the characters, due to the title glitch.

When I asked her about the title glitch and the acceptance of the quit claim, rather than a transfer warranty deed, a document that provides a clear title to the property free from any interest that may be held by other people, she tilted her head to the side and paused for a second.

She spoke as only a true California flower child could. "Well, you know . . . like, wow, I never really thought about that," she said. "Wow, geez, why'd they transfer something that way, you know? Like, I was relying on [the quit claim], so . . ." That testimony proved immensely valuable to our case and gave us ground to build on as we moved forward.

The last issue for the defense after we discovered the glitch in the title was the fact that the cartoon characters were just that—characters, not real people. To figure out the degree to which the cartoon characters were based on the real people, Scott and I deposed Joseph Barbera.

I was in awe of Barbera's creativity. He had created and founded some of the finest classic cartoons ever made, such as the Flintstones, Yogi Bear, Quick Draw McGraw, Augie Doggie, and Doggie Daddy. I loved these characters growing up, so it was such a pleasure and an honor to get to meet the creator of so many of my favorite childhood shows.

In person, he was an amazing, astute, and brilliant man. I got a real kick out of asking him questions about animation, how it works, and how it had changed over the years. Barbera talked about the animation process, as well as the profits it produced. I was surprised by how expensive animation is in producing a cartoon. I planned to make that one of my major points if King World owed damages.

Throughout the deposition process, Barbera was a true gentleman and gave us as much information as he could.

We also got to take the deposition of other animation artists like Iwao Takamoto and Bob Singer, who created cartoon characters from *The Jetsons* and *Scooby-Doo*. Takamoto and Singer were also involved in the design of the Little Rascals cartoons.

When I asked Singer about how the characters in the Little Rascals were created, he immediately said that it was really easy. He described the process to me. He said that he would take photos of the original Little Rascals and sketch them into cartoon characters, based on the actors' appearances.

"We have their photos, and we take the photo of them and then we begin to simplify to make it into a cartoon character," he explained.

He offered to show me what he meant. He pulled out a photograph of Porky. He then pulled out a picture of the cartoon Porky and compared them side by side. He pointed out the likeness and inspiration.

"So, in fact, the animation characters really are Porky Lee or Spanky McFarland?" I asked.

"Yes, it's definitely them," he said. "That's how we do it."

So we crossed off as a possible defense that the cartoon characters weren't really the actual people.

Singer, too, could not have been more polite. "You guys are the best lawyers we've ever had to deal with. You're even better than our own company's lawyers," he laughed. "Before you go, is there anything else I can do for you?"

Scott and I exchanged looks. Suddenly, I felt like a kid in a candy shop.

"We love the Hanna-Barbera cartoons," I said, speaking for the both of us. "What did you have in mind?"

"Well, who's your favorite?" Singer said, addressing me.

I told him that my favorite cartoon, hands down, was Yogi Bear. I knew my brother Peter's was Quick Draw McGraw. I also knew how insanely jealous he would be if I got a souvenir out of this case and he didn't. So I relayed that to Singer.

"Well, I'll see if I can get a little something with Yogi and Quick Draw for you and your brother," he said with wink.

We were walking on clouds as we left Hanna-Barbera. I almost felt like a cartoon character myself, hopping from fluffy animated cloud to fluffy animated cloud, with big stars swimming around my head.

The case came down to the fact that the quit claim King World received from Hanna-Barbera did not cover the necessary rights. Our position was that King World must pay our clients all of the profits it made because King World never had the right to use their likenesses in the first place. Unfortunately, based on the accounting available, the cartoon was not very successful. In the end, we were able to get a respectable settlement for the Little Rascals. I dare say they made more from the settlement than they did as little kids on *Our Gang*.

But for me, the best part came shortly after the case was settled. I received a package from Hanna-Barbera and inside were original drawings of Yogi Bear and Quick Draw McGraw. In mine, Yogi is saying, "Hey, hey, Mike, you guys got any parks up there in Colorado like Jellystone?" On my brother's, Quick Draw says, "I'll do the thin-nin' around here, Buba Boy!"

Those drawings are treasures that my brother and I continue to hold on to and show off in our offices. Everyone who walks in asks about them. They're memories of a wonderful time, representing some wonderful people.

Bob Singer's "Yogi Bear" gift to me

CHAPTER 20

ON THE BRINK

There were three times when my law firm could have gone under—three very tense, very worrisome times. Fortunately, all three times we managed to pull through. The first was in the early days of my collection work. The third came in 1999 when we dove head first into mass torts—a move that actually propelled us to becoming one of the most successful firms in the country. But the second time was a cold, hard mystery that took some unraveling.

In 1991, we discovered we were leaking cash. For the life of us, we could not figure out where it was going. Yes, we were paying overhead for some twenty lawyers and another forty-five additional support staff. We were advancing costs to mount cases. But there was something else that was siphoning money from us.

The red herring was a partner we had hired to run an office in New Mexico. Through our in-house office manager, Ashley Morris, we discovered that he was charging personal items like clothes and electronics on our company credit cards. I went to him and explained we did not do business that way. On a side note, after he reimbursed us, he was not able to practice law due to an alcohol problem. We ended up closing that office and letting him go.

After this issue with the New Mexico lawyer was settled, we discussed the situation with Morris. Yes, she told us, that was the leak, and now it's fixed. Crisis averted or so we thought.

The problem was, Morris turned out to be the problem. She was running a clever embezzlement scheme, which is why it took us some time—and a bit of luck—to figure it out.

As the in-house office manager and bookkeeper, Ashley Morris handled all of our payables and receivables. This was in the days before computerized checks, so all of them were typed out or written by hand. We had some checks and balances in place to protect us from fraud. The central one was that we would have one person okay a payment and then a different person would sign the check.

In addition to this check-and-balance procedure, we also had it set up so that our accountant verified that the canceled checks returned to us from the bank matched our payments. For example, if the firm wrote a check for $5,000 to an expert on a case, the accountant was supposed to look at the check and make sure that the payment matched the invoice.

Here's how the scam worked: Morris would receive an invoice from an expert for, say, $2,000. She was supposed to have me or one of the other partners sign off that it should be paid. But before getting our okay, she first made a copy of the invoice, unsigned, thereby giving her a duplicate of the invoice. She would have one partner sign one invoice and then go to another partner and have him sign the duplicate. This gave her two check authorizations. Then she would make one check out to the expert and make a second check out either to herself or her husband.

Initially, she started off small, $100 or $200 at a time, here and there. But as time passed and we didn't catch on, she grew bolder and bolder. When the canceled checks were returned from the bank, she would simply pull out the extra check written to her, and then go balance the account on the computer as if only one of the checks had been cashed. Meanwhile, by computer she was producing financial reports that appeared on the face of it to be incredibly strong. Problem was, when we called the bank, they informed us that we were losing money.

Here we were, trying to build our practice, and somehow our money was disappearing. We had a mysterious cash flow problem on our hands, and no one had any idea how to solve it.

Strangely, my wife Kathy and I were at Universal Studios in LA when she said, "Let's go to this psychic at Universal. It will be fun!" I said okay. The psychic looked at my palm and brought out the tarot cards. She said, "Something is wrong at your business." I thought, "Cash flow in New Mexico," immediately, but she said, "You do not know about it yet, but will find out soon. Also, do not worry because your business will end up being more successful than your wildest dreams."

Within two weeks came a tip. I was in North Carolina taking a deposition on a case when I received a call from Kathy. "Something really odd is happening at the firm. I gave one of the part-time night typists your number. She's going to call you and tell you something you really need to hear about." Perplexed, I told her to have the woman call me immediately. The night typist was a part-time worker who came in after hours to type up pleadings and letters. I could hear the nervousness in her voice on the other end of the line.

"Hi, Mr. Burg," she began. "I felt like I needed to call you because something really strange happened with my paycheck." I asked her what had happened.

She told me that when she opened the envelope, she realized that the number was more than double what it should have been. Being the honest person that she was, she went to talk to the in-house office manager, Ashley Morris. She told Morris about the mistake in her paycheck and felt wrong taking more money than she had rightly worked for and deserved. Morris laughed it off and said, "Consider it a Christmas bonus."

"It just didn't sound right to me," the night typist told me over the phone. "It didn't *feel* right. I thought I should call you and tell you." I thanked her and hung up to contemplate my next move. I thought to myself, this is bad, something serious is up.

As soon as I was done with the deposition in North Carolina, I flew back to Denver and called my partners into a meeting. I laid out all the information I had. One partner, David Hersh, took the lead in solving the problem. We agreed we would give everyone lie detector tests. We collectively decided that we would have a full office meeting at which we announced to all of our employees that over the next few days everyone would be subjected to a lie detector test.

Next day, sure enough, Ms. Office Manager did not show up for work. Not only had Morris disappeared, but she had also taken two months of returned checks with her. As a final salvo, she locked us out of our own computer accounting system.

The jig was up, but we were still in trouble. We called the police, and we also tried to call Morris multiple times, but it was no use. She was gone. She had, however, left some belongings in her office, so we hired nighttime security guards to patrol the place in the event she came back.

Next, we opened a full investigation. Because we were not sure who else, if anyone, was involved, we started talking to employees who could have feasibly been involved. First up was the accountant.

I called him into my office. "What's going on here?" I said to him, and fully expected an adequate answer. By this time, we had looked over some of the past checks that she had not taken and started seeing her and her husband's names printed in her prim handwriting, first on just a few, and then on many.

"What the hell?" I blared at the accountant. "Aren't you supposed to be monitoring this? What do we pay you for?"

"Are you accusing me of stealing money from you?" he asked.

"No," I said. "I'm accusing you of not doing what you're supposed to be doing—monitoring our finances!"

That afternoon he resigned. Surprise, surprise. So then we were out an accountant, as well as an office manager. And we were still locked out of our own computers.

David Hersh, Scott Eldredge, Peter, and I decided we needed to put our heads together and figure this out before it sank the entire firm. Everything else was put on hold for the moment. The first thing I did was run down to the bank. We had a $100,000 line of credit at the time with Central Bank and Trust (today, it's an eight-figure line of credit). I met with John Harliss, a manager at Central Bank and Trust, and alerted him to the embezzlement situation. I told him that I did not know how much we had lost, but I suspected that it was a significant amount.

"We might need another hundred thousand on our line, maybe even more," I told him. "If we don't get it, we'll likely go under. And of course, we will pay every cent of it back. But for now, we need help."

Harliss, in his neatly pressed suit, gazed calmly at me over the cherry wood of his desk. "Mr. Burg," he said, "I know you. I know where you started. And I have no doubt in my mind that you will pay us back."

I breathed a sigh of relief. It felt so good to have earned the trust of this bank, and the community at large. I thanked him.

"And you have my word that if you need another one or even two hundred thousand, I will give it to you," he said, standing to shake my hand.

Reputation matters. I wasn't about to try to hide anything from the bank. My view of banks has always been to be 100 percent transparent with them.

The pressure was off in the short term. We wouldn't be going under. It actually turned out that we did not even need to raise the line. Next we needed to hire a new accountant. We started asking around, trying to find someone who could comb through our books and discern what was real from what was not. We also hired a computer expert to try to break back into our computer system. It seemed as if we were on an upswing, starting to rebuild ourselves, when Ashley Morris struck again.

The month's canceled checks were scheduled to be delivered to the office, but somehow, Morris intercepted the mailman. She apparently claimed to be there to pick up our mail for us. She must have showed up right when the mail was being delivered.

Luckily, the mailman notified us that a woman had tried to pick up checks from him. Being the well-trained mailman he was, he did not give her the checks. We then put our security guard on alert and told him to watch for her.

The word started leaking out about what had been happening with our firm, and people began coming forward with information. The most egregious was that Morris had apparently started sporting an expensive designer wardrobe and had even bought a Corvette. Her line was that her grandmother had died and left her a sizable inheritance.

We started gathering evidence to turn over to the authorities in order to have her arrested. We finally received the checks that she had tried to pick up from the mailman. We had the bank go through the microfiche from our accounts. From the microfiche, we were able to determine that she had embezzled upward of $300,000 over a long period of time.

We were concerned about our trust account because that is where we keep money due to our clients from verdicts and settlements. The good news was that she had never touched our trust account. That wasn't just good news; it was great news. It meant that the problem only affected the firm's operating accounts, our own money.

The next issue was our new accountant. He overcharged us obscenely and ripped us off. He probably charged us three times what he should have, but we had to pay him because we needed to figure out if our balances were correct, in terms of our receivables and payables. We had no idea whether our payments had been going out, so we had the new accountant send out an audit letter saying that he was doing an internal review to see if the balances matched.

We also had to send out letters to insurance companies to see if Morris had been taking checks that we had never even laid eyes on and endorsed them over to herself.

Though it turned out that she did not, the only way to be certain and safe was to go through every single one of our payables and receivables to confirm it. We gathered enough evidence to go after her and get her arrested, prosecuted, and slammed behind bars.

One issue was that because she wasn't a bonded employee we weren't protected from thefts carried out by her. We carried a small policy for theft, but because she wasn't bonded, the recovery of the money she had stolen would prove difficult. We went after the first accountant, too, for not upholding his ethical and legal responsibility as a fiduciary to cross-check payments. He settled up with us for around $150,000, plus a bond payment from his insurance company.

At the end of the embezzlement day, we were a little over $100,000 out of pocket. The judge pointed out to us at the trial that Morris would be unable to pay us from jail, and asked us what our thoughts were.

Peter shook his head. "We think orange is a good color on her," he said. We wanted justice. We ended up working out a deal with the district attorney where Morris was supposed to be gradually paying us back.

She and her husband thought they were merely going to get probation, a slap on the wrist. They might have figured that it was just a white-collar crime, and that they probably wouldn't go to prison, but the judge put both her and her husband in orange suits for two to three years.

So we won a judgment against her and she went to jail, which was the main thing we wanted out of it. Justice was served, and the firm survived. And today we have a number of different checks and balances in place to protect the firm.

CHAPTER 21

STEAMBOAT SPRINGS EXPLODES

Steamboat Springs, Colorado, was buzzing with activity at the height of the ski season on Thursday, February 3, 2004. The idyllic Colorado town attracted vacationers from all over the state and the country. The Good News Building, located in the heart of downtown, was packed with the lunchtime crowd. Ladies were being beautified at the hair salon. The building's two restaurants were so busy that both were running on a wait. People waiting for tables were browsing in the gift shop.

Suddenly, without warning, a huge explosion rocked the building. Flames shot out of the lower windows. Within minutes, the area looked like a war zone. A raging fire broke out and spread to the restaurant's kitchen. Pressurized beverage containers began to explode like bombs. Terrified restaurant workers crawled through the rubble to escape.

Fire and rescue crews rushed to the scene. An entire side of the Good News Building collapsed. Four people working in the offices on the upper three floors jumped out of windows in fear that the entire building would collapse.

When the dust finally settled, amazingly, no one had died. Several people were hospitalized, and more than twenty people suffered serious injuries. Downtown Steamboat Springs was evacuated.

Gas service to all businesses and six hundred homes was shut down while investigators tried to determine what had happened. The preliminary indication was that a gas leak had caused the explosion; the pilot light of a basement hot-water heater had ignited leaking gas. The question of why this had happened became the central issue for the townspeople. They demanded to know who was responsible.

Days after the explosion hit the front pages of newspapers across the state, my firm was brought in. The legal case came to us through our insurance practice. Continental Insurance hired us to handle a subrogation claim to recover the loss on the property caused by the explosion. Though that was a business approach to protect the carrier's financial interests, everyone at the firm saw that the explosion and the harm caused to innocent victims was a human case. Yes, we had to represent our client. But wasn't there a larger responsibility?

As we discussed what had happened and what to do, my partner Kerry Jardine came up with a way to include the claims of individual victims in our case. Not only did this strengthen our case, it was the right thing to do. Peter, who had a strong relationship with Continental, presented the idea to them. The company was convinced and agreed to allow us to include other injured parties.

In the process of preparing the case, we met a local lawyer named Jim Heckbert. Jim had practiced in Arizona before semi-retiring to Steamboat Springs. He had a number of clients who were injured in the explosion. We all agreed to work together on the case because our interests were aligned. It was decided that Jim, Kerry, and I would be lead counsel for the plaintiffs. Peter Smith and Bill Grey from another firm were also part of the plaintiffs' team, though neither participated in the trial.

The defendants were Greeley Gas, the company that controlled the gas line at the time of the explosion, and U.S. West, the telephone company. U.S. West was at the center of the case. Eighteen years earlier, it had hired a subcontractor to lay telephone line. During that process, the subcontractor, A. A. Cox Construction, had damaged the gas pipeline. Rather than replacing the pipeline, Greeley Gas had wrapped it in field tape. Over time, the tape wore away and the gas line leaked.

U.S. West was represented by Tom Alfrey, a strong defense lawyer. Handsome and smart on his feet, Alfrey never used notes for any of his cross-examinations, openings, or closings. This kind of confidence moved juries. Greeley Gas was represented by Dave Kerber and Bill Saas, two very capable lawyers.

As our team prepared, we knew that this was going to be the biggest trial in the history of Steamboat Springs. In fact, the case was so big, with so many lawyers and so many parties, that the courthouse could not accommodate all of us.

The judge, Richard Doucette, was brought in from Hot Sulphur Springs, a nearby Colorado town. Because the explosion had occurred across the street from the Steamboat Springs courthouse, all the judges in Steamboat Springs were disqualified because they had witnessed the explosion.

Judge Doucette determined that the case would be heard in the mostly vacant, newly built airport just outside the city. A makeshift courtroom would be set up there, and the trial would proceed as usual. It seemed a little strange. I had never participated in a trial held anywhere but a courthouse.

One of the key lessons I learned in this case was that as an attorney you cannot rely on dogged preparation and on putting together a "bag of tricks" to get through every case. It is impossible to predict all the twists and turns that can occur over the course of a trial, and you can't assume that the same techniques will work every time.

All lawyers have their own comfort zones and ways in which they practice. I was, and am, no different. However, this case was one in which I had to throw out all of my preconceived notions of how to bring a case to trial. This wasn't a case that I could fit into my trial repertoire. The case pushed all the boundaries of everything I had learned from being a trial attorney, and I knew that to win I would have to push myself as well.

For starters, I had to leave my comfort zone entirely. As intimidating as courtrooms are for most people, they can be paradoxically comforting to an attorney. The courtroom is my safe haven. I know my way around a courtroom. I feel at home and comfortable there, no matter what the circumstances may be.

But in this case there would be no courtroom. I would be trying what was probably the biggest case of my career to that point in an airport. I had no idea what to expect. The "courtroom" had to be created, like a film company building a set for a movie. None of us knew what it would look like, much less how it would actually work on a day-to-day basis. Could a trial take place outside of a courthouse? I guess we were about to find out.

To make matters worse, I was diagnosed with a malignant melanoma three weeks before trial. The melanoma was removed surgically, and I was cleared just four days before the trial began.

No law school that I know of teaches a class in "how to try a case in an airport." Yet, here I was trying a case in an airport. If a lawyer is not willing to adapt and be nimble on his or her feet, these types of challenges can unseat even the most seasoned professional.

The first and most critical step is knowing your case. With a case that would certainly have oddities based on the venue alone, this was paramount. I knew that having a full handle on the case was critical to the outcome of the trial.

Our team, along with our outstanding paralegal Becky Draper, spent a great deal of trial prep time figuring out the logistics of the actual trial, which is something that you cannot do on the fly. We spent hours upon hours poring over the facts of the case and trying to understand what had *actually* happened—steps that must be completed well before the start of any trial. When it comes down to trying a case of this magnitude in these very unusual circumstances, it was critical to have prepped thoroughly so that we would be ready to roll with the punches of the moment.

As puzzling cases go, this case probably contained more puzzle pieces than any case I had previously worked on. There were many elements involved that ranged from when the gas line was pierced; why it wasn't repaired; how and why the explosion happened; what the damages would be against the gas company for not making its lines safe; to what damages would be assessed against the telephone company's contractor that fractured the gas line.

The trial was scheduled to last for seven weeks, but from the outset of the pretrial conference, it became obvious that this case was going to go on much longer than initially anticipated. Judge Doucette called the lawyers together for a pretrial discussion. There were no settlement offers on the table, because none of the defendants felt that they were responsible. Greeley Gas claimed that they had done nothing wrong. U.S. West claimed they did not damage the line that caused the catastrophic fracture and the release of natural gas. There was also the issue of how the cracked gas line was ignited. We believed that it was a gas hot-water heater pilot light in the Good News Building, but the defense was conceding nothing.

Because of the magnitude of the explosion and the ensuing terror, the case was highly dramatic and well publicized. *The Steamboat Pilot*, a local newspaper, covered the case in exhaustive detail. When Court TV asked for permission to film the trial, Judge Doucette asked our opinion on the matter of cameras.

My view, despite feeling comfortable in front of a camera from my acting days, is that having cameras in the courtroom changes everything. I watched the O. J. Simpson trial and realized that almost everyone, from the judge to the witnesses, seemed to play to the camera. All the participants were trying to bolster their own personalities, almost like self-promotion, conscious or not, rather than actually trying to help the court arrive at justice. From that case, I formed my opinion that cameras should not be permitted in court-rooms, because they alter the course of the trial. All sides asked that cameras should not be allowed in the Steamboat case, and Judge Doucette agreed.

As promised, the courtroom was a makeshift setup in the cavern-ous space of the unused airport. A legitimate-looking bench was installed for the judge, flanked by the flags of the United States and Colorado. There were row upon row of folding chairs set up to accommodate the massive gallery for people who showed up to watch the proceedings. The way our voices and footsteps carried in the large space took some getting used to. I tried to look at it as though I was on stage and playing to one of the largest audiences I had ever had in my life.

The search for the jury came first. Kerry, Becky Draper, and I set up camp in Steamboat Springs. Knowing that we would be there for at least seven weeks, we rented three one-bedroom condos and a four-wheel-drive truck.

Voir dire, the process during which lawyers question the poten-tial jurors, was basically unlimited. Often, judges will impose limits on voir dire, such as time limitations, a restriction on the types of questions that can be asked, or the number of peremptory chal-lenges a lawyer can use in excusing potentially unfavorable jurors.

This is a part of trial where the attorney really needs to know the ins and outs of his or her case. You must dissect the individual issues to determine the most incisive questions to raise with the jury pool, particularly if a judge limits your time.

Questions you should absolutely have figured out ahead of time include questions such as these: What are the primary issues in this case? Are there red flags that might signal that a potential juror should be dismissed? What are the potential biases that could alter a juror's ability to judge the case fairly based on the evidence?

All of these issues should be addressed well ahead of time so that when you walk into the courtroom—or in this instance, the airport—you appear calm, unruffled, and, most of all, prepared for anything.

In this case, the lawyers were allowed to ask as many questions as we wanted. We used a five-page questionnaire to ask the potential jury members questions, ranging from their opinions of corporations taking responsibility to their thoughts on people suing for personal gain.

Jury selection lasted five days. We went through over three hundred jurors before we found a jury of six that all sides agreed to seat. Depending on the state and the type of case at trial, juries can range from six to twelve jurors. Because of the projected length of the trial, we also selected three alternates.

Interestingly, the foreman of the jury, while in utero, had lost his father to a gas explosion. Under normal circumstances, this would have biased him and caused the defense to use a peremptory challenge to remove him. However, because he indicated that he listened to and supported Rush Limbaugh and despised both trials and lawyers, the defense left him on the jury.

During my voir dire, I looked at the very nervous jurors and realized why they were nervous. This was the biggest case in Steamboat Springs' history, and they were all about to play a very crucial role.

I asked if they were nervous. They all looked at me and nodded their heads yes, tight-lipped.

I told them I was nervous, too. "Wanna know why?" I asked. They stared at me expectantly. "This is my first trial, too . . ."

Surprised, even puzzled looks crossed their faces. How could a rookie lawyer be handling such a big case? After two beats, holding their eyes the whole time, I continued, ". . . in an airport." That got a laugh out of them.

Breaking the ice is critical. After that, the jury understood that I was there to tell them the truth about what had happened. In this case, I needed them to follow me every step of the way.

CHAPTER 22

READY FOR TRIAL

The opening statement sets the tone for every trial. This is the time when the lawyers first introduce the jury to their side of the case—where they succinctly present all their knowledge to a group of people who don't know anything about the case. Most important, it is the introduction of the client to the jury and the client's reason for seeking justice.

Generally, opening statements are brief. Judges typically do not allow much time, probably because they don't like long-winded lawyers. The goal is to give the jury as much information in that time as you possibly can, and to deliver that information smoothly and in an orderly fashion that makes logical sense.

Demeanor is often everything. You have to be pleasant and likable, but also engaging. This is another way in which acting lessons and stand-up comedy came in very handy. Being trained as an actor has been extremely useful in helping me communicate effectively with a jury. Acting teaches audience engagement, and the jury, for the purposes of the opening statement, is your audience.

That said, I never actually *act* in trial. If there were even a hint of me morphing into Al Pacino's character in . . . *And Justice for All*, the jury would smell a fraud. If they believe you are just saying things to get into their good graces, then you will lose every time. Sincerity and passion are key: without a heavy dose of genuine feeling the jury will never buy your arguments.

I use opening statements a little differently from most other lawyers. While I bolster my client's case, an important aspect of opening statements is to begin poking holes in the case of my opponent. It is never too early to start dismantling the other side's argument. This has to be done cleverly so that it does not detract from a straight-ahead presentation of my client's case.

For me, opening statements are not merely when each side stands up and gives an overview of his or her case and outlines what will be presented. Rather, this is where the trial actually begins, meaning that this is my first chance to start convincing the jury away from my opponents and their views, and toward me and my views. This is the time to begin to offer objections, should there be things introduced that are not relevant to the case that have not been properly disclosed, or that might otherwise challenge the rules of civil procedure.

In this case, U.S. West had spent a lot of money assembling a model of the fiberglass trench that showed the location of all the gas pipes. During the defense's opening statement, U.S. West attorney Tom Alfrey began talking about the trench. Immediately, Jim Heckbert, my co-counsel, jumped up and objected.

"Your Honor, I object," Jim said. "None of these measurements are correct. This does not represent the actual trench."

Alfrey then made a big mistake—one of the few he made during the trial. He decided to let Jim tell him where the errors were. Aspect by aspect, Jim methodically picked apart the model trench. He told them where all the mistakes were in their model, and why they should not be allowed to use it because it was so flawed.

Ultimately, Judge Doucette let Alfrey continue to use the fiberglass trench in his opening. Wisely, Alfrey never brought it up again for the rest of the trial. However, to turn the tables, I used the trench in my closing. I made it clear to the jury that U.S. West and Greeley Gas were trying to fool them, because the trench their lawyers talked about during their opening was a "magic" trench that they had made disappear.

Issues like this come up in any trial. It's important to take careful notes, even if some are only mental, and to not allow those inconsistencies to pass by unnoticed. Had we not objected, and had we not been the ones to insist on being walked through the dimensions and the history and all the other issues we had with the trench, it could have become a viable tool to use later. In fact, the jury might have relied on the faulty trench throughout the trial.

But in a fortuitous twist, the defense presented something that allowed us to start pointing out the deficiencies in their case early on. They had not called a single witness, they had not asked a single question, and yet, thanks to my team's competence and attention to detail, they had already lost a certain amount of credibility with the jury.

The other mistake with the trench issue, which we mentioned above, is that a lawyer should never allow the other side to offer any explanation or reading of his exhibits or models. In cases like this that involve so much technical jargon, it is very important that each witness provides testimony that educates the jury: education is key.

Because this particular case required learning about a complex issue (gas lines and how they are installed and maintained), I knew that I could not step into the courtroom and talk to the jury as if they knew everything that I knew about those issues. The fact is, they probably knew nothing about gas lines and their maintenance. I know I knew very little before the case.

Both sides brought in experts to discuss the gas lines. But again, I had to be careful not to put a witness or an expert on the stand and have them testify to issues that would go right over the heads of the jurors.

Our side began by bringing in the fire department, which had footage of the devastating fire from the explosion. The footage showed flames shooting more than one hundred feet in the air. Some of the people from the fire department were first-responders on the day of the explosion and had personal stories. Witnesses, one by one, testified about what happened to them as a result of the explosion. One restaurant worker recalled crawling out through the rubble with flames nipping at her heels.

We called two or three experts to the stand who were former employees of the U.S. Department of Transportation (DOT) to discuss the use and installation of natural gas and gas lines and the DOT regulations. We had some cause and origin experts who testified relating to the catalyst of the explosion. Finally, we called gas experts to testify about the duties of gas line installers. Most important, at every step, we broke down the complicated, technical jargon into lay terms, to be sure the jury understood what was being discussed.

Another factor in a case with heavy testimonials is that people are apt to lose interest. When a juror is sitting hour after hour listening to guys in suits ramble on about technical information, they will inevitably grow bored no matter how hard they try to pay attention. With a trial that stretches several weeks, presenting a lot of boring testimony can be detrimental to your case, even if the more tedious testimony is actually bolstering your claims.

For the jury's sake, when introducing testimony through an expert, it is always best to use the plainest language. I try to break the information down into small, bite-sized chunks for the jury to take in little by little, instead of overwhelming them with a barrage of technical mumbo jumbo. If they don't understand what is being said, it makes for very long, uninteresting days—and that makes them less inclined to pay full attention. And if they're not giving the case their full attention, it is quite likely they will miss vital information from testimony, which will obviously impact their ability to effectively evaluate the claims.

The jury in the Steamboat Springs explosion case managed to pay attention during the entire case, and it was clear to them that the use of natural gas can be extremely dangerous.

We had more experts come in to speak about the actual procedure of laying the pipeline. When the pipeline system was put in place, each piece of pipe had to be treated as if it were nitroglycerin, making sure that it was padded, coated, and laid into the trench with the greatest care.

The DOT also required the gas company to survey and examine the line once it was laid and covered. If there was any chance that their gas line could be hit or had been damaged in any way, the gas company was required to inspect the line and, if need be, replace it. But that had not been done under the Good News Building. The gas line had been damaged and sloppily wrapped in padding and field tape. Even if the gas company did not damage the line, it was required to inspect and replace it, if necessary.

Little by little, the jury began to understand the extreme dangers posed by gas lines, and how the gas line had to be understood by those who installed it, understood by those who maintained it, and understood by those who oversaw its functions. It was not something that could be simply installed and then forgotten about.

In addition to the fire department and the DOT, both sides of the case called metallurgy experts to testify on what had happened to the pipe. We had to look not only at the process and procedure by which the lines were constructed, but also at the physical components of the pipeline and how it was affected by time, natural elements such as freeze-thaw, and maintenance issues.

Both sides had experts to comment on the DOT standards. There were a multitude of regulations and guidelines in place for gas lines, and we needed experts in those areas to help us explain these issues to the jury.

The expert on DOT regulations for the defense was William Clayton, who lived in Houston, Texas. Clayton had spent most of his career working for Atmos Energy, the parent company of Greeley Gas. In fact, he had been involved in creating the DOT standards for gas lines.

Jim and I were both able to cross-examine Clayton. When it was my turn, I asked him about the duties of the gas company. I focused on a situation in which they knew their line was vulnerable and could be hit. I asked him: shouldn't it be the gas company's responsibility to protect the line from any kind of damage, and to check it as frequently as needed before it is buried again?

Amazingly, he agreed with me. He indicated that once the gas company knew the line could be hit, it had the obligation to inspect and replace the line. That was a big point for us.

As Clayton left the courtroom after his testimony, I asked him if he would ever testify against a gas company. He told me that if I could find the worst gas system in the country, the answer would be yes. I filed that away for future consideration.

About halfway through the trial, U.S. West attorney Tom Alfrey, being the competent lawyer he is, understood that this case was not going well for the defense. He shifted his strategy and began to point fingers at Greeley Gas.

While U.S. West's contractor may have been responsible for hitting the line with its backhoe, it was Greeley Gas that could have prevented the accident altogether if only they had gone in and replaced the line after it had been damaged.

Alfrey's tactic helped us tremendously during the trial. Both Jim and I were able to go after the defense witnesses with regard to their obligations based on the DOT standards. We hit them hard with the obligations that they failed to uphold with regard to the gas line maintenance. Alfrey confirmed our position by taking them to task on redirect (the time allowed for a lawyer to follow up on questions asked by the other counsel).

During this very intense trial, there was the occasional moment of lightness. One of the funniest things that occurred came in the middle of a heated cross-examination. A woman in a thick fur coat came waltzing into the empty airport lugging three suitcases and asked where she could check in for her flight. Everyone had a good laugh, because the airport wasn't even operational.

The case pushed past the seven-week mark and into nine weeks. As the case drew to a close, we had to prepare for our closing arguments. Both Jim and I were to give individual closings. Jim went first and did a convincing job. He laid out the technical foundation of our case. When it was my turn, I focused on the moral responsibility of Greeley Gas.

Closing arguments are among the most important parts of a trial. The lawyer has spent days, or in this case weeks, laying out the case, spewing all sorts of data at a jury that has tried to absorb it all in a very condensed period of time. By this point, the jury is tired, the lawyers are tired, the judge is tired. Even the bailiff is ready to move on to the next case on the docket to bring some new faces into the courtroom.

But for those of us who are trying a case, this is crunch time. At this stage, a lawyer cannot let his guard down precisely *because* the trial is so close to the end. In many ways, closing arguments can inject a trial with a new kind of energy.

Closing arguments can make the difference in the outcome of the case. All of the information has been laid out for the judge and jury. They know everything they need to know. The lawyer must have a handle on all the testimony, witnesses, and exhibits that have elicited any sort of objection, which objections were sustained, which were overruled. He must have clarity on what types of testimony or statements to avoid in order to ensure that there are no admonishments from the judge. Being interrupted by the judge is not the kind of final impression any lawyer wants to leave with the jury.

It is challenging to pull all that information together into a brief, succinct statement to use as the final image presented to the jury. But I attempt to turn it into a positive. I see it as my final chance to leave the jurors with a lasting impression of my case.

In this particular case, I had one cross-examination point that I really wanted to make clear to the jury. I had asked the Greeley Gas employees at trial, "How many more time bombs are buried beneath the streets of Steamboat Springs, just waiting to explode, as a result of your company failing to make its inspections?" That drew an objection, which was sustained.

"Well, then," I said, rephrasing my question, "how many more explosions can the city of Steamboat Springs expect?" The answer to that question was allowed. Amazingly, the Greeley Gas employees responded that they did not know.

What! That was terrifying—and incriminating. It was a chilling moment in the trial, because the jury knew and understood, at that moment, that Greeley Gas had not done their required work. The company knew that there was real danger afoot under the streets of Steamboat Springs, the city in which they lived, raised families, and felt comfortable. It was exactly the sentiment that I wanted to leave with the jury.

Of course, as a plaintiff's lawyer, no closing argument is complete unless you talk about money, real money. You cannot give the jury approximations or dollar ranges. You must ask, outright, for the exact amount of money you want them to award your client. In order to convince them to give your client the desired monetary compensation, a plaintiff's attorney needs to have evidence and testimony to back it up—all of which, by the way, should have been laid down throughout the trial. Damage conversations should never be brought up during closings, only returned to.

During my closing, I told the jury that besides giving us compensatory damages, they needed to send a message to Greeley Gas. They needed to let Greeley know that the negligence of their company toward basic safety in Steamboat Springs, Colorado was intolerable.

I asked the jury to match the punitive damages with compensatory damages, which is the maximum allowed in Colorado. For theatrical effect, I also asked that when they filled in the amount of money for punitive damages that they physically write the number really big so that it would go to the parent company in Houston to see.

"Maybe then they will understand that Steamboat Springs will not allow this kind of behavior," I concluded.

After four-and-a-half days of deliberation, the jury came back with a verdict of over $6.4 million in damages. They gave us an equal amount in punitive damages, and they wrote it really, *really* big, just the way I had asked.

It was an exciting victory. But more important, a few things occurred as a result of that case that had an even more lasting impact than the verdict. First, the jury members personally went down to the city council of Steamboat Springs and demanded that they dig up all the gas lines and replace them. What choice did the city have? Greeley Gas employees had basically said that the place was a ticking bomb. The city council concurred.

Interestingly, the lot where the Good News Building once stood remained vacant for nearly ten years. The building was fully razed. But finally, as part of the healing process and the long arm of commerce, a new building went up to house a business perfectly suited to the resilience and temperament of the community: Steamboat Ski and Bike Kare.

I also became friends with Jim Heckbert. We had a hand-in-glove working relationship on the case and played off of each other effortlessly at trial. Years later, Jim joined our firm, a first-class free agent deal if ever there was one.

You never know who is watching when you try a case. Every case you try could be the reason you get that phone call. As a result of the Steamboat Springs case, we were introduced to a firm in Wyoming that would change our direction. That firm was Simpson, Kepler & Edwards, founded by one of the true lions in the history of the U.S. Senate, Alan Simpson.

CHAPTER 23

ANOTHER TOWN EXPLODES!

Big cases build reputations, and that reputation becomes the life-blood of a law firm. I always had national aspirations for my firm, though I never chased cases for that reason. Rather, I went all out on every case. But news of large victories travels quickly around the legal community.

One of my largest victories had come in the Steamboat Springs, Colorado, gas explosion case. As a result of the press and television publicity on that case, I received a call from a lawyer in Cheyenne, Wyoming, in need of an experienced lawyer to handle another explosion case. His name was Rick Wolf. He called us to ask how soon we could be ready. The answer was: very quickly. My team consisted of explosion pros ready to go another round.

In 1997, Rick was working with Bill Simpson, a partner in Simpson Kepler & Edwards, the law firm of former U.S. Senator Alan Simpson, on an explosion case that had occurred two years before the Steamboat Springs explosion. In this case, Rick and Bill were representing a young couple named Randy and Melissa Hynes. Randy was a missionary, a man devoted to spreading the word of God, who had moved to Cody, Wyoming, from his small, conservative church in Greenville, Indiana. He and Melissa had hopes of creating a new congregation for their faith.

The circumstances of the gas explosion were similar to the Steamboat Springs case in that they were caused by gross negligence on the part of the gas company in maintaining its lines.

The young couple lived on the second floor of a four-story apartment building in Cody. One day, a neighbor noticed a slight flame being emitted from the electric baseboard heater in his apartment on the first floor. The neighbor called the fire department, which came to investigate. Unsure what the problem was, the assistant fire chief went to the basement to shut off the electricity. When he shut off the breaker, a spark was emitted and the entire building exploded.

Amazingly, no one was killed. However, Randy and Melissa Hynes were badly burned, as was the man who lived on the first floor.

The odd thing about the explosion was that the apartment had electric heat, so initially it was a mystery how there had been a gas explosion in an all-electric building. But it turned out that building had been full of gas from a leak in the underground gas pipes, which were old and brittle. Because it was very cold when this occurred, the leaking gas had followed the path of least resistance into the building, along the underground electrical lines.

After that initial phone call, it was at least another six months before we heard again from Rick. Then one day I received a call from both of them, indicating that Melissa's father, Reverend Donnie Bates, was interested in meeting me and my partners. We arranged a meeting at our offices in Denver with Reverend Bates, my partners Kerry Jardine and Peter Burg, and Rick Wolf and Bill Simpson, both of whom I was meeting for the first time.

In addition to being devoutly religious, the evangelical Reverend Donnie Bates turned out to be an astute, well-educated businessman who knew how to conduct himself in a legal setting. We learned from Donnie more about the extent of the damage done to the Hynes. The couple had suffered brutal burns: over 60 percent of Randy's body had been burned in the explosion. Melissa suffered as well, with burns covering more than 25 percent of her body.

Kerry and I laid out how we would handle the case. We also walked the group through how we had won the Steamboat Springs case, not to mention a quick reminder of the $6 million verdict we secured. Bill was very solicitous of us coming aboard. "We're under attack on all fronts," he said. "We're looking to you guys as the cavalry that will keep us in this battle."

After the meeting, Reverend Bates pulled me aside. He said he wanted to talk in private. We went back into my office and closed the door. He expressed concern as to whether or not Rick Wolf had the firepower to handle this case.

Rick had been brought in by Bill Simpson, who had handled a criminal matter for Randy Hynes. In that case, Randy had shot a moose without a license, a serious offense in the moose country that is Wyoming. Bill had swooped in to the rescue and worked out a deal for Randy to get him off with probation for killing the moose.

I told Reverend Bates that they both seemed like very capable lawyers, and it was not in my nature to be pushing lawyers off their own cases. Reverend Bates then leaned against my desk and asked in a light, inquisitive voice, "Michael, what religion are you?"

I was taken aback. I didn't really see what this had to do with the case. Additionally, my religious views are complicated and have changed over the course of my life. I suspected that this had less to do with a kind of therapeutic confessional and more to do with determining whether or not the Reverend really wanted us to come in and work on the case.

"With all due respect, Reverend, my religion is between myself and God," I said.

He looked me in the eye. "Michael, this is your case now," he said. "You do what you want. If you want to fire Simpson and Wolf, do it. We are going to sign an agreement with you, and you can do whatever you want."

I had no interest in firing Rick Wolf or Bill Simpson. Not only were they the ones who had brought us in on the case, but they both seemed like competent lawyers and people who my team and I believed we could work well with. My firm, however, took the lead in the case, based on our previous success with the Steamboat Springs case.

When we looked at the Cody case, on the surface it appeared to be cleaner and easier to win than the Steamboat Springs case. In Cody, there were gas lines that ran under the street in front of the apartment building where Randy and Melissa lived.

We brought in an expert, Joe Romig, to examine the lines and determine the cause and origin of the explosion. Joe was a Rhodes Scholar and had been an All-American football player at the University of Colorado. We also brought in some of our old experts from the Steamboat case, and even our old nemesis, William Clayton.

Clayton had testified against us in the Steamboat Springs case, but I decided to ask if he would take a look at the gas lines in Cody. I wanted him to judge if Cody's gas system would qualify for the worst gas system in the United States. He agreed to take a look and met us in Cody, along with Bill Simpson, to investigate the gas line.

The gas system in Cody was ancient. The pipes dated back to World War II and had become brittle with age. The gas lines were laid haphazardly. At points in the distribution system, some were in the middle of the street, while others were above ground and hooked onto buildings with flimsy little hooks where cars could easily hit them and cause explosions. The entire setup was a disaster waiting to happen.

After inspecting the lines, Clayton delivered his verdict. "I think it's fair to say that this is, in fact, the worst gas system I have ever seen in the United States of America," he declared. He agreed to be our witness.

Clayton had an odd request: he did not want us to pay him for his work. He was willing to testify pro bono for two reasons. The first was that he wanted to go hunting in Wyoming.

I was perplexed. He wanted to forgo a fee so he could go hunting? Bill Simpson immediately understood. Apparently, the cost of a hunt ran anywhere from $5,000 to $20,000. And so Bill arranged a hunt for Clayton in lieu of payment for his expert testimony. The second reason was that he had worked for gas companies his entire life. He felt that the Cody system was an embarrassment to the gas industry.

The defense counsel was Tom Gorman, a well-known figure in Wyoming. He had played football at the University of Wyoming. He marketed himself as never having lost a case. Tom made it clear up front to Rick Wolf and Bill Simpson that if they wanted to settle this case, he would not be willing to pay more than $100,000. We turned him down.

As we began to take depositions, I got to know Gorman. He was, not to put too fine a point on it, a blowhard. One day when we were on the same flight back from an out-of-town deposition, he sat down next to me and looked me in the eye.

"Michael Burg," he said, "no Jewish lawyer is coming into Cheyenne, Wyoming, and getting a verdict over $1 million. If you want to settle this case, then come talk to me, and we'll see if we can get it done. I'm not saying we'll pay a million, but if you think you can try this case and beat me, you've got another think coming. I've never lost a case, and I'm not going to lose this one to you."

After his little soliloquy, he tensely held eye contact for another beat before he got up from the seat beside me and walked away. I suddenly found myself a little concerned about what kind of trial we were getting ourselves into in Cheyenne.

The case had been assigned to Judge Clarence "Bud" Brimmer. He had served as Wyoming Attorney General and been appointed to the bench by President Ford. Our opponents immediately filed a motion to try to prevent us from talking about the Cody gas system in its entirety, and to restrict us to talking only about the specific area in which it broke. This was clearly an evasive move, but surprisingly the pretrial magistrate ruled that they were correct, and that the rest of the system was irrelevant to our case. We appealed to Judge Brimmer in the hopes that he would override the magistrate and let justice have its fair chance (thankfully, and rightly, he did).

Next came the question of how to divide up the witnesses. Kerry and I agreed to carry the load, but we also wanted Bill Simpson and Rick Wolf in there somewhere—we only had the case because of them. The problem was that Rick was becoming negative. He kept pushing for us to settle rather than go to trial. At one point he suggested settling for $200,000, which would have only covered our costs.

Under Wyoming state law, a civil case requires twelve jurors and their decision must be unanimous. The overall reputation of juries in Wyoming was so conservative that it was thought to be almost impossible to be awarded a large verdict. Both Rick and Bill told me that a verdict of $500,000 in Wyoming was like a $5 million verdict anywhere else. Though that may have explained Rick's low-aiming goal, I wasn't buying it.

Rick's negativity bothered me, as negativity from one of our own usually does. We were supposed to be focused on winning the case, not talking about the most graceful way to lose. Moreover, he seemed to take the opposite position of mine on every issue. If I said the sky was blue, he said it was gray. If I said the light was green, he said it was red. I felt that his attitude about the case would come across to the judge and jury.

I sat down with Bill Simpson to express my concerns. "I think we need to sideline Wolf," I said point-blank. "I just don't think we can afford to have any negativity. The jury will pick up on it. But you, Bill, you'll still be carrying a significant portion of the trial."

Bill looked me in the eye. "I agree with Wolf about settling," he said, "but I will do my best and I will talk to Wolf." He made good on his word.

The trial lasted five-and-a-half weeks. Our jury was a random pick out of a bag of marbles. We had a rancher sporting a ten-gallon hat, some government employees who looked bored, and several working and nonworking types between them.

Leading up to the trial, with all the work we and our experts had done, there was still one piece of the puzzle that we had not gotten a chance to examine: the broken pipe itself. Tom Gorman, the defense lawyer, had been keeping the pipe from us. Our metallurgy expert had been permitted to examine the pipe, but the rest of us had never seen it.

We made a motion to see the pipe. The judge allowed it. Finally, I could hold in my hands the broken pipe that was the cause of my clients' injuries, and the reason for the entire trial. It was surprisingly small and lightweight. There was a nasty gash where it had broken.

When I was done examining it, I put it down on the plaintiff's table. I kept an eye on Gorman. Every time he started heading over in my direction, I picked it back up again.

Finally he marched up to me. "Are you going to give me that damn pipe back?"

"I'll give it to you when I'm ready," I said.

The steam was practically spewing out of his ears. His fists balled. I could see his face redden.

"Give me the pipe or I will take it from you," he said through gritted teeth, clearly trying to maintain his composure. I wanted to laugh but instead bit my lip.

"You may be from Grable, Wyoming," I said in a light, but calculating tone, "but I grew up in Chicago, and if you want to come try to get this pipe, come and pry it from my hands."

Admittedly, I loved to taunt, to boast about my Windy City roots, to dare people to fight me. The Fabulous Kangaroo Brothers were back again, boxing gloves up. In the end, Gorman and I didn't come to blows. I decided to behave and relinquished the pipe.

The trial started and proceeded without incident. There was a moment of levity when discussing Randy Hynes' post-traumatic stress disorder. He had taken to drawing moose. I used this during the case as an example of his emotional trauma. I put up a few of his drawings for the jury to see. When it was Gorman's turn, he tried to use this to his advantage. "Look at those drawings. He's an amazing artist! He hasn't suffered!"

I then had to get up and say, "No, no, you don't understand. The moose is *the only thing* he ever draws."

The witnesses came on, one after the other, talking about how horrific the explosion was. The doctors from the University of Utah hospital who had treated my clients were called as witnesses, and they held up beautifully on the stand. Finally, William Clayton, the gas expert, was called to the stand. He was the picture of calm authority.

"Mr. Clayton," I began, "did you testify against me in the trial in the Steamboat Springs explosion case?"

"Yes, I did," he said.

"Did you testify on behalf of Atmos Energy?"

"Yes, I did."

"Mr. Clayton, how old are you?"

"I am sixty-two years old."

"And how many years have you worked in the gas industry?"

"It has been over forty years now."

"And have you ever testified against a gas company?"

"No, this is the first time."

"How many times have you testified for a gas company?"

"Oh, probably more than two dozen times."

"Do you remember," I continued, "when I asked you, after the Steamboat Springs trial, if you would ever testify against a gas company?"

He indicated that he did, indeed, remember.

"Do you remember what you told me your requirement would be?"

"Yes, I do," he said. "I said it would have to be the worst gas company in the United States."

"And did you examine the gas system here in Cody, Wyoming?"

He indicated that he had done so.

"And what did you find?"

"I found it to be the worst gas system in the United States," he said. "So here I am."

"And Mr. Clayton, are you getting payment for your time with regards to this case?" I asked, just because I wanted everyone to know.

"No," he said.

"But you're getting something, aren't you?"

Here Clayton cracked a smile. "Yep. I'm going hunting with Bill Simpson."

"But Mr. Clayton, why would you do all this work basically for free, and then also come and testify for this case?"

"Because I've dedicated my life to the natural gas system. I feel it is my obligation to come in here and testify when the gas system is the worst in the United States."

"Thank you," I said, stepping back.

I was confident that the deal was as good as sealed.

On the day of closing arguments the gallery was packed with eager and curious faces. There must have been two hundred people there. The anticipation was palpable. Everyone in the room knew, or at least legend had it, that Tom Gorman had never lost a case.

The night before, our team had discussed what we would ask for in damages. Rick Wolf cautioned me I could not ask for $1 million. In fact, he brought in a man who had had his nose burned off in a motorcycle explosion. The jury had awarded him $600,000, which they considered a weighty award. When I heard his story, I thought to myself that his case should have been worth millions.

I went around the room and asked everyone what they thought an appropriate compensation would be. Rick wanted to keep it under a million. Bill Simpson thought between $1 million and $2 million. Becky Draper, our top-notch paralegal, said $2 million to $3 million. Becky had grown up in Baggs, Wyoming. She knew how conservative Wyoming jurors were; yet she still thought we should ask as high as $3 million.

"So how much are you going to ask for?" Becky asked me.

I shrugged. "I won't know until I ask."

It was time for closing arguments. I prepared all night. I wanted to be sure the jury understood not just the seriousness of the problems with the gas line and how bad it was, but also how badly my clients were injured. I spoke about how this gas system had to be the worst in existence in the United States of America. I talked about the fact that these two innocent, young people were very badly burned, their quality of life and health severely altered due to this explosion. Then I switched gears momentarily.

"Every year, I'm in charge of making the turkey for our Thanksgiving dinner. Last year, I pulled the turkey out of the oven and accidentally pressed my unprotected thumb against the searing hot pan. As a result of the burn, a blister formed. Let me say, when that blister popped, I was in so much pain, and I'll admit to being a big baby about it. But still, it really hurt. I put aloe on it. I treated it the best I could, but I still felt the pain."

I paused here, and turned to the jury. "What's it worth to have those blisters over a third of your body? On your chest? On your genitalia? On your legs? What's it worth to Randy and Melissa Hynes? Just imagine the pain. I know I barely can. That little blister from last Thanksgiving is enough pain for me, and that was just on my thumb, not over a large percentage of my skin. No amount of money could compensate them for what they have gone through, thanks to this company's irresponsible maintenance of its gas line. If there was some kind of magic box that we could put Randy and Melissa in, and put their verdict in the box as well, and the magic box could, as compensation, put them back in the same physical state they were in prior to the explosion, they would take that verdict over any amount of money. But unfortunately, that magic box does not exist. What does exist are courts of law and the awarding of monetary damages."

As I gave my speech I noticed one juror, the rancher in the ten-gallon hat. I suspected that he would be one of the most conservative in the box, so he was my bellwether. The golden rule is, you will never get what you ask for from a jury. No matter what you ask for, they will always reduce it in an effort to strike a compromise.

When my speech was winding down, I looked the rancher in the eye and said, "And do you know what we're asking you to do? We're asking you to award what we think the damages are in this case: $8.5 million."

A hush fell over the courtroom. The moment, giving the speech, fighting for my clients, asking for the massive compensation, had completely swept me up. I was lost in my passion, unaware of the existence of anyone else in the room beside the jury. Only a gasp from the gallery brought me back. I looked the jurors in the eye, one after the other. Nobody blinked. Nobody looked away.

The trial concluded. On my way out of the courthouse, one of the security guards approached me and told me it was the finest closing argument he had ever heard. I nodded my thanks and kept on going.

The jury went out. Rick came up to me. In a bleak and somewhat frantic tone, he informed me that he thought I had lost the case. "You asked for too much money," he said. "We're not getting anything." His negativity persisted. I just shook my head at him, consoled by the knowledge that it's never over until the jury returns.

A day-and-a-half later the jury returned with its verdict. We had won the case. They awarded us $5.6 million, one of the largest verdicts to ever come out of the U.S. District Court in Wyoming. I was elated, and so was the whole team. We were all smiles and hugs and pats on the back.

Judge Brimmer approached me after trial and shook my hand. He said that Gerry Spence, the legendary lawyer for whom I have the highest regard, had been in his courtroom many times. "But I think that was the finest closing argument I've ever heard," he said.

Tom Gorman, knees wobbly, refused to come over and shake my hand. He just kept looking off into space, wondering how it happened, how he had lost to the Jewish lawyer from Colorado. The loss had clearly hit him like a two-by-four.

Bill Simpson, Kerry Jardine, and a now grateful Rick Wolf, everyone from the team, all went out and celebrated that night with a nice dinner and drinks all around. It was an amazing day. It was an amazing verdict.

Gorman later appealed to the 10th Circuit claiming that the verdict was excessive, but the circuit upheld the decision, saying that while the verdict was significant, it was certainly not excessive. It was what Randy and Melissa Hynes deserved.

On a lighter note, humorist Dave Barry put a quote from my closing in his top ten most ridiculous quotes of the year: "The people of Wyoming won't stand for their towns being blown up." Hey, I'll take what I can get if Dave Barry is quoting me.

Two weeks after the trial, I received a letter in the mail from Bill Simpson. The letter said that I had changed Bill's life as a lawyer. It was yet another incredible compliment from another incredible man to make me incredibly proud. I had a feeling that things might be changing for me—that my firm's profile was on the rise.

CHAPTER 24

MEET THE SIMPSONS!

The intercom buzzed. "Senator Alan Simpson is on the line for you," my assistant, Gina Clement, announced. I picked up the phone.

"This is Al Simpson," the voice on the other end said with authority. "I gotta tell you that my sons think you are the greatest thing since sliced bread, and I think it's important that I come down and talk to you about this potential deal that's on the table to merge our firms."

I had never met Al Simpson. There was no deal on the table. Our firm had just won the explosion case in Wyoming with Simpson's firm. Simpson's son, Bill, had been the lead for their firm. Since the case, Bill and my partners and I had talked about putting our firm together with Bill's to expand our reach into Wyoming. But Al Simpson's name was never involved in any of the discussions about our joining forces.

I was thrilled to sit down with Al Simpson. We set up a lunch at Alexander's for me, Al, and Peter. Over butter and bread, we sat down, pressed the white napkins on our laps, and began the meeting.

Al Simpson was a colorful storyteller. It turned out that his firm had a wild, Wild West backstory. Al's grandfather, Bill Simpson, held two amazing distinctions. The first was that in 1894 he successfully prosecuted Butch Cassidy for stealing horses from a German aristo-crat. Cassidy was convicted and served eighteen months in prison, the only time the notorious outlaw ever served time.

The elder Bill Simpson's second distinction was that he was the only lawyer in the history of Wyoming ever charged with first degree murder. It happened in 1924. He had a dispute with a man who had been on the other side of a lawsuit. The man tried to attack him. In self-defense, Bill shot the man on the street in downtown Cody. He was tried twice, both times resulting in a hung jury. The state decided not to pursue the case a third time.

Al's father, Milward, had defended Bill. When Al had joined his father's firm in 1950, Al suggested the firm be called Simpson & Father, much to his father's dismay. Al continued to practice in the firm and was elected to the U.S. Senate in 1978. His sons, Bill (the namesake of his wily grandfather) and Colin, later joined the firm.

The most surprising thing about Al was his sense of humor. I had expected a straitlaced former senator, but instead got a sharp-tongued provocateur. "You know," he said at one point, "I've just left the Senate. I'm the director of the Kennedy Institute of Government at Harvard. It's a pretty big deal to be at Harvard. Most of those guys there graduated cum laude." He paused. "I graduated thank the laude."

He also joked about law school. He said that when you are trying a case or standing on the floor of the U.S. Senate, nobody asks you what your GPA was. "I used to tell all the swells from the Ivy League that I was eighteenth in my law class," he said. "They would agree that was pretty good. Then they'd ask how many were in my class." He smiled. "Eighteen."

We talked about his life and his accomplishments, both in the public and private spheres. He had served in the Senate for eighteen years, eight of those as Minority Leader.

"Look," he said, "I will not go patting my old colleagues in the Senate to get fifty or a hundred thousand to fund your firm. I'm not going to whore myself out like that. I'm not going to do those sort of things. It's just not right, so don't ever expect me to do that." He fell silent and took a sip of his water.

Wow. Peter and I were not expecting that to come out of his mouth. We didn't even know he was thinking of being involved in the deal in any way, shape, or form. But now he was setting conditions on his involvement, so clearly he was going to be involved in the merger. Peter and I remained silent. Both of us were trying to come up with the right thing to say.

Al broke the silence. "I've spent my whole life making sure my name is worth something," he repeated, adding the kicker: "Don't fuck it up."

The decision was made: we would merge the firms.

"Senator Simpson, this is really unbelievable," I said.

"Call me Al," he said.

I told him this was a great honor and declared we would call the firm Simpson Burg.

"Simpson Burg sounds like some small town in Wyoming my great-grandfather started," he said. "No, it's gotta be Burg Simpson." And that was that. We shook hands, and the deal and name were done.

The night after we sealed the merger deal, Peter and I were so excited about it that we called our parents and told them the extraordinary news. In true parental style, they were both on the phone when we told them the incredible news: we had merged firms with former Senator Alan Simpson. There was silence on the line. I waited for a response. Peter waited. We thought for sure there would have been more of a reaction.

Finally, my mother said, "Does he know you're Jewish?"

I laughed. I wished Al had been on the line. "Yeah! He doesn't care. It's fine."

In late 1999, we rechristened the firm Burg Simpson Eldredge Hersh & Jardine. But like almost all firms with a string of names, it became known by the first two, Burg Simpson.

Burg Simpson senior partners
Back row: Peter Burg, Scott Eldredge, David Hersh
Front row: Michael Burg, Kerry Jardine, Alan Simpson

The merger sent ripples of shock through the Denver legal community. People wanted to know how the merger with Alan Simpson was even possible. How does a Republican like Simpson get involved with what was becoming a plaintiff firm? The whole thing felt very surreal at the time.

Our arrangement with Al was that he could do whatever he wanted in regard to the firm. We didn't expect him to do any heavy lifting because he already had so much on his plate. He said that if we tried cases in Wyoming he would come in and help us pick the jury, things like that. He just wanted to be involved.

But the instant national exposure he gave us was a boost. We now had an iconic former senator in our firm. It helped us gain a national footprint. The Simpson name added credibility and legitimacy, as well as sending the message that we were a serious firm.

The addition of Bill Simpson was also huge. He is an incredibly fine trial lawyer who handles both criminal and civil cases. He reminds me of a combination of Jimmy Stewart and Abe Lincoln, a noble hybrid that any jury automatically takes a liking to.

On the surface, the political marriage was odd. I had grown up a bleeding-heart liberal. Although my politics have become more conservative, particularly on fiscal issues, I still characterize myself as a Democrat.

I supported Colin, Al's son, when he ran for the Wyoming House of Representatives in 1999. He was elected and ended up serving twelve years, including two as Speaker of the House. In 2000, he ran for governor, but finished fourth in the primary. The more conservative elements of the Republican Party in Wyoming attacked him, as well as Al, for being way too moderate to be governor of a state like Wyoming.

Al's old friend Dick Cheney refused to support Colin, which I think impacted Al negatively. It hurt him because they had been friends for so long. Al had helped Cheney get elected to Congress back in the day, as well as pushing when Cheney got on the Bush-Cheney ticket, which led to him being vice president for eight years.

But the truth is that Al is a pragmatist. He always says "country first." He rails against what's going on in our nation's capital today. He was friends with Democrats like Ted Kennedy. They worked together, and while they didn't agree on everything, they were able to work together very successfully on what they did agree on. He used to say that he and Senator Kennedy disagreed on maybe 40 percent of issues, but they worked together on the other 60 percent to get something done.

I believe that if Al Simpson were in his sixties instead of his eighties, he would make a powerful presidential candidate. A man like Al is what this country needs, someone who puts country first—not party, but country—someone who wants to fix the problems and address the tough issues. That was what the Simpson-Bowles Commission on Fiscal Responsibility, in advising the president, did to address the issue of our massive debt. Like Al said, by pressing on that issue, he pissed off so many people that nobody wanted to do anything. Republicans also criticized him for working with the Obama administration. When he supported gay rights and gay marriage, the backlash he received for it from other Republicans was astounding. But he always stood up for what he thought was right, and that is what makes him special.

Today, Al Simpson is eighty-four years old and maintains a very active lifestyle, traveling around the country to speak. He's incredibly smart and knowledgeable, and to my mind, he is one of the greatest patriots ever to live in this country.

When we first signed the merger, my friend, the prominent mass torts attorney Mike Papantonio, expressed his congratulations. He also gave me one very telling piece of advice that has proved to be true. He said, "The more successful you get, the bigger the bull's-eye on your back."

For Al, that has always been true; for me, it was becoming true. But I knew that if I was going to take a bullet in the back, I'd rather do it with Al Simpson as my law partner.

CHAPTER 25

MASS TORTS:
THE WORLD SERIES OF LAW

The cost of pursuing mass tort actions generally exceeds the recovery any single case can attain, which is why they are bundled. It is not uncommon in these cases for lawyers to spend millions of dollars establishing liability in order for thousands of clients to receive individual awards. Awards can range from thousands to millions of dollars, and everything in between. These differ from class action lawsuits, in which all parties have suffered the same injury.

Lawyers all over the country advertise for mass tort cases. Toll-free numbers are used in television ads to solicit cases. Many, if not most of these lawyers have no intention of trying to work up the cases, nor do they have the ability or finances to follow through. Instead, their goal is to build an inventory of clients through advertising, and then try to settle the cases directly with the defense. In this way, they get thousands of potential litigants to disappear by simply settling the cases.

Unfortunately, these newcomers to mass torts are often clueless regarding the complexities of mass tort litigation. They simply have no idea of how difficult and costly it is to mount successful mass tort cases against multinational corporations. It can take years of litigation, millions of dollars, and tens of thousands of hours of attorney and paralegal time. They also have no concept of how hard real mass tort firms work in building a legal team to take hundreds of depositions and review millions of pages of documents in a single mass tort case, most of the time without any realistic hope of a quick settlement.

In 1999, after we extricated ourselves from defense work, we were looking for an opportunity to break into the business in the right way and with a winning case. At the time, we had thirty-five lawyers in the firm. To a degree, we knew that we were throwing our talents to the wind, but it was an adventure, something new, something none of us had ever done before, and we were excited to get going.

Mass torts are also a great way to represent the underdog against behemoth corporations that will do anything to make billions of dollars. To us, moving into mass torts was akin to making a stand and fighting for the little guy, something I have always prided myself in doing.

We knew we had to choose our cases wisely because, frankly, prior to that time, there had been a fair number of mass torts that had not panned out very well for the lawyers who took them on. For example, I had heard of two or three firms going bankrupt from pursuing costly litigation against makers of breast implants. We needed to be very careful and very diligent about which cases we took on and the attention to detail we paid them.

Kerry, Peter, and I looked at a case regarding the drug Fen-Phen, talked it over, thought about it, and decided that it looked legitimate enough to pursue. In December of 1999, we took the plunge and became involved.

Fen-Phen, the drug combination of fenfluramine and phentermine, was developed as a medication to lessen addictions to substances such as alcohol and cocaine, but also as an anti-obesity medication. The phentermine did not interact negatively, but unfortunately, the fenfluramine led to severe and horrific heart valve problems that often resulted in death.

Fen-Phen was an interesting substance in particular because it left a fingerprint-like indicator of a very specific type of heart damage called valvular heart disease. Specifically, the disease leads to the dysfunction or dissolution of the mitral valve, a crucial passage in the heart that controls blood flow. The condition was directly linked to Fen-Phen, so it made for a great mass tort candidate, as every case corroborated the dangers of the drug.

We wanted to go out and dig up as many Fen-Phen cases as we could because it seemed like a good opportunity. This began before we had merged firms with Al Simpson, but while we were still in contact with them as a result of the Wyoming explosion case. Bill Simpson connected me with other lawyers in Wyoming, and through them we discovered that there was a hotbed of Fen-Phen cases that had not yet been brought to legal attention.

It turned out that there were more women taking Fen-Phen per capita in Wyoming than in any other state. We had hit the gold mine. And that was only Wyoming.

We mobilized our attorneys and our networks nationwide and were able to find around 350 cases total by the middle of March 1999 for the first phase of the litigation. It was a relatively large bet for us at the time, but my time in Las Vegas had taught me when to bet and when to fold. This seemed like the time to bet.

Kerry Jardine took the lead in finding all the cases. He and Bill Simpson negotiated slots on radio and newspaper ads looking for people who took Fen-Phen. Kerry came back to us with the initial survey results of over three hundred people who had taken Fen-Phen, all of whom had responded to our newspaper or radio ads. Results came in from all over the country, but Wyoming remained the hot spot.

Peter and I were shocked by the volume of Fen-Phen cases Kerry brought in to us. How could we possibly handle that many cases? It seemed insane, and for a while we were freaking out, worrying about how to handle what grew to more than 450 cases.

By March, we had developed a two-phase plan for our Fen-Phen cases, dubbed "Fen-Phen One" and "Fen-Phen Two." For Fen-Phen One, the cases had to be in by March of 2000. Cases after that date would be thrown in with the second Fen-Phen phase.

With all of the cases we had gathered, we were confident that we would be able to move forward, but there were a lot of steps ahead of us.

Kerry discovered an expert in the field by the name of Jerry Alexander, based out of Kansas City. We met him at a seminar during the research portion of the Fen-Phen case and were impressed by his knowledge of the drug. I explained our mission to him and asked if he was interested in helping our cause. We worked out a deal where he would receive 5 percent of the fees.

For a couple of months, Kerry and I traveled to Jerry's office in Kansas City to confer with him. He was a solo practitioner who operated out of a dark, dank office that reminded me of my early days when I couldn't find work at a firm for the life of me. I would venture into the bowels of his office and find him sitting at his desk, poring over documents, articles, and test results by the dim light that filtered in through the room's single, tiny window. He reminded me of a Fen-Phen mad scientist. He knew everything about Fen-Phen, from the chemistry to the physiology. He knew how to look at echo-cardiograms and figure out which cases would make for the best ones to bring to trial.

Even though we had a knowledgeable expert and a plethora of cases, we were not the only players in the mass tort game working on Fen-Phen. This made it imperative that we learn as much as we could about the mass tort field of practice, who the other players were, the good guys, the bad guys, and who else we needed to know to get ahead.

As we proceeded with Fen-Phen, we found that without even trying we attracted a following and an interest. When the other lawyers working on Fen-Phen found out that a firm nobody had ever heard of had 450-plus cases, they started lining up to take us to lunch.

By May, we had settled a number of cases and started seeing checks roll in for the first dozen or so clients. We saw that this area of law was very profitable, but more important, we realized how much we were helping our clients, so we pushed ourselves and made it through our entire inventory by the middle of October.

Fen-Phen was a very special case for us for many reasons. It was a crazy combination of luck and extremely hard work. We never had another case that moved as quickly. It was mostly a matter of impeccably perfect timing. For example, with a later mass tort case, Yaz/Yasmin, the mismarketed birth control pill, we spent $15 million to $20 million before we ever got anywhere close to discussing a settlement. With Yaz, it took two-and-a-half years to reach the discussion point of settlements, but with Fen-Phen it was a mere ten months from start to finish.

As a result of how quickly and successfully we handled the cases, Fen-Phen changed our trajectory in the mass torts community. By the end of the Fen-Phen case, we had established ourselves as players in the mass tort game after only our first mass tort case.

There had been fifty other firms working on Fen-Phen cases at the time, hoping to move up the ladder from those that gather cases to the executive committee on the next action. Those firms had been working at it for four to five years. Here we swooped in, got the job done, and found ourselves moving up the ladder more quickly than we could have ever imagined.

All of this was wonderful for our firm, but it also meant big steps for me. Professionally, I found myself first on the executive committee for future mass torts, and then in the position of lead attorney for the entire litigation, directing a team of my own. Personally, I was helping people and that felt good. I was fighting the good fight, fighting for the underdog, and seeing the reality of helping people—and doing it successfully.

We were co-counsels with other firms for the Fen-Phen cases, as is traditional with mass tort cases. Co-counsels were Levin Papantonio, led by the godfather of mass torts, Mike Papantonio, and the firm

of Mark Robinson, a California product liability attorney who had
tried the landmark Ford Pinto case. It was a remarkable opportunity
and a great personal challenge, but it served as a great way to prove
my worth to myself and my new colleagues.

Before we had finished settling the Fen-Phen cases, our next mass tort
case, which involved the drug Zyprexa, began. In 2000, Zyprexa was
the third largest selling drug in the United States, racking up almost
$5 billion per year in sales. Zyprexa (olanzapine is the generic name)
is an antipsychotic approved by the Food and Drug Administration
(FDA) for the treatment of schizophrenia and bipolar disorder. A
side effect of the drug is that it causes weight gain of ninety to one
hundred pounds over a relatively short period of time, thereby often
triggering diabetes.

Eli Lilly and Company were also marketing the drug "off-
label"—meaning, outside its intended and approved use by the
FDA—as the new Prozac. Doctors prescribed Zyprexa to everyone from children with attention deficit disorder to housewives with
depression and anxiety. We knew Zyprexa wouldn't be as easy as
Fen-Phen had been to challenge, but the drug was clearly harming
people who were taking it off-label, as well as the unfortunate people
who were bipolar and schizophrenic and also becoming diabetic.

Every mass tort case has an executive committee of lawyers
leading the way for the national and international cases. One of
the lead lawyers on Zyprexa was a colorful New York lawyer named
Mel Weiss. A client of mine knew Mel and made the introduction. I
flew to meet Mel at a mass tort conference in Chicago. Every major
mass tort firm was there. As I prepared to walk into a huge room full
of intimidating strangers, I felt a flutter of something akin to stage
fright. It was like my first night doing stand-up comedy. But as soon
as I walked into the room, Mel jumped up from his table and walked
across the room to hug me hello.

I had met Mel previously through a client of mine in Denver. At my client's request, I had flown to New York and met Mel with Peter, Kerry, and Bill Simpson. We had set up a fishing trip for Mel on the Snake River in Wyoming with Al and Bill Simpson, something that he had really appreciated.

At that time, Mel was the king of mass torts. Everybody respected him, and if you were in with him, it meant you were a player. While Mel asked me how I was and caught up on the Simpsons, out of the corner of my eye I could see the other guys looking at me, their expressions reading: *Who the hell is that guy? And how does he know Mel Weiss?*

As a result of Mel's friendship and partnership, I ended up on the executive committee and the fee committee for Zyprexa. We took worldwide depositions. Ramon Lopez, another attorney on the executive committee, and I took some especially key depositions in Indianapolis, where Eli Lily is headquartered. Our team reviewed millions of pages of documents from around the globe. As a result of the work of our leadership with Mel, Ramon, and Chris Seeger, we were ultimately able to achieve a settlement for every single one of our clients, for a total of $690 million, something that even in retrospect still seems near impossible.

Though we were able to award money to our clients, we could not cure their diseases. But thankfully, as a result of the hard and tireless work done by all the firms involved, a settlement was entered in which our injured clients were fairly compensated for their injuries.

⋉∭⋊

Fen-Phen and Zyprexa solidified our place in mass torts. We went from the bottom to the top of the executive committee, and then to leadership. The next case was Ortho Evra, and I took the lead on that one, appointed by Federal Judge David Katz of Toledo, Ohio.

Ortho Evra is a birth control patch that seemed to have problems regulating hormone release. Some women would still become pregnant, while others would suffer massive strokes. Either way, the medication was not working the way it was prescribed.

Studies showed that women using the patch were receiving 60 percent more estrogen than the medication advertised. Rather than disclosing the problem and changing the patch, they hired a doctor to hide behind named Andrew Friedman.

Friedman had worked for a while as a researcher at Harvard, as well as at Brigham and Women's Hospital in Boston. After graduating from Amherst College, he was hired by a pharmaceutical company to do studies on Lupron, a medication to treat endometriosis and severe PMS. He had three studies on the drug published in peer-reviewed magazines.

One day, Friedman's assistant went to Friedman's boss and said that he had never seen the data on the published studies. When confronted by his boss, Friedman made excuses and distributed the blame. To cover himself, Friedman put fake medical notes in his patients' records at Harvard and at Brigham and Women's, saying that the women participated in a study that they had not taken part in. He then turned the fake notes over to his boss.

But Friedman wasn't quite as smart as he thought he was. His boss looked the notes over and told him that he had a problem. He had printed the fake results on a printer that showed it came from a copy machine that did not exist at the time the study had supposedly been done. He gave himself away with a sloppy error. Caught, he admitted that he had faked the data, as well as the entire study. He was fired from Harvard and Brigham and Women's Hospital and had his medical license suspended for two years.

Sixty days later, the jobless Friedman received a call from Johnson & Johnson offering him a job as a consultant for the Ortho Evra patch. He accepted. Did he pause to inform his new employers that his medical license had just been revoked due to negligence and laziness on studies on a medication of equal importance and with equal impact on women's health? Of course not. He did not have to disclose that information, because they knew all about it when they hired him. He was the man Johnson & Johnson wanted for the job.

Friedman became the medical face of the Ortho Evra patch. Within eight months, he was named director of women's health at Ortho-McNeil, Johnson & Johnson's subsidiary that produced Ortho Evra. He earned a massive amount of money in a position he should not have been in—one he held at the cost of the health and even the lives of thousands of women.

Being the lead in Ortho Evra, I assigned myself to take his deposition. It is probably one of my favorite depositions, right up there with the Little Rascals case, but for a much different reason.

There were three cameras in the room where the deposition was held, one on me, one on the defense lawyer, and one on Friedman. Shortly after I started, Friedman began sweating. Soon, he was perspiring like Albert Brooks' character trying to anchor the news in *Broadcast News*.

I bore down hard on this guy, whom I was determined to expose as a fraud. "You admitted, in your transcripts with the state, that you both lied and cheated," I said, referring to the Lupron papers. "I want to ask you, which was worse, the lying or the cheating?"

"They're both bad," he said.

"Yes, but which was worse?" I pressed.

Before he could answer, I kept going. "Were you nervous?" I asked. "Was it easier the second and third studies that you phonied up?"

He shifted nervously in his chair. My suspicion was that if one, two, or three of the studies had been faked, then it was likely that others had been, too. I was calling into question his entire career.

Friedman regrouped. As an excuse for faking the data, he cited chronic knee pain. He launched into a story about playing tennis at Amherst that had caused the knee pain, which was supposedly the reason he didn't have enough time to complete the studies and faked his data. For added drama, he also claimed that his son had been diagnosed with attention deficit disorder (ADD) at the time, and that, too, had taken him away from the lab.

There was no way I was going to let this guy off the hook.

"You played tennis at Amherst?" I asked.

"Yes, I did," he said confidently.

"Let me ask you something. When you were at Amherst playing tennis did you ever call a ball that was in out, or one that was out in?"

He shook his head. "I would never do that."

"Oh, I see. So you waited until people's lives were at stake before you started to lie and cheat. Is that correct?"

He couldn't respond. He had nothing to say. There was a telling photograph taken during the deposition that must have been snapped right at that point. In it, I am wearing a big, excited smile. Friedman is stormy-faced and sweating. In the background, the defense lawyer's hand is raised in an obvious objection.

My team and I dug up a wealth of information while researching Friedman. His trouble had started at an early age, when he was on vacation in Europe for a summer between years of college. We located correspondence between him and the dean of Amherst, in which Friedman requested to know the dimensions of his dorm room so he could buy the appropriately sized Persian rug.

We knew a tidbit like that probably wouldn't make it into the trial, but it was still a funny fact. I wanted to know if Johnson & Johnson knew what Friedman had done in the past. Their representative said they knew. They knew! And they still made him director.

"Everybody deserves a second chance," they told me.

To me, that makes them just as corrupt and dirty as he was. They ignored the facts and the 60 percent correction on estrogen levels in their information, and they hid behind him to protect themselves. It was absurd, because this is Johnson & Johnson, the baby company, the nurse company. They actually hired an already corrupt guy to back a dangerous product.

In my mind, Friedman remains the poster boy for pharmaceutical companies that get themselves in trouble. We need good pharmaceutical companies, honest ones, and we need them working on products that are going to help people. Friedman was eventually repositioned, though he remains at Johnson & Johnson. His professional profile boasts that he is the Head of the Global Labeling Center of Excellence at Janssen, a subsidiary of Johnson & Johnson pharmaceuticals. I guess I would rather have him handling labels than women's health.

I was the lead lawyer on the Ortho Evra case. From there, we began to look at other birth control drugs that were resulting in adverse events listed by the manufacturer and the FDA. A giant red flag went up when we studied Yaz, a birth control drug manufactured by Bayer.

Yaz (also marketed as Yasmin) differs from other birth control pills because it contains a different type of chemical, created by Bayer, called drospirenone. We saw that thousands of women using the birth control drug were developing potentially fatal blood-clot related injuries, such as deep vein thrombosis (DVT), pulmonary embolism, gallbladder disease, and strokes.

We studied the pharmacology of the pill to determine why so many women were suffering from these conditions. Two studies had come out that reported on testing and studying Yaz, and both studies concluded that the drug was as good, if not better, than the previous generation of the drug, and that there was no excessive link to harmful issues. This didn't jibe with how many women had been harmed.

Something was clearly wrong with the drug. When other mass tort law firms were reluctant to get involved because of the studies, we smelled a rat. The partners in the firm took a vote, and we decided to proceed. Not only did we dive into the deep end of the pool, we actually put some weights around our shoulders by deciding to go after *all* of the credible cases we could find. We doubled down, which is what we do.

We spent millions of dollars conducting research, hiring medical experts, gathering cases, and flying around the country taking depositions. Fortunately, a breakthrough came early on when one of our experts discovered that the two studies that claimed Yaz had no greater adverse effects than other birth control pills were not independent studies. In fact, they had been conducted by former Bayer employees whose offices were within fifteen miles of the Bayer plant.

Then we discovered that drospirenone was affecting progestin, which is a balancing agent that is supposed to prevent clots. Many of the women using Yaz, who were having greater amounts of blood clots, strokes, pulmonary embolisms, deaths, and heart attacks than women using other birth control pills, also had low estrogen levels. In the opinion of our medical experts, the synthetic progestin created by Bayer at that time was not doing its job and balancing the clotting of estrogen.

Bayer was also marketing Yaz off-label, implying that it helped with PMS symptoms—and even a type of acne. We discovered during the case that the FDA had warned Bayer that it could not sell Yaz in this manner.

We were the first firm involved in researching Yaz and in filing cases. Other mass tort and other law firms that had been gathering cases joined us to give the action the greatest leverage against Bayer. As the lead Yaz firm, we managed three hundred law firms that were involved with some 26,000 cases.

When we first filed the action, Adam Hoeflich, Bayer's lead counsel, told the judge that Bayer was never going to pay a dime on any case. In the end, we got Bayer to pay approximately $2 billion to the harmed women without ever having a single trial. We were able to help women who had pulmonary embolisms, strokes, and heart attacks, and women who had been completely disabled, obtain compensation for their injuries. To me, that was the most important part of the case.

CHAPTER 26

THE "CRAP AND VOMIT" CASE

*"The difference between a successful person and others is not a lack of
strength, not a lack of knowledge, but rather, a lack of will."*
—Vince Lombardi

The fall of 2007 was an exciting time in Denver, Colorado. The
economy was roaring, the stock market was hitting all-time
highs, and the local baseball team, the Colorado Rockies, were in
the midst of one of their greatest pennant winning streaks in the
history of the game. They won twenty-one of twenty-two games to
propel them from a last place team to the World Series. I remember
sitting in my office one day with some of the partners on our lunch
break, when I came across an article in the local paper's financial
section. The article was about two exotic financial investment instru-
ments known as "residential mortgage-backed securities" and "collateralized debt obligations."

I knew nothing about these types of investments at the time, and
the descriptions in the article seemed like a blur to me, but I could
tell they were important. In the article, experts discussed how these
"securitized products" were a ticking time bomb, and how recent,

across-the-board ratings downgrades from safe investments to junk could have a negative effect on the economy. Based on these down-grades, the experts estimated that somewhere between $50 and $100 billion would evaporate from the economy.

It sounded incredibly ominous, but too complicated to under-stand from reading one newspaper article, so I flipped to the sports section. Talk faded into banter about RBIs and ERAs and the Rockies' World Series quest. I never expected to give these invest-ments another thought until a week later, when I received a phone call from my son, Scott.

At the time, Scott worked for Pursuit Partners, a Connecticut-based hedge fund run by Tony Schepis and Frank Canelas. Scott was calling to tell me that Pursuit believed they may have a viable case involving the type of investments I had just read about a week earlier.

Trillions of dollars of the world economy depends on the via-bility of these types of investment vehicles. On the surface, they seemed appealing. Collateralized debt obligations, or CDOs, Scott explained to me, are investments made up of bundles of pooled assets, typically mortgages, bonds, or loans, which are then repack-aged together in slices of assets called "tranches," and sold to inves-tors. In that way, an investor could invest in one thousand different mortgages and receive a "slice" of each homeowner's mortgage pay-ment, thus lowering the risk of investing in one or two bad ones. Investment banks would bundle thousands of assets together, have the securities rated as safe investments by the ratings agencies, and then sell them to investors on the open market.

Pursuit, Scott told me, had purchased certain residential mortgage-backed securities and CDOs that were rated as safe investment-grade securities at the time of sale. A few weeks later, they were downgraded to "junk," which wiped out Pursuit's entire investment of $45 million.

Something didn't add up. No matter who Pursuit turned to, they couldn't get any straight answers and, perhaps more important, they couldn't find anyone who was willing to stand up and ask the right questions.

Scott told me that Pursuit had already approached law firms in New York and Connecticut, but none of the blue chip firms would touch the case. The potential defendants were UBS, the largest investment bank in the world, and the ratings agencies Moody's and Standard & Poor's (with whom Pursuit later reached a confidential settlement), behemoths later described as "too big to fail" after the economic collapse. These huge financial institutions also had the biggest and best defense law firms in the world on their side. The response Pursuit heard time and again was, "You want to sue who?" and "They will bury you!" But prompted by Tony and Frank, Scott asked if I would look into the matter and consider having Burg Simpson represent Pursuit.

This was the very definition of a David versus Goliath fight. Never one to shy away from a challenge, I agreed to have a look. Little did I know at the time that I was about to embark on a case that went to the core of the largest Wall Street collapse in our lifetime. By the time it was over, $7 *trillion* had disappeared from the economy.

My law partner David TeSelle and I flew to Connecticut to meet with Pursuit and to discuss the details of the case. I really need to pause to emphasize this point. David and I knew nothing about securitized investment products other than what my son had told me. And what Scott told me, I understood only on a basic level. I had never taken on Wall Street. I was never a banker or a creator of securitized products. But here's what I did know after our meeting with Pursuit: under all of the talk of "indentures" and "offering memoranda," and "defaults," "triggers," and "side pockets," at its core, there was a simple wrong that appeared to need to be righted. Millions of dollars of these securities had been sold as safe investments when, in fact, they weren't safe and had default "triggers," which caused investors to lose all their money overnight. I rolled up my sleeves and dedicated myself to learning everything I could about residential mortgage-backed securities, CDOs, and securitized products, just like when I was a kid and learned about RBIs and ERAs and batting averages, so I could bring to light what was happening on Wall Street.

After hearing the basics of the case, David TeSelle and I agreed that it looked like there was a viable claim. When we expressed this to the Pursuit team, Frank Canelas turned pale. He feared that we were going to confirm what he was most concerned with: if what David and I suspected turned out to be true, and the ratings weren't corrected, there would be a massive collapse of the entire financial system. He told us it would be a drain of trillions upon trillions of dollars. If these downgrades stayed in place and were not reversed, the world economy was going to take a massive hit. This was in October 2007, and the reverberations of these catastrophic downgrades would not ripple through the market until the spring of 2008, when the massive stock market collapse occurred.

To this day, I joke with David TeSelle that if I was a smarter man and more in tune to such things, I might have started shorting CDOs, and the entire U.S. economy then and there, based on Frank's prediction. I would've made a fortune. I am sure, looking back, that some people were one step ahead and did just that. But rather than shorting the case for my own personal benefit, I chose to pursue a case for justice, not just for Pursuit but for every American who wanted to hold accountable those responsible for the economic collapse.

The first thing our team did was get to work. We knew virtually nothing about CDOs, credit ratings on securitized products, and default "triggers" when we took the case. We had to learn it all, and that is part of what makes Burg Simpson so remarkable and successful: even if we don't know a single thing about a case or what it involves, we will figure it out. We will put in the hours to acquire all the information we need to know, from the technical details of laying down and securing gas lines as we did in the Steamboat Springs and Wyoming gas explosion cases, to understanding the complex jargon and inner workings of the depths of the financial markets. For the Pursuit case, we put in hundreds and hundreds of hours to learn and become conversant regarding investment banks, broker-dealers, and CDOs, and to figure out how to ultimately present the case to a jury in a way that they could understand it.

We read the documents and called the trustees and the people who had drafted the documents in question. We needed to understand whether UBS was legally entitled to take the "waterfall" payments that their clients had paid for. In a "waterfall" payment scenario, the payments flow down, like to a waterfall, from the most risky to the least risky. So I called them and asked. We called all the biggest investment firms in San Francisco, Chicago, New York, and Washington, DC, too, but nobody had any idea how these type of payments worked because they had never seen a situation like this before. We reviewed the documents and told UBS that we did not believe they had the right to take the waterfall payments. UBS disagreed, claiming that they did have the right under the CDO documents. Then they declared a default, claimed insecurity under the CDO documents, and took the "waterfall"—the stream of payments intended for the CDO bondholders below them—for themselves.

What was crazy to me was that the CDO documents did contain default provisions and protections for the senior noteholder (UBS in this case) to protect them if massive numbers of mortgage-holders stopped paying their mortgages. But here's the deal: only a small percentage of mortgage holders actually defaulted on their mortgage payments at that time. There was still a significant stream of cash flow being generated for investors in the CDOs. Despite the fact that the ratings agencies downgraded the CDO bonds to junk status, the ratings-based "triggers" in the deal documents gave super senior noteholders such as UBS the power to take all of the cash flow for themselves and deny it to other investors who had paid tens of millions of dollars.

If a CDO creator was selling these securities as safe, investment-grade securities and knew they were not, or knew they would soon be downgraded to junk status, this may give rise to a viable claim. Based upon the close, special relationship between the ratings agencies and the banks, we began to put together our case.

We were ready to file our complaint, but given the New York state federal courts' bias toward Wall Street, and the number of rulings that had emerged in favor of big banks and against the consumer, we decided to file in Connecticut state court. Most of the decisions that had come down from the New York federal court were very pro-Wall Street. In addition, at that point the New York state courts were holding that the Martin Act required that any securities or fraud claims had to be brought by the state attorney general, not by private firms.

By the time we filed, in the early spring of 2008, the mortgage-backed CDO market collapse had already occurred, just as Frank had predicted, and everything had gone to hell in a handbasket.

In preparing our case in Connecticut, we engaged a local counsel, Fred Gold of Shipman & Goodwin. Everything was on track with Shipman & Goodwin until the firm found out just how serious we were about filing the case against UBS and Moody's. They backed out. We then engaged Gary Klein with Carmody Torrance Sandak Hennessey, who turned out to be a reliable and dedicated local counsel.

UBS was represented by Williams & Connolly, the powerhouse Washington, DC, firm founded by Edward Bennett Williams. The firm has consistently been rated the top white-collar criminal defense firm in the country. It has represented everyone from President Clinton in his impeachment, to Colenel Oliver North in the Iran-Contra Affair, to the drug company Merck in the Vioxx cases.

Once we filed the case in front of Judge John Blawie, we moved immediately for a prejudgment remedy (PJR), which was part of the reason we filed in Connecticut in the first place. A PJR calls for what is essentially a mini-trial in front of a judge long before the actual trial date, and even before discovery. The judge hears witnesses and reviews evidence. In the PJR, if the judge finds probable cause that one party is likely to win the case, he can then order the likely losers to post a bond.

Three days before the PJR, Williams & Connolly disclosed about 250,000 pages of documents to us. Despite the last-minute disclosure, we did not want to lose our hearing date, and knew the importance of pushing forward aggressively. Time was the enemy. We did not ask for a continuance for more time to review the documents. Instead, we immediately put every pair of eyes we could find in our office on the documents, dividing them up and scouring them for smoking guns. Sure enough, we found some just in time to use at the hearing.

This included the "crap and vomit" emails referred to in Judge Blawie's Order. We had a five-day mini-trial in Stamford, Connecticut.

At the conclusion of the PJR, Judge Blawie found we had established probable cause that Pursuit would win the case and ordered UBS to post a bond of $35 million, which would cover potential damages. In his order, Judge Blawie said:

> *The use of the term "triggerless," which was used by UBS to entice the Plaintiffs to purchase the same Notes they had earlier rejected, is akin to a representation by UBS that a gun being handed to the Plaintiffs is not loaded, when in fact UBS knew the gun was not only loaded, but was about to go off. The court takes UBS employees at their word when they reference their Notes, these purported "investment grade" securities which they sold, as "crap" and "vomit", for UBS alone possessed the knowledge of what their product, their inventory, was truly worth. While*

UBS would argue that such descriptors lack a precise meaning, the true meaning of these words are the true value of UBS's wares [which] became abundantly clear when the Plaintiffs' multi-million dollar investment was completely wiped out and liquidated by UBS shortly after the last of the Note purchases was consummated.

That is the difference between a risk that something might happen to change the value of an investment, which is both a fact of life and a risk shared by all parties to any securities transaction, and the undisclosed knowledge that something will happen. That type of nondisclosure, whether it is on the part of a seller or a buyer, can cross the line into actionable securities fraud, and the court finds probable cause to sustain a finding that in this instance, it did.

When we initially filed the case, others in the legal community thought we were off our rockers. They told us we were crazy to think we could prove our claims, and crazy for pursuing the case in Connecticut state court. But after the PJR ruling came out, and similar actions filed in more traditional forums were dismissed, things changed. *The Hedge Fund Report*, a financial trade magazine, called our decision to venue the lawsuit in Connecticut "inspired" and recommended that others with similar grievances follow the Burg Simpson path. Mass media picked up on the case due to the massive bond posting and began doing stories on the lawsuit. The case appeared as a "crap and vomit lawsuit" on Bloomberg Business, the *Financial Times*, and the *Wall Street Journal*.

Thereafter, we worked closely with the U.S. congressional committees investigating the Wall Street collapse, and much of our evidence was used in their reports. We met with, advised, and many times represented states, municipalities, and other government agencies that lost millions of taxpayer dollars from investment in these "toxic" CDO assets.

The case was a monumental moment for Burg Simpson. Not only because we were the first privately filed case to come out of the economic collapse and the first ones to have a lawsuit that a judge called viable, but also because we were changing the national narrative about the collapse. We were causing people to ask questions about how these mysterious securitized products almost collapsed the world economy. The same people in the legal community who first shook their heads at us when we brought the claim were now blown away by it, asking, how did we know about all of this way back then? The answer was that at the time, we didn't know all about it. We resolved to move ahead, ready to do everything we could to bring this matter to conclusion and find justice for our clients. Nothing in this case was going to be easy, but little did we know exactly how hard it would be.

Next, we hired the preeminent expert in the world on these issues, Dr. Anthony Saunders, a professor at New York University and a member of the Nobel Prize for Economics nominating committee. His expertise in the details of finance and CDOs, as well as his impeccable credentials and professorial manner, were critical to our building a successful case. We take the complex and confusing, and make it understandable to everyday people—that's our role. But without A-plus experts like Dr. Saunders to show that the simple story we create is actually backed by the facts and the law, defense lawyers would be free to use the confusion and complexity of cases like this to fool the judge and jurors with smoke and mirrors.

The case was on Judge Blawie's complex commercial docket for 2011. As the court date was approaching, we were working tirelessly, preparing to take on the giants of big banking and big business. Suddenly, however, Judge Blawie was taken off the case and the targeted trial date was vacated. This was a real surprise.

The new judge assigned to the case was Judge Barbara Brazzell-Massaro. After setting the case for a new trial a year later, she dismissed our case entirely for lack of standing (an issue Judge Blawie had already decided in our favor). The judge reasoned that the CDO's were bought by the Broker-Dealer (Pursuit) but the damages, if any, were to the Fund. More specifically, she ruled that since Pursuit's broker-dealer arm bought the CDOs from UBS and then immediately sold them into the Pursuit investment funds, the Pursuit investment funds were not defrauded because it did not buy them directly from UBS. And the entity that did execute the trade, the Pursuit broker-dealer entity, had no losses because they immediately sold the same bonds to the investment funds. In other words, even if UBS did defraud the broker-dealer, there was no remedy. The broker-dealer had no claim because they simply executed the trade and took a fee, so they had no losses. The funds that suffered all of the losses, the court reasoned, were not the ones defrauded. A real Kafkaesque nightmare for sure.

Complicated issues aside, the ruling, issued late in the day on November 6, 2012, stunk. It was the day Barack Obama was reelected president of the United States and we were thus deprived of any media coverage. That was a true punch to the gut. All the people, time, resources, and energy devoted to this case for five years had been thrown away in an instant. When I received the news I felt sick, but we did not quit. We knew that to get the case to trial now would take years, perhaps even appeals all the way to the Supreme Court, but we were not going down without a fight. So we picked ourselves up, dusted ourselves off, and committed ourselves to figuring out a strategy on how to turn this loss into a huge win.

We knew that under Connecticut law, a case could not be dismissed for lack of standing without an evidentiary hearing to consider the actual facts relevant to standing. This court had not held such a hearing, so we moved for reconsideration. The motion languished for many months, but was finally granted. Reluctantly, the court gave us our hearing, setting it again many months into the future.

Many naysayers at the time questioned our strategy. Why ask the court that dismissed your case for a hearing where you know the judge will just hold the hearing to comply with the law, and then dismiss you again? Don't you know how this works? But we believed in our strategy. We believed we were right on standing, and we had the confidence and belief that we could execute a hearing strategy to either overcome the overwhelming odds with this judge or create a strong record for appeal.

In January 2014, the hearing was held. Our expert witness, Professor Saunders, illuminated for the judge that acquiring CDOs was not like purchasing stocks, and that the only purpose of the broker-dealer is to purchase the assets that are going into the fund under the agreement of all parties within the fund. In this way, it is a unitary system. Yes, there were several entities, but they all made up the Pursuit Hedge Fund.

Six months after the hearing concluded, and twenty months after the case had been dismissed, Judge Brazzell-Massaro issued her order. She completely reversed herself, reinstated the case, and ordered it to be set for trial. Needless to say, that was a very good day for us and our clients. Shortly thereafter, we were assigned to our third judge, Judge Kari Dooley, and this time it seemed that we were going to get a fair shot at seeing the courtroom with our case.

Judge Dooley moved with speed and alacrity. She held a half-dozen hearings on various motions that our opponents filed to try to have parts of the case thrown out. The sign of a good judge, she promptly ruled on all motions, set deadlines and kept them, and moved the case forward toward trial. Some motions we won, some we lost, but her rulings were fair and just. Our country would be a better place if all judges were as diligent and competent as Judge Dooley. Ultimately, she denied the summary judgment motion requested by the defendants and set a firm trial date. We finally could see the light at the end of this long tunnel.

Yet, despite having won the PJR, overcome the dismissal, defeated the summary judgment motions, and having clearly demonstrated that we were prepared and ready for trial, we still could not get an offer of settlement from the defendants.

In August, we began jury selection. On our side of the courtroom were myself, David TeSelle, and David Hersh from our firm, our local counsel, one associate attorney, and one paralegal. On the other side, UBS had twelve lawyers, and Moody's had another five. It felt like our small but adept team was there to fight an army of attorneys and paralegals, us versus all of them.

During jury selection, we met with the lawyers from both sides about settling the case. On the Thursday of the second week of jury selection, after already spending nearly two full weeks selecting the jury, we resolved the case with Moody's. The following Monday, we met with UBS and resolved the case with them as well. On Tuesday, we all went to Judge Dooley, and instead of continuing to pick the jury, we were able to tell her that the case had been settled. After eight years of fighting, we reached a resolution for our clients, Pursuit Partners. It was an incredible feeling to have taken the case to a final conclusion.

This was a case about trying to find the truth about what happened to some of the $7 trillion that vanished from the world economy. Here we were, just a bunch of guys out in Denver, Colorado, who were concerned with the corruption on Wall Street that had affected every single person in this country.

It did not matter that we didn't know anything about CDOs when we started. We were prepared, willing, and dedicated to learning everything we needed to know about the subject to win the case, just as we are when we take on complex medical cases involving faulty drugs. We learned it so well that David TeSelle, David Hersh, and I all took depositions with the world's finest experts and professionals who work with these secured priced products for a living, and we were able to ask questions that made sense and understand the answers. We studied and learned all about these products, some of the most complex economic concepts in the world, and learned it well enough to deliver justice for our clients.

The case represents a core philosophy of Burg Simpson: we don't quit. We are not afraid to put in the hard work and the hours, and to fight for eight years on one case if that is what it takes. We will do whatever we need to do within the bounds of the law to win for our clients, especially when it means standing up for the underdog, for the guys who would never win without the help of tenacious, committed, and hard-working lawyers. It is nothing less than an honor to fight for those who need us.

CHAPTER 27

NOT SO FINE WINE

I love wine, but by no means am I an oenophile. Like most people, I never thought much about what was in the wine I drank, assuming it was fermented grapes—at least until the spring of 2015. I got a call from a Denver attorney named Darrell Waas, with whom I had worked on prior cases. Darrell said, "I've got this crazy possible case, but if anybody knows what to do with it, it's you." Before he even told me about the case, I knew it sounded like something for me. Once I heard what he had to say, I was certain it was for me.

Darrell had been retained by Kevin Hicks, the cofounder of BeverageGrades, an independent testing lab in Denver. In an effort to explain to people the scientific difference of what goes into a $10 bottle of wine versus a $50 bottle of wine, Kevin tested the content of 1,306 different types of wine and found that 83 of them showed dangerously elevated levels of inorganic arsenic. During this process, he noticed that some of the cheaper wines had very high arsenic readings—as high as 50 parts per billion (ppb). This was shocking information, considering that the drinking water standard is only 10 ppb. How could there be so much more arsenic in wine?

After testing and retesting to confirm his results, he approached the wineries. The companies with these high arsenic levels refused to talk to him. Concerned for the safety of consumers, Kevin contacted Darrell. I immediately agreed to take a look at the case.

First, we had the wine retested by an independent lab to verify Kevin's findings. The results were eventually confirmed by two additional independent labs. In some cases, the levels were up to 500 percent or more than the maximum safe daily limit. Medical experts have determined that the risks of arsenic exposure include cancer, diabetes, and cardiovascular ailments.

I then conducted a great deal of research into arsenic and found that the difference between inorganic and organic arsenic is important. Inorganic arsenic is five times more deadly than the organic. Organic occurs naturally in the soil, while inorganic arsenic comes from soil that has pesticides and additives. By the end of our research, it was clear that these wines, some of which came from trusted household names, had toxic levels of arsenic not produced by the soil. Some of the popular wine brands named in the lawsuit included: Franzia, Ménage à Trois, Sutter Home, Wine Cube, Charles Shaw, Glen Ellen, Cupcake, Beringer, and Vendage. The wines named in the lawsuit are primarily inexpensive white or blush varietals, including moscato, pinot grigio, and sauvignon blanc.

We also found that the wines in question are barely wines at all. In the red wines, the producers add what can best be described as an alcohol-infused purple goo. The white wines, considered "sweet wines," are full of clarifiers to make the color appear more palatable. Many of these wines retail for under $5 a bottle, and some come in a refrigerator-ready, lined cardboard box.

This stuff was completely different from most wine made in California. Most winemakers have a pride of craftsmanship in their production, but these low-end, toxic wines are mass-produced to keep up with demand, and at a price point much lower than that of mainstream wineries.

We began to mount our case. I brought in Levin Papantonio, the firm that had been integral in bringing Big Tobacco to the settlement table in Florida, and a partner of ours in several mass tort cases. I also engaged the California firm of Kabateck Brown Kellner because the case would have to be filed in California. The case represented a health risk to the public, so we also involved the California Attorney General's office.

On March 19, 2015, we filed a class action lawsuit on behalf of California consumers against the twenty-six wineries that manufactured the eighty-three toxic wines in question. The case was big news, not only in California but also nationally. The day we filed, *CBS This Morning* covered the press conference and ran a segment on the lawsuit. We also did an interview on *Charlie Rose*. The following day *Good Morning America* also ran a piece on the case.

Even though this wine was harming consumers, we filed under Proposition 65, the California label law that requires manufacturers to list on the label what is in their products. The fine is up to $2,500 per incident, which translates into a staggering sum. Even at $500 per incident—per bottle—the case would come to some $6 billion in damages.

The most important aspect of the suit, however, was getting the eighty-three types of wine pulled from the shelves before they caused cancer and other ailments to the consumer. The FDA and other administrative agencies no longer have sufficient funding from Congress and can no longer protect consumers. In keeping with our long history of fighting for the consumer and for the little guy, I was proud that my firm could step in. In keeping with our long history, this is exactly what we do.

EPILOGUE

THE ROLE OF A LIFETIME

I admit that I am a little star struck. That really comes out when Kathy and I attend the Screen Actors Guild Awards. As a result of our prior involvement in the film and television industry, my wife and I have been to the SAG awards ten times. When Kathy was on the SAG national board and played a part in creating the awards show, we always had great seats on the floor, front and center of the stage, sandwiched in between the stars and nominees.

The walk down the red carpet was a real kick. Fans in the stands yelled at Kathy and me to turn so they could take our pictures.

The SAG awards are very intimate. At the main floor of tables, actors hang out with actors. I have long since abandoned my acting and stand-up career, so for me it was a treat to attend and to mingle with so many star-studded names in person. I have met and conversed with Paul Reiser, Helen Hunt, the complete cast of *Friends*, Michael Douglas, Catherine Zeta-Jones, Dustin Hoffman, Robin Williams, George Clooney, and Nicole Kidman, to name a few.

At the after-party one year, we were hanging out with the *Friends* cast. They were all in a great mood, because it was the year that they made $1 million an episode. Spirits were high and the liquor was flowing. Talking to David Schwimmer, I learned that he went to

Three stars: Kathy with Noah Wyle and George Clooney in their *ER* days

Northwestern, just as a fun fact. And Jennifer Aniston—don't get me started. She was very sweet and reminded of me a little doll.

I asked Matt LeBlanc if they were coming back for another season. LeBlanc goes, "Are you kidding me? For a million dollars an episode how can we not come back for another season!"

It was interesting talking to professional actors, hearing about what their next moves and projects were. It took me out of my world as a lawyer and back to my acting days. Well, not all the way back, as this group was light-years beyond where I reached.

Another crazy SAG story is the time I saw Catherine Zeta-Jones smoking a cigarette while she was clearly pregnant. That made me crazy.

I also loved meeting the cast of *The Sopranos*. They received multiple nominations every year, so every year we would reunite with them. One year they were sitting at the table next to ours. I struck up a conversation. I told them how much I appreciated their work, how much I admired them, and about how I myself had grown up in Chicago with a father in the liquor business. I felt like I had met the real-life *Sopranos*.

"I think I know you guys already!" I joked.

One of the actors, Tony Sirico, stopped me. "Hey, buddy," he said, "we're just actors. Don't be talking to us about the real guys in Chicago!"

We shared a laugh over that one.

Kathy and I took tons of pictures at the SAG Awards, too. A couple of them are on display in my office or at home. My wife and I have pictures of us with Dustin Hoffman and Robin Williams. Of course, my wife has one with her and George Clooney.

Not only were we invited to the SAG Awards, but we also received invitations to the after-parties as well, thanks to my wife's continuing involvement with SAG. The *People* magazine after-party was a night I will never forget, thanks to a very special interaction with one of the most gorgeous actresses I've ever laid eyes on.

When we entered the party, it was packed with faces that we didn't recognize. I spotted Geoffrey Rush, one of my favorite actors. I let him know how much I admired his work and we got to talking for a few minutes. As I was talking to him, I had this feeling that somebody was lingering off to my left, just out of my peripheral vision. When the conversation with Rush ended, I turned around to see who it was.

It was Nicole Kidman. I wasn't prepared for my reaction. Her blonde hair was styled up in an elegant bun, and she looked dazzling in a slinky red dress. Swirling her drink in her hand, she said to me, "Are you an actor?"

"Technically yes," I said. "But I'm really a trial lawyer."

"Oh," she said. "So you act in court?"

I laughed. "Yeah, I do act in court, but I'm also a member of SAG."

"Well, that's very interesting," she said. "Tell me about what kinds of cases you do."

I started explaining to her the long-story-short of mass torts. She gazed at me with those piercing blue eyes, her head tilted slightly to the side. How could a woman like Nicole Kidman still be talking to me? My heart raced every time either one of us spoke: it raced for her because she was, well, Nicole Kidman, and it raced for me because I was sure I sounded like an idiot.

When I had finished up my lawyer spiel, she alluded to the fact that she needed a date for the Academy Awards. It may be one of the proudest offers I've ever received—Nicole Kidman asked me to the Academy Awards. Well, she at least *hinted* at inviting me.

The next thing I knew my wife had popped up behind me.

"Nicole, this is my wife, Kathy," I said.

They shook hands very politely, but I noticed a slight change in Nicole's facial expression. The flirtation was over. She had definitely been flirting with me, which is something that I'll probably brag about forever. By the way, my wife did say, with a smile, that I could go to the Academy Awards with Nicole Kidman, but she would have to come along as a chaperone! I was no longer the awkward eighth grader who couldn't get a date. That did wonders for my ego.

Whenever I tell stories like my Nicole Kidman encounter, I am often faced with incredulous responses, particularly if I lace in other stories. Responses are along the lines of "Really? You played golf with Michael Jordan? Basketball with Sinbad? You went to President George W. Bush's inaugural and had dinner with his father? You represented the Little Rascals and members of the Denver Broncos? You were serenaded by Debbie Reynolds in Vegas on your twenty-first birthday? You auditioned for the *Breaking Away* TV series? You did stand-up in the same club with Roseanne Barr? Bullshit! Who are you anyway?"

With Kathy and President Obama

I will tell you who I am. I'm Michael Burg, one of the most accomplished trial lawyers in the country. And yes, I did meet (and flirt with) Nicole Kidman, as well as have those other encounters.

If I had to compare my life to a movie, I would choose *The Secret Life of Walter Mitty*, a film starring Ben Stiller, where the main character leaves his office job to have a worldwide adventure. The spirit of exploration, both of the self and the world, speaks to me in that film. And, of course, I have to agree with my brother that *Forrest Gump* has some relevance too, in that Forrest just ends up surrounded by these incredible, powerful people by sheer chance and timing. It sounds a little campy, and I don't fancy myself to be at the same, shall we say, intellectual level as Forrest. But the movie depicts an incredible journey, and the journey always speaks to me.

My own journey has exceeded my own imagination. Sometimes I wonder how I made it this far; how I was this fortunate, how I achieved this crazy, amazing life I lead. After some contemplation, I always give the same answer: hard work and perseverance. My motto is: get up every time you get knocked down. If you always get up, you can always move forward.

There are a lot of ways that one can look at a life. Ultimately, though, it really does come down to pieces: the small parts of myself that have been collected over the years and that, collectively, make me the person I am, which in turn made me the kind of trial attorney that I am. I carry with me small parts of all my clients, pieces of real stories that motivate me. The pieces come in to my life just the same as the pieces are presented to a jury: one piece at a time.

I started out with what I like to call "the single blade of grass." One desk. No clients. A mountain of hard work in front of me. Since then, the lawn has become enormous, and it weaves itself across the country into our different offices and the national cases we work on. However, no matter how big that lawn becomes, the simple fact of the matter is this: I still have exactly what I started with in that small office at that first desk, given to me by my father. I still have a burning desire to be the best trial attorney I can be.

Law is the most honorable and noble profession available today. We are the enforcers of the rights of individuals, the protectors of the weak and the downtrodden. We provide compensation and justice for those deserving, and we educate those inclined to understand more about the complexities and importance of the world's most powerful legal system.

And so while part of me does miss being an actor, it is an honor and a privilege to serve the law. I love fighting for the little guy with every ounce of willpower and determination I can muster.

The Presidential Inaugural Committee
requests the honor of your presence
to attend and participate
in the
Inauguration of

Barack H. Obama

as President of the United States of America

and

Joseph R. Biden, Jr.

as Vice President of the United States of America
on Tuesday, the twentieth of January
two thousand and nine
in the City of Washington

Invitation to President Obama's inauguration

INDEX

A

acting, 109–110, 150–155, 157–167, 169, 197, 223
actors, 281–284
Alexander, Jerry, 254
Alfalfa Club, 8–9
Alfrey, Tom, 217, 224, 228
Allen, Bruce, 46–47
American Airport Development Company, 175–178
American Arbitration Association (AAA), 53
American Jurisprudence Award, 87
androstenedione, 47–48
animators, 204–205
Aniston, Jennifer, 282
anti-Semitism, 27, 29, 76–77
arbitrators, 53
Arguello, Christine, 145–146
arsenic, 277–278
Ashcraft & Gerel, 16
Atler, Larry, 111, 112–113
Atler, Zall & Haligman, 89, 90–91, 96, 111–115
Atmos Energy, 227

B

bad faith cases, 144–148, 181–190
Ballard Spahr, 175–178
Barbera, Joseph, 203–204
bar exam, 90–92, 93
Barr, Roseanne, 106
Barry, Dave, 244
baseball, 263
basketball, 33, 35–36, 40
    Nenê Hilario, 52–54
Bates, Donnie, 234, 235
Bayer, 16–17, 261–262
Beake, John, 41
bellwether trials, 15
Berry, Matt, 104, 107–109
Betzer, Sheri, 140, 141
BeverageGrades, 277
Biddle, Oliver, 175
birth, Burg's, 20
birth control
    Ortho Evra, 257–261
    Yaz/Yasmin, 16–17, 255, 261–262
Blank, Brad, 44–45
Blawie, John, 269
Boehringer Ingelheim, 17
Bragnalo, Rick, 41

Branney, Joe, 86–87
Brazzell-Massaro, Barbara, 271, 273
Breaking Away, 161–162
Brimmer, Clarence "Bud," 237
brothers, Burg's. *See* Burg, Frank;
    Burg, Peter
bullying, 25–26, 29, 76, 122, 183
Bundy, Bob, 193–197
Bundy v. Colorado National Bank,
    193–197
Burg, Frank, 2, 29, 58, 74, 234
Burg, Peter, 1, 2–3, 74, 257
  and embezzlement scheme, 211,
    212
  in gadolinium case, 15
  in Michael's firm, 173–174, 178
  and pet insurance case, 181–183
  as sports agent, 44
  and Steamboat Springs case, 216
Burg, Phyllis, 20, 26–28, 30, 34,
    76–77, 116, 164–165, 247
Burg, Scott, 66, 128, 170–171, 264
Burg, Stephen, 128, 170, 171, 197
Burg, Sydney, 20, 21–23, 34, 39, 57,
    116, 164–165, 247
Burger King, 131
Burg Simpson, creation of, 246–249
Burg Simpson Eldredge Hersh &
    Jardine, 248
Bush, George H. W., 10
Bustion, Dave "Stretch," 40

C
California, 157, 160–167, 278
cameras, 219–220
Canelas, Frank, 264, 265, 266, 268
car dealers
  Bob Bundy, 193–197
  R. Douglas Spedding, 65–71
Cardi, Phil, 182, 183–184, 185–186,
    188, 189, 190

Carmody Torrance Sandak Hen-
    nessey, 268
cases, favorite, 193–205
cases, turning down, 137–138
Cassidy, Butch, 246
CDOs (collateralized debt obliga-
    tions), 263–275
Cheney, Dick, 249
Chicago, 21–28, 239
childhood, Burg's
  anti-Semitism in, 29
  bullying in, 25–26, 29
  high school, 36, 57
  religious tensions during, 23
  school, 33–34
  sepsis, 19–20
  in South Side, 21–28
  sports during, 33, 35–36, 39–40
  in Wilmette, 28
children, Burg's, 4
  See also Burg, Scott; Burg, Stephen
Christopher, Kathy, 152–154,
    172–173, 209, 281, 283
Clarence Darrow for the Defense (Stone),
    83
Clayton, William, 227–228, 236,
    240–241
Clement, Gina, 245
clerking, 86, 87–89
closing arguments
  in Cody case, 242–243
  in Steamboat Springs case, 229–230
Cody, Wyoming, 233–244
collateralized debt obligations
    (CDOs), 263–275
collection work, 117–118, 122–128
college, 74, 77–80
Colorado
  anti-Semitism in, 76–77
  See also Denver; Steamboat Springs
Colorado National Bank, 193–197

Colorado Rockies, 263
Columbine High School, 171
comedy, 103–109, 223
Comedy Works, 104
comfort zones, 217–218
competition, 54–55
confidence, 31
Conflicts of Law course, 86
conspiracy, 186, 187, 188
Continental Insurance, 216
Coplan, Dale, 118
corporations, 252
    See also mass tort cases
court reporters, 191
courtroom, 95, 99
  in airport, 217–221
Crabb, James, 26–27

D

Dalan, Aaron, 46–47
Darrow, Clarence, 7, 83–84, 85
  Clarence Darrow Award, 7
dating, in college, 77–80
Davis, Marvin, 124
Davis, Walter, 8
death penalty, 83, 84
Debs, Eugene, 84
Debs v. the United States, 84
Dempsey, Jack, 4
Denver, 73–82, 85
  film and television production in,
    157
  See also Colorado
Denver, University of, 40, 74, 75, 77
Denver Broncos, 41–43, 194
Department of Transportation
    (DOT), 226, 227
Dial, Bob, 123–125
divorce, Burg's, 169–170
dog case, 131–136
Dooley, Kari, 273

DOT (Department of Transporta-
    tion), 226, 227
Doucette, Richard, 217, 219, 220,
    224
Douglas, Mrs., 33–34, 90
Doyle, William, 85
Draper, Becky, 218, 220, 241
drugs, 13–17
  Fen-Phen, 252–256
  Ortho Evra, 257–261
  Pradaxa, 17
  Yaz/Yasmin, 16–17, 255, 261–262
  Zyprexa, 256–257
drug suspensions, 47–48
Dunn, Jerry, 115, 117–118, 123
Dunn, Wendell, 126–127

E

economic collapse, 264–275
education, Burg's, 33–34, 36, 57, 74,
    77–80
Eldredge, Scott, 181, 200, 201, 202,
    204, 211
embezzlement scheme, 208–213
ethics test, 92
evolution, 83, 84
executive committee, 255, 256, 257
expense, of cases, 137–138

F

Fabry, Mike, 76
Fabulous Kangaroo Brothers, 2, 174,
    239
Farrell, Jo, 155, 158, 160
father, Burg's. *See* Burg, Sydney
Fen-Phen, 252–256
Fields, Totie, 62
finances, Burg's, 92–93, 111–112,
    128, 149, 169, 170
finances, of law firm, 207
financial crisis, 263–275

Finesilver, Sherman, 42, 91
Fisher, Jeff, 49–51
football, 36
  corruption in, 49–51
  drug suspensions, 47–48
  free agents, 44, 49
  Inside the NFL, 41
  Super Bowl bet, 194
  Ralph Tamm, 47–48
  U.S. Football League, 67
Forrest Gump, 285
fraternity, 77
free agents, 44, 49
free speech, 84
Frick, Ann, 53
Friedman, Andrew, 258
Friedman, Laurie, 59–61
Friedman, Milt, 58
Friedman, Sheldon, 115
Friedman, Tootsie, 59
Friends, 281–282
Fritz (dog), 131–136
Fusco, Joe, 58–59

G

gadolinium, 13–16
Gant shirts, 30
Garmica, Lenny, 27–28
gas explosions
  in Cody, Wyoming, 233–244
  in Steamboat Springs, 215–221,
    223–231, 233, 236
Gelt, Theodore, 89
Gemas, Leo, 133–134
General Electric, 14
general managers, negotiating with,
  46–47
Georgetown University, 84–85
Gold, Frank, 268
Gold Seal Liquors, 21, 58–61, 62, 63
Good News Building, 215, 227, 231

Gorman, Tom, 237, 239, 241, 244
Gould, Elliott, 164
grades, Burg's, 33–34, 36, 74, 75, 77
Grant, Lonnie, 151, 154
Greeley Gas, 216–221, 224–231
Groves, Justice, 91

H

Haligman, Ed, 111, 119, 169
Hal Roach Studios, 202
Hames, Gene, 184–185
handwriting, 34, 90
Hanna-Barbera, 200, 202, 205
Harder, John, 140–143
Harliss, John, 211
Hawley, Bob, 88
HBO, 41
hearsay rule, 186, 187
Heckbert, Jim, 216, 224, 228, 231
hecklers, 107
Hellen, Ted, 181, 186
Hersh, David, 210, 211, 274
Hicks, Kevin, 277–278
high school, 75
Hilario, Nenê, 52–54
Hoeflich, Adam, 262
The Hollywood Reporter, 157–159, 161
Holmes, Oliver Wendell, 6
Household Pet, 181–190
House of Pies, 80–81
hunting, 235, 236
Husband, John, 155
Hynes, Melissa, 233, 234, 242, 244
Hynes, Randy, 233, 234, 235,
  239–240, 242, 244

I

Ickovic, David, 139, 140
Inside the NFL, 41
insurance, 143–148, 181–190
insurance defense, 174, 178–179

Ireland Stapleton Pryor & Holmes, 86, 87–89

Isaacson, Rosenbaum, Spiegelman & Friedman, 115

J

Jackson, Mark, 41

James River Insurance Company, 143–148

Jardine, Kerry, 216, 220, 234, 235, 238, 244, 253, 257

Jefferson Bank and Trust, 125

JF Images, 155

jobs, in high school, 57–61

Johnson, Vance, 41–43

Johnson & Johnson, 258–261

Jordan, Michael, 8

Judaism, 89–90

   See also religion

jurors, 134, 136, 238, 242

jury, 100, 101, 189, 225, 226

jury selection, 220–221

jury trial, first, 131–136

K

Kammerer, Holly, 197, 199

Katz, David, 257

Katz, Seth, 17

Kennedy, Robert F., 4

Kennedy, Ted, 249

Kerber, Dave, 217

Kibrick, Syd, 201, 202

Kidman, Nicole, 283–284

King World, 201, 202, 205

Klein, Gary, 268

Kraus, Jeff, 139, 141

Ku Klux Klan, 77

Kwal Paints, 123

L

Las Vegas, 61–62, 66, 104

law school, 84–87

lawyer, trial, 84, 85, 87, 89, 99–102

lawyers, 5–7

leadership, 4

LeBlanc, Matt, 282

Lee, Gordon, 200, 201

Leopold-Loeb trial, 83, 84

Levin Papantonio, 15, 255, 278

Eli Lilly and Company, 256, 257

Little America, 78–79

Little Rascals, 7–8, 200–205

Lopez, Ramon, 257

Lord, Bissel & Brooks, 186, 187, 188

Los Angeles, 157, 160–167, 169

Loyola Ramblers, 35

Lupron, 258, 259

M

Maloney, Annie, 160, 161

Maloney, John, 41

manipulation, 46

Mann Act, 79, 80

Marsh, Thompson, 85–86

Martin Act, 268

Marx Brothers, 2

mass tort cases

   Burg Simpson's entry into, 252

   defined, 15

   executive committee, 255, 256, 257

   Fen-Phen, 252–256

   gadolinium, 15–16

   Ortho Evra, 257–261

   Pradaxa, 17

   Yaz/Yasmin, 16–17, 255, 261–262

   Zyprexa, 256–257

Matsch, Richard, 126–128

McFarland, George, 201

McGwire, Mark, 47

melanoma, 218

Meyer, William, 186, 187, 188

Miller, Kent, 144–145

modeling, 154

Moody's, 265, 274
moose, 235, 239–240
morality, 46
Morris, Ashley, 207–213
Morris, Gary, 125
Morris, William, 162–163
Mossman, Judge, 140, 141, 142, 143
mother, Burg's. *See* Burg, Phyllis
motivation, 54–55, 138
MRIs, 13–16
Munoz, Anthony, 44

N
Nattiel, Ricky, 41
natural gas
   in Cody, Wyoming, 233–244
   in Steamboat Springs, 215–221,
      223–231, 233, 236
negativity, 238, 243
Nelson, Robb, 44, 51–52
nephrogenic systemic fibrosis (NSF),
   13–16
Neufeld, Herb, 194, 195, 196
NFL. *See* football
nickname, 30–31
Nizer, Louis, 139
North Shore, 28
nose, bloody, 141–143
NSF (nephrogenic systemic fibrosis),
   13–16
Nugent, Terry, 44

O
O'Connor, Carroll, 162
O'Donnell, Mike, 175
opening statements, 223–224
Orion Group, 181–190
Ortho Evra, 257–261

P
Papantonio, Mike, 250, 255

parents, Burg's. *See* Burg, Phyllis;
   Burg, Sydney
Peluso, Tom, 41
peremptory challenge, 134
Perkins Coie, 140
pet insurance, 181–190
Phathong, Von, 198–200
Phillips, Wade, 41
philosophy, personal, 4
photographs, 1
PJR (prejudgment remedy), 268–269
political science, 75
politics, 249–250
Pradaxa, 17
Preeo, Bob, 175
prejudgment remedy (PJR), 268–269
preparation, 218–219, 274
principle, 132–133, 137
pro bono work, 137
process, 99–102
Pro Line Management, 37, 44–52
promises, delivering on, 80–81
Proposition 65, 278
Pursuit Partners, 264, 266, 269, 272,
   273, 274

Q
Quick Draw McGraw, 204–205
quitting, 139, 143, 272, 274

R
Racketeer Influenced and Corrupt
   Organizations act (RICO), 141
Rafferty, Troy, 15
Raful, Larry, 162
Rant, Tom, 68–70
religion, 23, 235, 237
   anti-Semitism, 27, 29, 76–77
remarriage, Burg's, 172–173
reputation, 211, 233
Reynolds, Debbie, 62

Rice, Condoleezza, 9, 10
Richardson, Sherry, 191
RICO (Racketeer Influenced and
    Corrupt Organizations act), 141
Ridge Runners, 29
Robinson, Kevin, 44, 51–52
Robinson, Mark, 256
Romig, Joe, 236
Rudd, Kelly, 142
Rush, Red, 35

S
Saas, Bill, 217
SAG (Screen Actors Guild), 152, 153,
    281
Santos, Joe, 52
Saunders, Anthony, 271, 273
Schepis, Tony, 264, 265
Schwimmer, David, 281–282
Scopes "Monkey" Trial, 83, 84
Screen Actors Guild (SAG), 152, 153,
    281
Screen Actors Guild Awards, 281–
    284
The Secret Life of Walter Mitty, 285
securities, 263–275
Seeger, Chris, 257
Selznick, Joyce, 161
sepsis, 19–20
Shapiro, Jules, 20
Shipman & Goodwin, 268
shoes, factory rejects, 23
Silver, Jack, 96, 97–98, 115, 116–117
Simpson, Alan, 231, 233, 245, 257
Simpson, Bill (grandfather of Alan),
    245–246
Simpson, Bill (son of Alan), 4, 233,
    234, 235, 236, 237, 238, 244,
    245, 249, 253, 257
Simpson, Colin, 246, 249
Simpson, Kepler & Edwards, 231, 233

Simpson, Milward, 246
Simpson, O. J., 219
Sinatra, Frank, 27–28, 70
Singer, Bob, 8, 204–205
Sirico, Tony, 283
solo practitioner, 121–129
The Sopranos, 282–283
Southern California, University of,
    162
Spakone, Jake, 58, 59
Spedding, R. Douglas, 65–71
speech, free, 84
Spence, Gerry, 91
sports, 35
    in Burg's childhood, 39–40
    Colorado Rockies, 263
    motivation in, 54–55
    See also basketball; football
sports agents, 41, 44–45, 46–47
sports law, lack of negotiation in, 41
sports management, 37, 41, 44–52
stand-up comedy, 103–109, 223
Starr, Ken, 88–89
Stavropoulos, John Yanni, 181, 186
Steamboat Springs, Colorado,
    215–221, 223–231, 233, 236
Steele, William, 175, 177
stepchildren, Burg's, 173
steroids, 47–48
Stone, Irving, 83
Strom, Earl, 37
Sturm College of Law, 3, 150, 173
Sun West, 139–143
"The Super Bowl Case," 193–197

T
Takamoto, Iwao, 204
Tamm, Ralph, 47–48
teaching, 93, 149–150
TeSelle, David, 143, 265, 266, 274
theft, 181

TIG/TransAmerica Insurance,
    178–179
timing, 109
TransAmerica Insurance, 178–179
trial, first, 95–99
trial lawyer, 84, 85, 87, 89, 99–102
Trump, Donald, 67
trust account, 212

U
UBS, 265–275
underdog, 252
    See also mass tort cases
University of Denver, 40, 74, 75, 77
University of Southern California,
    162
U.S. Department of Transportation
    (DOT), 226, 227
U.S. Football League, 67
U.S. West, 216–221, 224–231

V
VanderWerf, Gretchen, 88
Vannoy, Steve, 154, 155, 158
Van Schaack real estate company, 96
Vellano, Michael, 133–134
Vietnam War, 74
Voight, Jon, 164
voir dire, 220–221

W
Waas, Darrell, 277
Wall Street collapse, 263–275

water damage case, 96–99
waterfall payments, 267
Weiss, Mel, 256–257
White, Byron, 88
White, Debbie, 81–82, 85, 89, 92–93,
    128, 151, 154, 169–170, 171
White Sox, 39
White & Steele, 175
Wiley, Marcellus, 44–46
Wilkin, Dave, 175
Willfork, David, 132, 134, 136
Willfork, Lisa, 132, 136
Williams, Edward Bennett, 268
Williams & Connolly, 268, 269
wine, 277–279
winning, desire for, 54–55
wives, Burg's. *See* Christopher, Kathy;
    White, Debbie
Wolf, Rick, 233, 234, 235, 237, 238,
    241, 243, 244
Wood, Ris & Hames, 173, 174, 184
Wright, Louie, 44
Wyoming, 233–244, 249, 253

Y
Yaz/Yasmin, 16–17, 255, 261–262
Yogi Bear, 7, 8, 204–205

Z
Zall, Ron, 111, 113
Zeta-Jones, Catherine, 282
Zyprexa, 256–257

ACKNOWLEDGMENTS

When I met my wife, Kathy, my whole life changed, and together we took our journey from the bottom to the top. Kathy, thank you for always believing in me and encouraging me to write this book.

To my brothers, Peter and Frank. Without Peter's hard work and his partnership in all aspects of my life, none of this could have happened. And to Frank, thank you for leading the way, for fighting for what is right, toughening me up, and for always being by my side.

To our children, Scott and Stephen, and Reese and Samantha. All have grown up to be great leaders. All four of you make me proud of what I do and very proud of what you do, every day.

To my grandchildren, Sydney, Max, Emmett, Madeline, and Isaac, who light up my life and for whom I have tried to make America a better place.

To all my partners and shareholders, including Peter Burg, Kerry Jardine, Scott Eldredge, David Hersh, David TeSelle, Holly Kammerer, Tom Henderson, Seth Katz, Bill Simpson, Janet Abaray, Diane Smith, Stephen Burg, and all the other shareholders, thank you for working so tirelessly to help people in need.

To Al Simpson, who is one of the greatest patriots in the history of the United States, who always puts country ahead of party. You are the best!

This book would not be in print without the work of Gina Clement. My loyal legal assistant for almost twenty years, Gina keeps me going in the right direction, keeps me on schedule, and is always willing to set me straight when needed. Thank you for your editing and writing, which has made both my life and the book better.

Jenna Bernstein transcribed countless hours of tapes and helped shape the book. Her ability to sift through complex legal material and tease out the best stories was an invaluable contribution.

In addition to putting the deal together, Andrew Stuart again proved himself to be one of the most literate literary agents in the business as he guided the editorial and publication process.

Dorianne Perrucci did her usual terrific job editing the book. Her keen eye for storytelling and her attention to details are welcome traits for any author. She received an assist from copy editor Patricia Connolly.

BenBella Books is a first-class publisher, and the writers thank the entire team for their work on the book: Glenn Yeffeth, Adrienne Lang, Sarah Dombrowsky, Alicia Kania, Cameron Proffitt, Jessika Rieck, and Vy Tran.

Finally, Nick Reed and Ryan Azevedo took the finished production and crafted a masterful, multiplatform marketing campaign.

ABOUT THE AUTHORS

Mike Burg is a trial attorney who has dedicated his life to fighting for the underdog and to protecting the rights of Americans to a trial by jury. He is the recipient of numerous legal awards, including the Clarence Darrow Award, the American Association for Justice Heavy Lifting Award, and the Weidemann Wysocki Award. In 2016, he was named the Denver Lawyer of the Year for Product Liability Litigation – Plaintiffs, by Best Lawyers® in America. Additionally, he was named one of America's 50 Leading Trial Lawyers by The Legal 500 from 2012 through 2015 and was named Lawyer of the Year in Product Liability Litigation by *Best Lawyers® in America* in 2016. In 2013, Michael was named Lawyer of the Year by *Best Lawyers® in America* for Mass Tort Litigation/ Class Actions – Plaintiffs. *Law Week Colorado* named Mike the Lawyer of the Decade from 2000 to 2010. He is past president of the National Trial Lawyers (2010).

Mike has been appointed to numerous leadership positions by federal judges around the country in a variety of high-profile multi-district litigations. He actively practices law in the areas of catastrophic personal injury and commercial litigation and has won numerous verdicts for his clients, over twenty of which have been in excess of $1 million. In April 2016, Mike was inducted into the

Trial Lawyers Hall of Fame at Temple University Law School in Philadelphia, Pennsylvania.

Josh Young has co-written five *New York Times* best-sellers, two *Los Angeles Times* best-sellers, three books that were made into TV documentaries, and thirteen books that have been ranked no. 1 in their category on Amazon.com. He is the co-author of comedian Howie Mandel's *Here's the Deal: Don't Touch Me*; movie mogul Mike Medavoy's *You're Only as Good as Your Next One*; Dr. Sam Parnia's *Erasing Death: The Science That Is Rewriting the Boundaries Between Life and Death*; and Colin Tudge's *The Link: Uncovering Our Oldest Ancestor*, which has been translated into five languages. He is the co-author of survivalist Matt Graham's *Epic Survival: Extreme Adventure, Stone Age Wisdom, and Lessons in Living from a Modern Hunter-Gatherer* and of Wayne Rogers' iconoclastic business book *Make Your Own Rules: A Renegade Guide to Unconventional Success*. Additionally, Josh is the author of *And Give Up Showbiz?: How Fred Levin Beat Big Tobacco, Avoided Two Murder Prosecutions, Became Chief of Ghana, Earned Boxing Manager of the Year, and Transformed American Law*.

On the film side, Josh served as production consultant on *White House Down* (2013). As a journalist, Josh was a contributing editor at *George* magazine, *Entertainment Weekly,* and *LIFE Magazine*. His work has appeared in the *New York Times,* the *New Republic, Details,* the *Sunday Telegraph* (London), and *Los Angeles Times*. More information is available at www.joshyoungauthor.com.